The Primary ICT and E-learning Co-ordinator's Manual

Book 1: A guide for new subject leaders

The Primary ICT and E-learning Co-ordinator's Manual

Book 1: A guide for new subject leaders

James Wright

P·C·P

Paul Chapman
Publishing

First published 2007

Paul Chapman Publishing
A SAGE Publications Company
1 Oliver's Yard
55 City Road
London
EC1Y 1SP

SAGE Publications Inc
2455 Teller Road
Thousand Oaks, CA 91320

SAGE Publications India Pvt Ltd
B1/I1 Mohan Cooperative Industrial Area
Mathura Road, Post Bag 7
New Delhi 110 044

SAGE Publications Asia-Pacific Pte Ltd
33 Pekin Street #02–01
Far East Square
Singapore 0487 63

Library of Congress Control Number: 200694 0061

British Library Cataloguing in Publication data
A catalogue record for this book is available from the
British Library

ISBN-978-1-4129-3562-3
ISBN-978-1-4129-3563-0 (pbk)

Typset by Pantek Arts Ltd, Maidstone, Kent
Printed in Great Britian by the Cromwell Press,
Trowbridge, Wilts
Printed on paper from sustainable resources

Contents

Qualifications and Curriculum Authority copyright material
is reproduced under the terms of HMSO Guidance Note 8.

Preface

In recent years the traditional position of information and communication technology (ICT) co-ordinator within the primary school setting has expanded and evolved beyond recognition. No longer is it simply a matter of organizing appropriate software and timetabling access to a suite of computers to deliver a discrete curriculum. As ICT has demonstrated its impact upon all areas of the curriculum, school networks need to be effectively managed and resourced, staff need to be trained, pupils need to be guaranteed a technological entitlement. Concurrently the expansion of the Internet has brought with it a host of E-safety concerns that schools need to address such that all ICT and E-learning co-ordinators must possess or develop a long-term strategic view that can steer them through this complex process.

The Primary ICT and E-learning Co-ordinator's Manual is a two-volume work that covers all areas of this demanding brief in the form of two distinct 'manuals'. Book 1, 'A guide for new subject leaders', is directed primarily at new subject leaders and details a 33-task schedule of activities spread carefully over the co-ordinator's first year. Book 2, 'A guide for experienced leaders and managers', develops the co-ordinator's journey into the second year but may also be a useful starting point for more experienced leaders and school managers.

Each book follows a group of virtual co-ordinators from various school settings as they are mentored through a systematic series of activities that guide them through the school year. Through their weblog (blog) discussions we witness their development into effective subject leaders as they each attempt to integrate the book's 33 guided tasks and ultimately produce a sustainable strategy for E-learning.

Whilst the co-ordinators in the weblog are fictional characters they are based on the author's real experience of working with hundreds of primary co-ordinators in his advisory work across two local authorities. As Senior Adviser for ICT with Warrington Children's Services, James worked with a wide range of schools in order to develop their strategic leadership of the subject, before moving to Lancashire where he currently works as a school improvement partner and link adviser with strategic responsibility for schools ICT. James previously taught and co-ordinated ICT across the primary age range and has written and developed a wide range of training materials including headteacher and subject leader seminars including 'School Self Evaluation for ICT', 'Assessing Standards in ICT' and 'E-safety and Every Child Matters'. He has supported the British Educational Communications and Technology Agency (BECTA) both as a BECTA 'expert' and in a consultative role upon the local authority self-review framework and is an accredited ICT Mark assessor.

Readers may contact James directly via his companion website at www.james-wright.org through which co-ordinators may join live blogs supporting the implementation of both manuals.

Blogging

21st August

Alex

Posts:

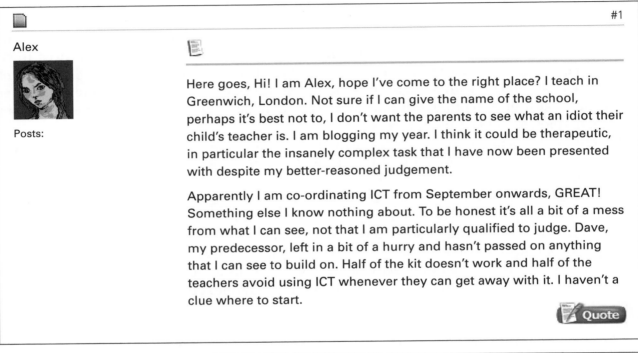

Here goes, Hi! I am Alex, hope I've come to the right place? I teach in Greenwich, London. Not sure if I can give the name of the school, perhaps it's best not to, I don't want the parents to see what an idiot their child's teacher is. I am blogging my year. I think it could be therapeutic, in particular the insanely complex task that I have now been presented with despite my better-reasoned judgement.

Apparently I am co-ordinating ICT from September onwards, GREAT! Something else I know nothing about. To be honest it's all a bit of a mess from what I can see, not that I am particularly qualified to judge. Dave, my predecessor, left in a bit of a hurry and hasn't passed on anything that I can see to build on. Half of the kit doesn't work and half of the teachers avoid using ICT whenever they can get away with it. I haven't a clue where to start.

Quote

Toby

Posts:

Hi, Alex, Toby here, Swindon. You need to relax, just focus on your class and do what you can with the subject co-ordination. Are you an NQT?

Quote

Alex

Posts:

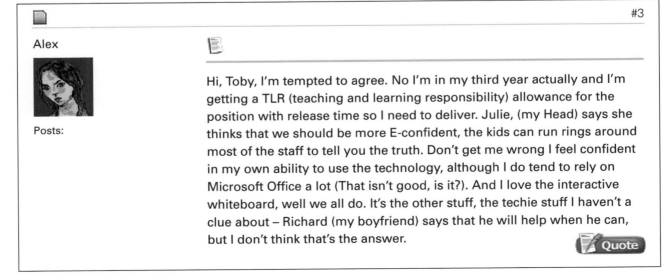

Hi, Toby, I'm tempted to agree. No I'm in my third year actually and I'm getting a TLR (teaching and learning responsibility) allowance for the position with release time so I need to deliver. Julie, (my Head) says she thinks that we should be more E-confident, the kids can run rings around most of the staff to tell you the truth. Don't get me wrong I feel confident in my own ability to use the technology, although I do tend to rely on Microsoft Office a lot (That isn't good, is it?). And I love the interactive whiteboard, well we all do. It's the other stuff, the techie stuff I haven't a clue about – Richard (my boyfriend) says that he will help when he can, but I don't think that's the answer.

Quote

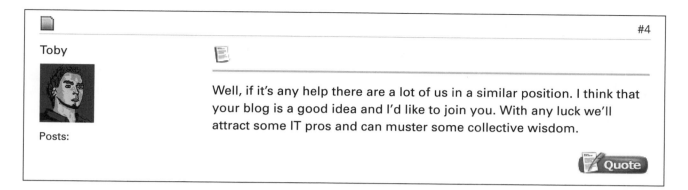

#4

Toby

Posts:

Well, if it's any help there are a lot of us in a similar position. I think that your blog is a good idea and I'd like to join you. With any luck we'll attract some IT pros and can muster some collective wisdom.

Quote

24th August

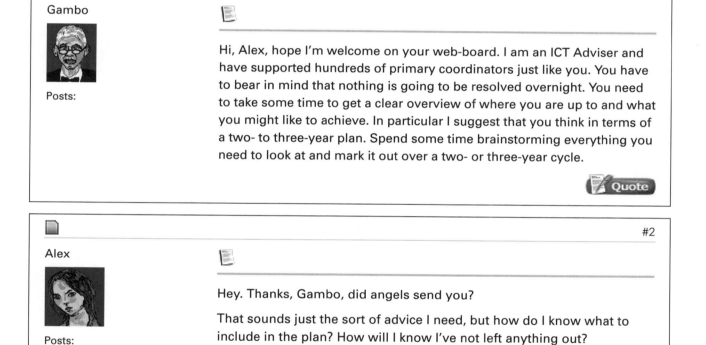

#1

Gambo

Posts:

Hi, Alex, hope I'm welcome on your web-board. I am an ICT Adviser and have supported hundreds of primary coordinators just like you. You have to bear in mind that nothing is going to be resolved overnight. You need to take some time to get a clear overview of where you are up to and what you might like to achieve. In particular I suggest that you think in terms of a two- to three-year plan. Spend some time brainstorming everything you need to look at and mark it out over a two- or three-year cycle.

Quote

#2

Alex

Posts:

Hey. Thanks, Gambo, did angels send you?

That sounds just the sort of advice I need, but how do I know what to include in the plan? How will I know I've not left anything out?

Quote

25th August

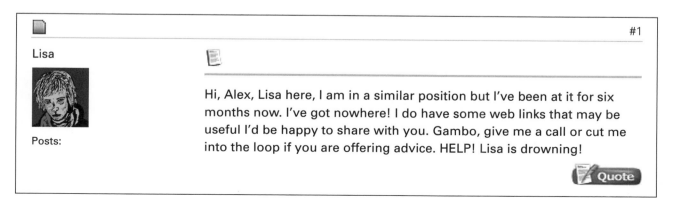

#1

Lisa

Posts:

Hi, Alex, Lisa here, I am in a similar position but I've been at it for six months now. I've got nowhere! I do have some web links that may be useful I'd be happy to share with you. Gambo, give me a call or cut me into the loop if you are offering advice. HELP! Lisa is drowning!

Quote

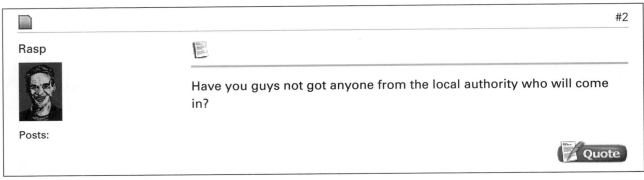

Rasp

Posts:

Have you guys not got anyone from the local authority who will come in?

#2

Quote

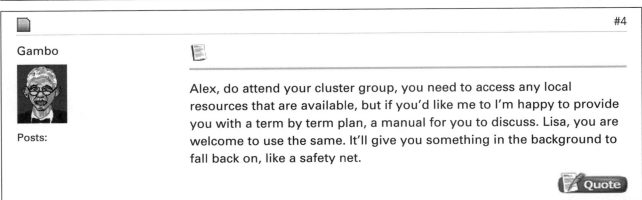

Alex

Posts:

I have a co-ordinator cluster meeting to attend in October, Shall I wait?

#3

Quote

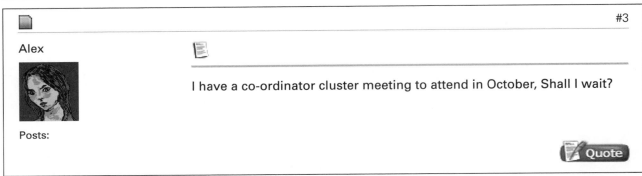

Gambo

Posts:

Alex, do attend your cluster group, you need to access any local resources that are available, but if you'd like me to I'm happy to provide you with a term by term plan, a manual for you to discuss. Lisa, you are welcome to use the same. It'll give you something in the background to fall back on, like a safety net.

#4

Quote

26th August

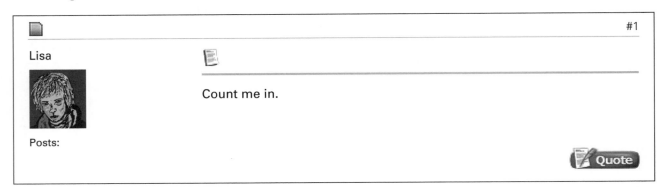

Lisa

Posts:

Count me in.

#1

Quote

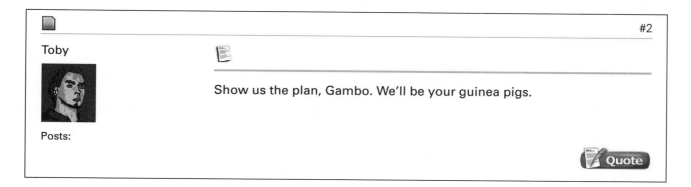

Toby

Posts:

Show us the plan, Gambo. We'll be your guinea pigs.

#2

27th August

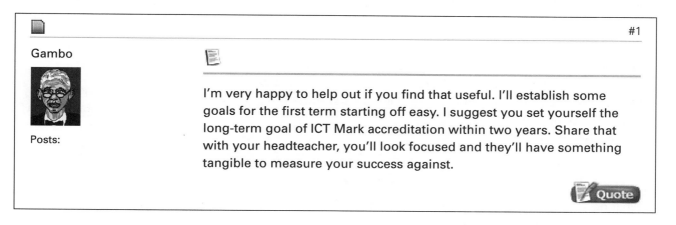

Gambo

Posts:

I'm very happy to help out if you find that useful. I'll establish some goals for the first term starting off easy. I suggest you set yourself the long-term goal of ICT Mark accreditation within two years. Share that with your headteacher, you'll look focused and they'll have something tangible to measure your success against.

#1

28th August

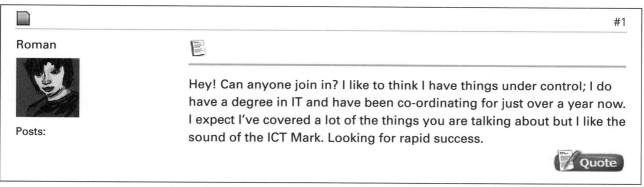

Roman

Posts:

Hey! Can anyone join in? I like to think I have things under control; I do have a degree in IT and have been co-ordinating for just over a year now. I expect I've covered a lot of the things you are talking about but I like the sound of the ICT Mark. Looking for rapid success.

#1

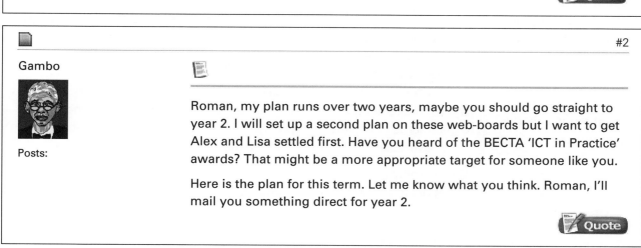

Gambo

Posts:

Roman, my plan runs over two years, maybe you should go straight to year 2. I will set up a second plan on these web-boards but I want to get Alex and Lisa settled first. Have you heard of the BECTA 'ICT in Practice' awards? That might be a more appropriate target for someone like you.

Here is the plan for this term. Let me know what you think. Roman, I'll mail you something direct for year 2.

#2

Table 1.1 Autumn Term Plan

AUTUMN TERM			
SEPTEMBER	OCTOBER	NOVEMBER	DECEMBER
FACT FINDING What is available? When was it produced or updated, e.g. ICT Policy, Scheme of Work, Development Plan. Any INSET that took place. Dig out the last Ofsted report. If it was pre-September 05 it will have a subject report for ICT as well as reference to ICT across the curriculum. Any key issues?	**HARDWARE/SOFTWARE AUDIT** Set up your own system for recording the kit that you have. My advice would be to set up a spreadsheet, note where each machine is located, when it was bought, any warranty etc in place. You might also want to include the serial numbers etc. Make sure it is security etched. Often the office may have this info anyway as part of its audit returns. If you are really efficient you'll also note what software is on each machine and tie it in to a licence somewhere. I think you will need to book around 2 half days of release to complete this this term.		**MICROSOFT LICENSING FRAMEWORK** Many schools may haemorrhage money paying for Microsoft licensing – It has proved something of a black art. This is a good early hit to score. Audit your needs and use the BECTA framework to get a best value deal.
VISION What do you want ICT to mean for your school? Put together a vision that will motivate the staff and pupils. (You should find one at the top of your policy to start off with – Does that one actually mean anything to you?)	**STRATEGIC AUDIT, SELF REVIEW FRAMEWORK** You need to get a structured overview of the subject in this first term and you might as well use a national framework to help you to do so. Don't expect to have all the answers at this stage but this will give you the overview and it will begin to produce a sketch development plan. Ideally get someone from the authority to come in for half a day to get you started. I think you will need to book around 3 half days of release to complete this this term.		
LEADERSHIP Who is leading the subject? Is it collegiate and does it involve senior management? Get this established it'll help in terms of budget access to staff meetings etc. At least one meeting needed here; it's likely to be after school I'm afraid.	**TECHNICAL SUPPORT AUDIT** Who is supporting your network? What service is being provided? What is it costing? Contact the LA, cluster schools to get a sense of what is available. Above all make sure it's not down to you!	**DISCRETE ICT OVERVIEW** As a discrete subject, what exactly is being taught? How is it being taught? For how long? What about differentiation and progression? This activity is to give you an initial overview of this vital area, to flag up some key issues and gaps in provision. Later in the year I shall chat to you about a more root and branch review of the scheme of work.	

Available on the net at http://www.sagepub.co.uk/wrightbk1

29th August

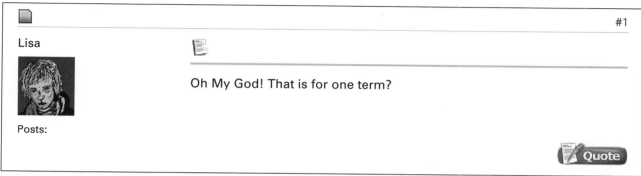

Lisa

Posts:

#1

Oh My God! That is for one term?

Quote

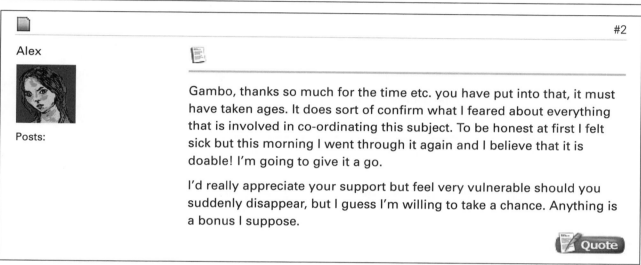

Alex

Posts:

#2

Gambo, thanks so much for the time etc. you have put into that, it must have taken ages. It does sort of confirm what I feared about everything that is involved in co-ordinating this subject. To be honest at first I felt sick but this morning I went through it again and I believe that it is doable! I'm going to give it a go.

I'd really appreciate your support but feel very vulnerable should you suddenly disappear, but I guess I'm willing to take a chance. Anything is a bonus I suppose.

Quote

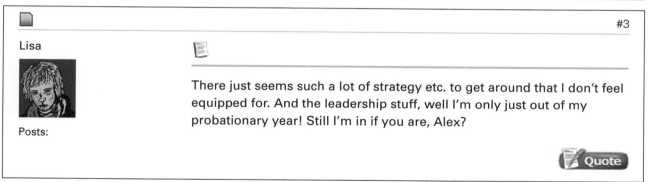

Lisa

Posts:

#3

There just seems such a lot of strategy etc. to get around that I don't feel equipped for. And the leadership stuff, well I'm only just out of my probationary year! Still I'm in if you are, Alex?

Quote

30th August

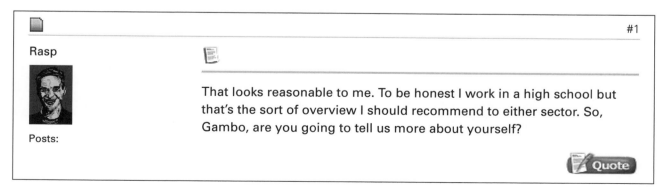

Rasp

Posts:

#1

That looks reasonable to me. To be honest I work in a high school but that's the sort of overview I should recommend to either sector. So, Gambo, are you going to tell us more about yourself?

Quote

31st August

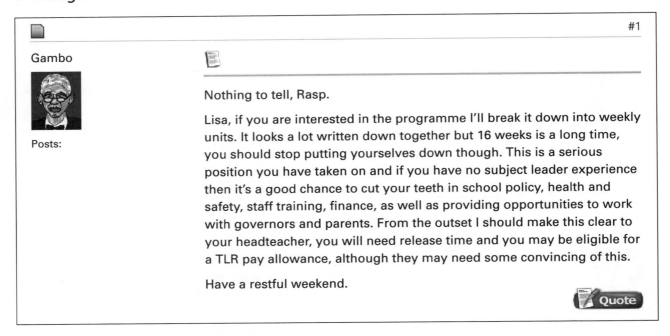

Gambo

Posts:

Nothing to tell, Rasp.

Lisa, if you are interested in the programme I'll break it down into weekly units. It looks a lot written down together but 16 weeks is a long time, you should stop putting yourselves down though. This is a serious position you have taken on and if you have no subject leader experience then it's a good chance to cut your teeth in school policy, health and safety, staff training, finance, as well as providing opportunities to work with governors and parents. From the outset I should make this clear to your headteacher, you will need release time and you may be eligible for a TLR pay allowance, although they may need some convincing of this.

Have a restful weekend.

Quote

Chapter 1 • *September*

3rd September

Week 1, Task 1 – Fact Finding and Creating a Subject Leader File

The first task for any co-ordinator is to assemble a subject leader file if one has not been provided. This is going to be your bible, something you can take along to meetings and show to the head-teacher, even to the Office for Standards in Education (Ofsted) to demonstrate how the subject is managed and, more importantly, is led. Keep an electronic version also, you might as well learn to think and work digitally if you are not already.

Assembling this folder is going to provide you with your first opportunity to scratch the surface of the subject and to find out what has gone on before. There are a number of formats that you may wish to follow, including any that you may have used previously or that are preferred by the school. However, given that there is now a national 'road-map' for ICT development, it makes sense to adopt this from the outset. Therefore I recommend that you arrange your documentation in line with the BECTA self-review framework categories. Therefore, set up the following sections and collate any existing documentation within this format.

1 Leadership and Management
2 Curriculum
3 Learning and Teaching
4 Assessment
5 Professional Development
6 Extended Opportunities for Learning
7 Resources
8 Impact on Pupil Outcomes.

In the front of the folder make a list of the documents and note when they were last updated. Try to get everything that you find into this system; if there is a lot of existing paperwork around the school, set up a filing system that replicates these categories. Above all try to do it this week, as it is a great way to take control of the strategy in your first week and to avoid simply getting bogged down in cables and machinery.

4th September

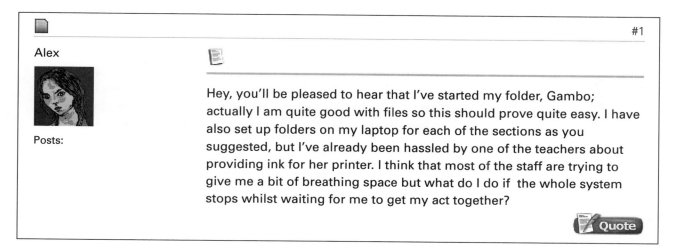

#1

Alex

Posts:

Hey, you'll be pleased to hear that I've started my folder, Gambo; actually I am quite good with files so this should prove quite easy. I have also set up folders on my laptop for each of the sections as you suggested, but I've already been hassled by one of the teachers about providing ink for her printer. I think that most of the staff are trying to give me a bit of breathing space but what do I do if the whole system stops whilst waiting for me to get my act together?

Quote

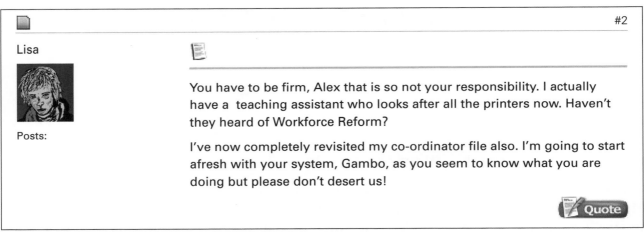

Lisa

Posts:

#2

You have to be firm, Alex that is so not your responsibility. I actually have a teaching assistant who looks after all the printers now. Haven't they heard of Workforce Reform?

I've now completely revisited my co-ordinator file also. I'm going to start afresh with your system, Gambo, as you seem to know what you are doing but please don't desert us!

Quote

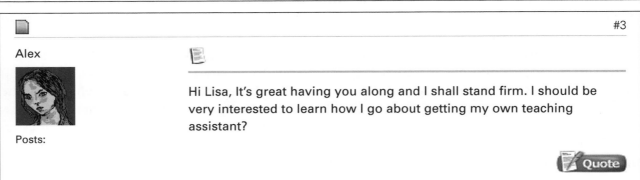

Alex

Posts:

#3

Hi Lisa, It's great having you along and I shall stand firm. I should be very interested to learn how I go about getting my own teaching assistant?

Quote

5th September

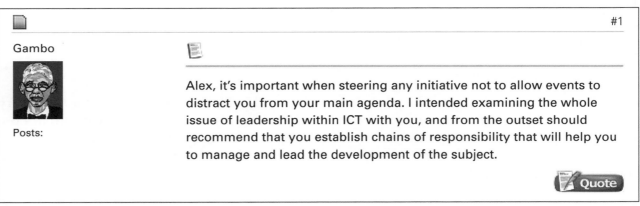

Gambo

Posts:

#1

Alex, it's important when steering any initiative not to allow events to distract you from your main agenda. I intended examining the whole issue of leadership within ICT with you, and from the outset should recommend that you establish chains of responsibility that will help you to manage and lead the development of the subject.

Quote

Toby

Posts:

#2

I've tweaked my file a little, I am backdating the review dates etc. as well it's quite an eye opener, a lot of the material is way out of date, and I mean years out of date. Gambo, I actually enjoy messing around with the equipment and have half a day to do so, do I have to give it up?

Quote

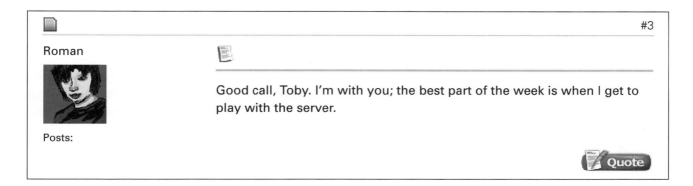

Roman

Posts:

#3

Good call, Toby. I'm with you; the best part of the week is when I get to play with the server.

Quote

6th September

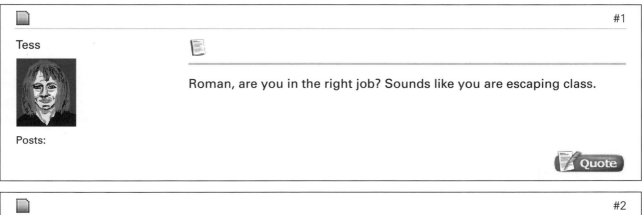

Tess

Posts:

#1

Roman, are you in the right job? Sounds like you are escaping class.

Quote

Roman

Posts:

#2

Tess, I just enjoy the break. Variety is the spice of life you know.

Quote

7th September

Gambo

Posts:

#1

In my experience every school is unique, but you have to ask yourself why you are given release time and whether it's good value for you to be doing the technician's job. There is plenty of strategic business for you to attend to, I should review this especially if I were your headteacher.

Quote

10th September

Week 2, Task 2 – Vision

Hopefully you have already been thinking about this and may have found an existing 'vision' for E-learning within your current ICT policy. There are going to be a wide variety of meetings and contexts within which you will need to 'sell' your ideas. There may be opposition from some quarters – staff, parents – as to where all of this technology is leading and you will need some strongly held core beliefs to draw upon. That is why it is worth spending a little time now putting your vision together.

In principle you need to decide how ICT can engage learners and enhance teaching and learning within your school.

Here is one example:

At ********** we recognize and value the use of ICT as a teaching and learning tool for both children and adults and seek to encourage pupils to become autonomous and independent in its use. We aim to develop a whole school approach to ICT that ensures continuity and progression and which develops the following core beliefs:

1 We believe that the rapid development of technology in the home, the workplace and the wider community has had and will continue to have an immense impact on the lives of individuals. Children need to develop a variety of ICT skills, which allow them to harness the power of technology and use it both purposefully and appropriately.

2 We believe that ICT is an important medium for learning and study at all educational levels and that through the effective use of ICT pupils and adults may enhance and extend learning opportunities and provide a powerful and motivating means to improve attainment in all curriculum areas.

3 We believe that the effective use of ICT allows pupils to communicate their ideas in a creative manner that reaches out beyond the classroom and which carries with it ethical implications and consequences.

The school ICT network is not only important for the children but for all learners at the school, including staff, governors and parents. As an essential skill for life I believe that school facilities have to serve that purpose. Hence, as the debate regarding the need for schools to retain an ICT suite is raised against the expansion of mobile equipment, I remain a supporter of the suite for exactly that purpose. I use this as an example of the vision directly impacting upon practice, strategy and actions.

Take a little time to formulate your ideas at this early stage before you are engulfed by the practicalities of managing the subject. Use your vision statement to encapsulate your core values. You may wish to emphasize the inclusive use of ICT, or the manner in which it promotes different styles of learning. Alternatively you may wish to talk about its balanced and effective use as a deterrent for overuse. Talk to colleagues so that you are not out on a limb; the school's ICT vision should mesh closely with its broader values and ethos.

Also now is a good time to develop your grasp of where E-learning is going. Begin to read around your subject and sample the thoughts of some leading writers in the field such as Marc Prensky or Alan November. Marc Prensky: 'Don't bother me Mom, I'm Learning' is rapidly becoming a formative ICT document (www.marcprensky.com): as is also Alan November's 'Empowering Students with Technology' (www.novemberlearning.com). Take time to develop your own views about where the technological revolution is ultimately going to lead.

11th September

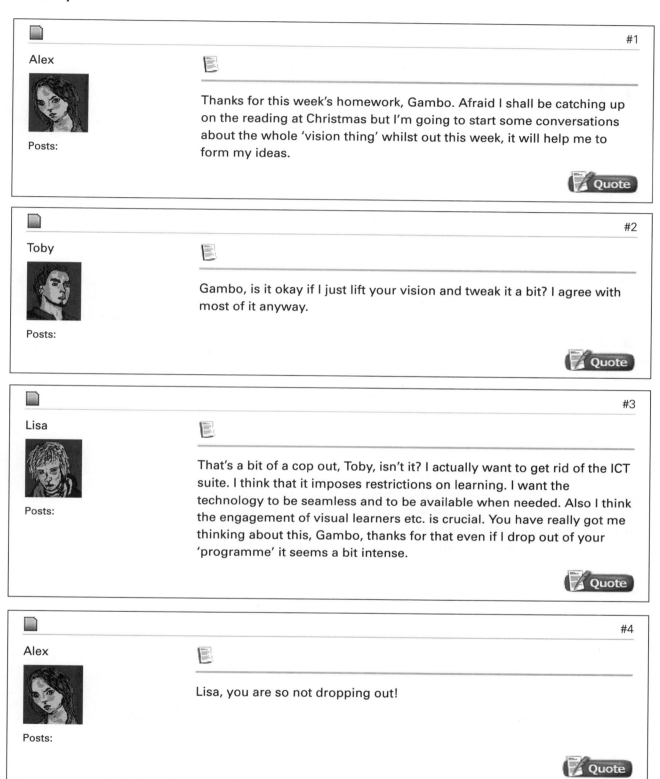

#1

Alex

Posts:

Thanks for this week's homework, Gambo. Afraid I shall be catching up on the reading at Christmas but I'm going to start some conversations about the whole 'vision thing' whilst out this week, it will help me to form my ideas.

Quote

#2

Toby

Posts:

Gambo, is it okay if I just lift your vision and tweak it a bit? I agree with most of it anyway.

Quote

#3

Lisa

Posts:

That's a bit of a cop out, Toby, isn't it? I actually want to get rid of the ICT suite. I think that it imposes restrictions on learning. I want the technology to be seamless and to be available when needed. Also I think the engagement of visual learners etc. is crucial. You have really got me thinking about this, Gambo, thanks for that even if I drop out of your 'programme' it seems a bit intense.

Quote

#4

Alex

Posts:

Lisa, you are so not dropping out!

Quote

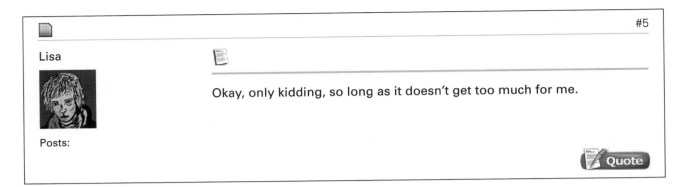

13th September

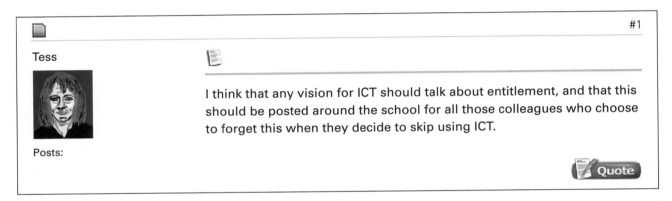

17th September

Week 3, Task 3 – Leadership

Figure 1.1 provides a model of leadership for ICT within the primary school. At the top is a role I refer to as the E-learning co-ordinator although the title in itself is not important; what is important is the requirement that this person is a member of the school's senior management team. The E-learning co-ordinator will have overall responsibility for the self-evaluation of ICT and for

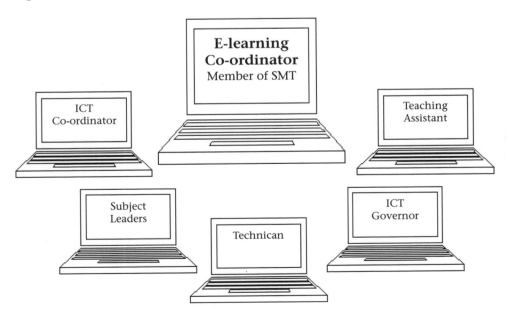

Figure 1.1 A model for E-learning leadership

Available on the net at http://www.sagepub.co.uk/wrightbk1

realizing the school's E-learning vision. They will be the lead figure in monitoring provision and progress and the main contributor to the school's self-evaluation form (SEF) with regard to ICT.

So who is this person? As ICT co-ordinator it may be you or it may be the role that you aspire to. The most likely scenario is that the ICT co-ordinator in effect leads the subject but feeds back to the E-learning co-ordinator, who may be the deputy headteacher, perhaps the headteacher or an assistant headteacher in a large school. The title may be largely nominal but there are key areas in which any ICT subject leader must be able to access senior management support, not least when we come to discuss E-safety and the role of the Internet safety co-ordinator.

You need to know who this person is within your school as they are going to make a crucial contribution to your success, or otherwise. Do not become isolated in the role of co-ordinator. I advocate a team of around six individuals (or roles) who are going to contribute to the ICT strategy. Furthermore, a team provides a sustainable system, one that will not simply collapse once the co-ordinator leaves. It is a very common scenario for a primary school to raise its profile off the back of a rising star as ICT co-ordinator; everything begins to take off, then suddenly they leave and the whole system collapses. You need to establish a collegiate approach that will sustain itself should individuals leave. That is the true test of its success. Your task is to be clear about the ICT team for your school, and who does what. I look forward to your feedback and will post again tomorrow to develop these ideas.

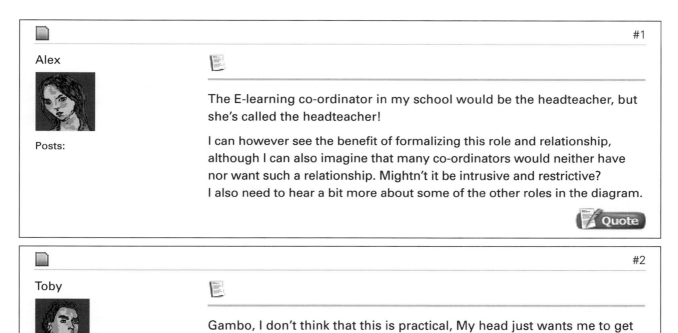

	#1
Alex	

The E-learning co-ordinator in my school would be the headteacher, but she's called the headteacher!

I can however see the benefit of formalizing this role and relationship, although I can also imagine that many co-ordinators would neither have nor want such a relationship. Mightn't it be intrusive and restrictive?
I also need to hear a bit more about some of the other roles in the diagram.

	#2
Toby	

Gambo, I don't think that this is practical, My head just wants me to get on with it and I should say that he is pretty supportive if I need something funding.

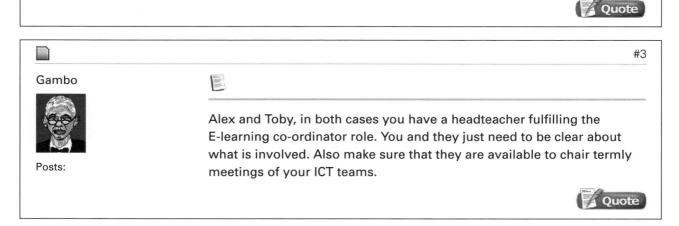

	#3
Gambo	

Alex and Toby, in both cases you have a headteacher fulfilling the E-learning co-ordinator role. You and they just need to be clear about what is involved. Also make sure that they are available to chair termly meetings of your ICT teams.

18th September

Other subject leaders

Each subject leader is responsible for developing the use of ICT within their subject area. If they are not doing this in your school then you will end up picking up the pieces and ICT will become marginalized. Establish this from the outset and you will be doing the school a big favour. Produce an action plan with the headteacher (E-learning co-ordinator) for each subject to be put 'on action' in terms of ICT. Incorporate monitoring observations and ask them to produce a plan for software and resource spending to present to the E-learning group's termly meeting. (Note the advantage of having some senior management authority behind you. If you become isolated none of this will be achieved.)

Technicians

I advocate that the school sets up a two-tier technical support service. First, you will need some form of formal contract or relationship with contractors who will ultimately manage your resources. I will address this in detail shortly; you do not want to worry about this during your first month in charge. Secondly, you should have some internal provision, probably in the form of a teaching assistant (TA) who has received some training to look after day-to-day technical duties. However, all we are determining at this point is who these people are in your school and tying them into the loop so that you are clear about communication and the monitoring of these systems.

ICT governor

Every school should have an ICT (E-learning) governor. It is not statutory but it is the hidden message that is relevant; it says that this is an important subject. Generally speaking you will not be able to be selective as governors will not be queuing up for the job, but you should try to bring one into your E-learning group.

It may be the case, as in many school's that you have real ICT expertise within your governing body. If so it is vital that you get this sorted out now. They will either be a total asset or a handicap that will hang over you throughout your time at the school. This is worth expanding upon.

There are many schools in which the ICT governor in effect co-ordinates the subject. They may use their own commercial experience and knowledge to interfere in the day-to-day management of the subject and to overrule every decision that you make. I believe that no matter how experienced they are they are never in a position to take over in this way. It is essential when setting your vision for E-learning that a clear pedagogy, grounded in sound primary education, embraces all that you aim to achieve. Make this clear and your governor will understand their role.

That said they will have extremely valuable expertise to share, but so have you. Establish an effective working relationship from the outset and then benefit from their support. The ICT governor should meet with you and the wider team on a regular basis with particular involvement in E-safety and all Health and Safety procedures relating to ICT.

To conclude, establish your team, decide upon a suitable meeting cycle and meet as soon as possible to discuss your vision and the results of your fact-finding review.

18th September

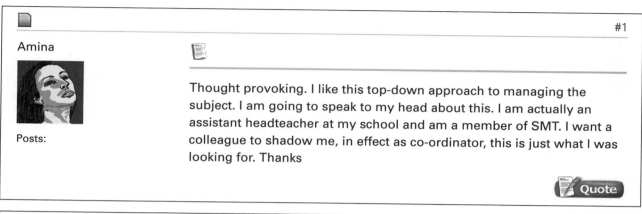

Amina

Posts:

#1

Thought provoking. I like this top-down approach to managing the subject. I am going to speak to my head about this. I am actually an assistant headteacher at my school and am a member of SMT. I want a colleague to shadow me, in effect as co-ordinator, this is just what I was looking for. Thanks

Quote

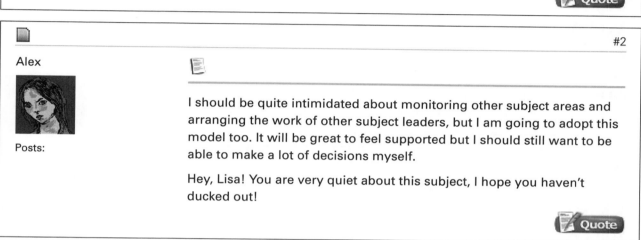

Alex

Posts:

#2

I should be quite intimidated about monitoring other subject areas and arranging the work of other subject leaders, but I am going to adopt this model too. It will be great to feel supported but I should still want to be able to make a lot of decisions myself.

Hey, Lisa! You are very quiet about this subject, I hope you haven't ducked out!

Quote

19th September

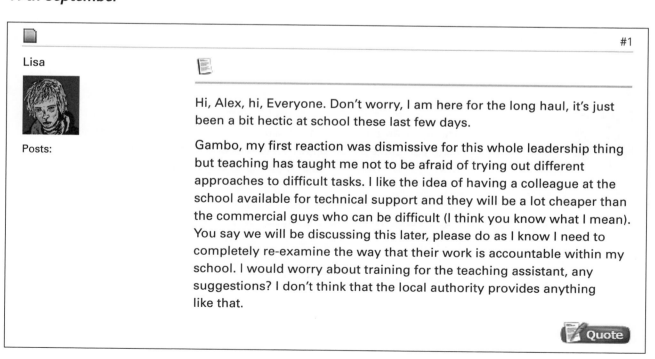

Lisa

Posts:

#1

Hi, Alex, hi, Everyone. Don't worry, I am here for the long haul, it's just been a bit hectic at school these last few days.

Gambo, my first reaction was dismissive for this whole leadership thing but teaching has taught me not to be afraid of trying out different approaches to difficult tasks. I like the idea of having a colleague at the school available for technical support and they will be a lot cheaper than the commercial guys who can be difficult (I think you know what I mean). You say we will be discussing this later, please do as I know I need to completely re-examine the way that their work is accountable within my school. I would worry about training for the teaching assistant, any suggestions? I don't think that the local authority provides anything like that.

Quote

#2

Alex

Posts:

Hi, Lisa, hope you are out of the heat at school now, you sound very focused!

Quote

#3

Toby

Posts:

Welcome back, Lisa! Work–life balance? Time management?

Quote

#4

Lisa

Posts:

Toby, I'll remind you of that when it's your next parents' evening.

Gambo, we've got two weeks to set up the meeting, right? I feel as though I am actually gaining control of events and beginning to set the agenda. Thanks!

Quote

#5

Alex

Posts:

Thanks, Gambo, I'm going to work on this over the next week or so. I also feel I have accomplished a lot already. Look forward to seeing the new plan for October. Lots of audits to begin I believe?

Quote

Chapter 2 • October

1st October

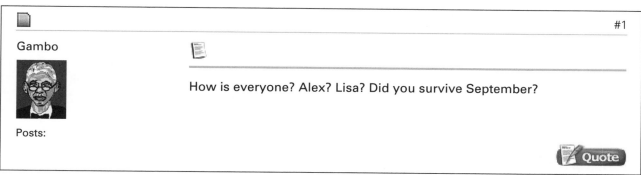

Gambo

Posts:

#1

How is everyone? Alex? Lisa? Did you survive September?

Quote

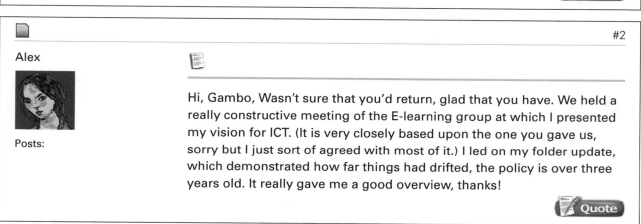

Alex

Posts:

#2

Hi, Gambo, Wasn't sure that you'd return, glad that you have. We held a really constructive meeting of the E-learning group at which I presented my vision for ICT. (It is very closely based upon the one you gave us, sorry but I just sort of agreed with most of it.) I led on my folder update, which demonstrated how far things had drifted, the policy is over three years old. It really gave me a good overview, thanks!

Quote

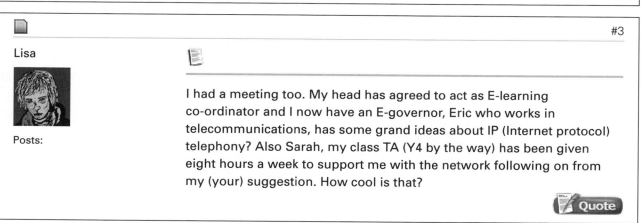

Lisa

Posts:

#3

I had a meeting too. My head has agreed to act as E-learning co-ordinator and I now have an E-governor, Eric who works in telecommunications, has some grand ideas about IP (Internet protocol) telephony? Also Sarah, my class TA (Y4 by the way) has been given eight hours a week to support me with the network following on from my (your) suggestion. How cool is that?

Quote

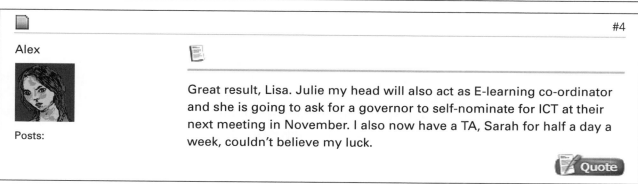

Alex

Posts:

#4

Great result, Lisa. Julie my head will also act as E-learning co-ordinator and she is going to ask for a governor to self-nominate for ICT at their next meeting in November. I also now have a TA, Sarah for half a day a week, couldn't believe my luck.

Quote

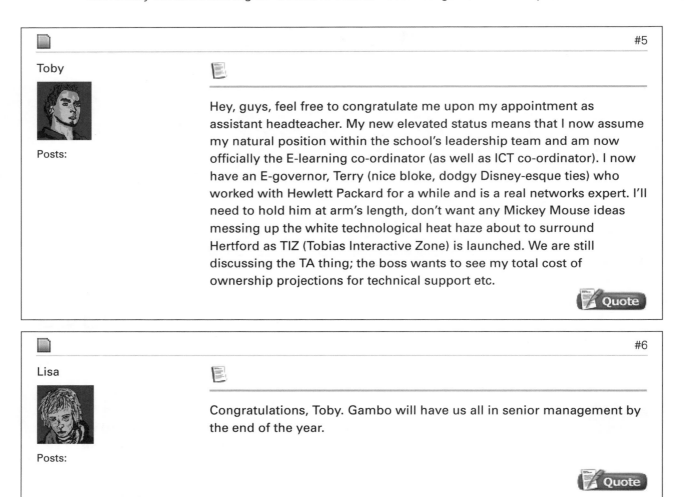

Toby

Posts:

#5

Hey, guys, feel free to congratulate me upon my appointment as assistant headteacher. My new elevated status means that I now assume my natural position within the school's leadership team and am now officially the E-learning co-ordinator (as well as ICT co-ordinator). I now have an E-governor, Terry (nice bloke, dodgy Disney-esque ties) who worked with Hewlett Packard for a while and is a real networks expert. I'll need to hold him at arm's length, don't want any Mickey Mouse ideas messing up the white technological heat haze about to surround Hertford as TIZ (Tobias Interactive Zone) is launched. We are still discussing the TA thing; the boss wants to see my total cost of ownership projections for technical support etc.

Quote

Lisa

Posts:

#6

Congratulations, Toby. Gambo will have us all in senior management by the end of the year.

Quote

2nd October

Throughout October you are going to commence three major audits:

1 A full network infrastructure review incorporating both hardware and software.
2 A strategic self-review to analyse where the school is developmentally in terms of E-learning.
3 A technical support audit to determine your network requirements in terms of time and costs and to assess the extent to which present provision is meeting these needs.

The three audits may be conducted concurrently as the findings from one will help to inform the other. They will take time and need to be completed thoroughly. In fact the strategic self-review will last until the end of term. Therefore, during October we shall tour the school to identify and register all hardware components; become familiar with the self-review online matrix and the rationale behind its usage; and complete the technical support review. Let us begin with the hardware audit.

Week 5, Task 4 – Hardware Audit

Whilst in theory you have a month to complete this task, there are other things to do so let us see if we can complete the hardware count this week. This is your opportunity to take ownership of the school network. That means knowing exactly what you have, its specification, where it is located, its maintenance history and serial number, and so on. If you have a TA you might get them to work with you on this. To clarify, I am not advocating that you have a technical overview or specific responsibilities for the hardware. I am suggesting that in a purely practical sense it is good to know what kit you have and that a bit of time invested now will pay dividends later on. This is not only for your benefit but will serve you well when applying for funding. What we

Table 2.1 Hardware audit template

Location:						
	Make S/N	Network	Date new	Specification	Monitor S/N	Supplier
Computer 1		Y/N		Processor GHz		
				Hard drive: Gb		
Computer 2		Y/N		Processor GHz		
				Hard drive: Gb		
Computer 3		Y/N		Processor GHz		
				Hard drive: Gb		
Computer 4		Y/N		Processor GHz		
				Hard drive: Gb		
Computer 5		Y/N		Processor GHz		
				Hard drive: Gb		
	Make S/N	Type	Date new	Specification	S/N	Supplier
Interactive whiteboard						
Data projector						
Printer						
Digital camera						
Other 1						
Other 2						
Other 3						
Notes						

Available on the net at http://www.sagepub.co.uk/wrightbk1

want, in effect, is an overview of the school so that you can make projections about where the ICT is going to occur, this year, next year, in three years' time.

Start with a plan of the school and conduct a systematic survey traversing the school and cross-referencing your plan with all hardware that you find. Complete a spreadsheet as you go around if you can take a laptop or personal digital assistant (PDA) with you. Ideally ask your TA to accompany you for an afternoon, thereafter get him or her to take over but do not lose ownership of the task. Remember to include teacher laptops and any management or administration machines.

Table 2.1 is an exemplar template that you may wish to complete for each area. The time this will take obviously depends upon the size of the school network. Include everything, such as any server details, routers, switches, and so on. By the end of the month you should have a comprehensive list of everything on the network, mapped against a diagram of the school. Next month we will use this spreadsheet to complete a software audit and to begin to plan how the network will expand and develop over the coming years as well as to identify what the technical support requirements are and so begin to produce some tentative funding projections.

3rd October

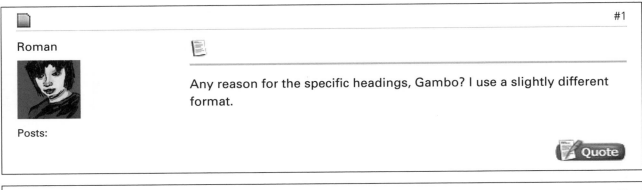

Roman

Posts:

Any reason for the specific headings, Gambo? I use a slightly different format.

Quote

#2

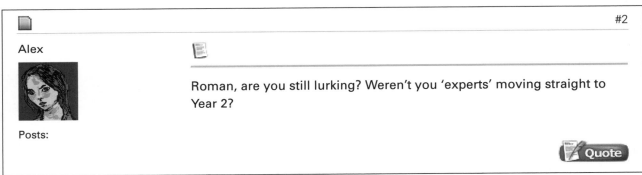

Alex

Posts:

Roman, are you still lurking? Weren't you 'experts' moving straight to Year 2?

Quote

#3

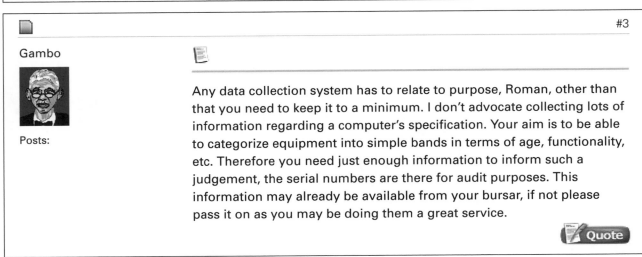

Gambo

Posts:

Any data collection system has to relate to purpose, Roman, other than that you need to keep it to a minimum. I don't advocate collecting lots of information regarding a computer's specification. Your aim is to be able to categorize equipment into simple bands in terms of age, functionality, etc. Therefore you need just enough information to inform such a judgement, the serial numbers are there for audit purposes. This information may already be available from your bursar, if not please pass it on as you may be doing them a great service.

Quote

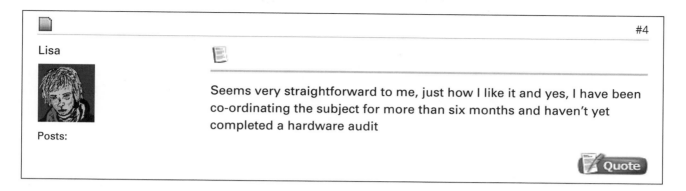

4th October

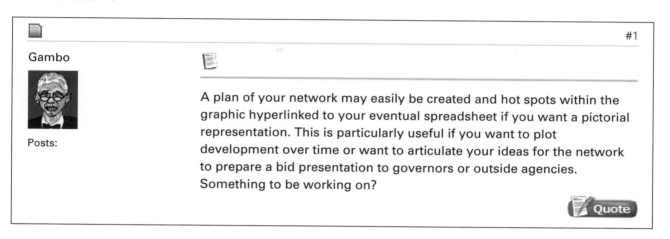

9th October

Week 6, Task 5 – Technical Support Audit

Despite modern information technology (IT) networks having been in schools for several years now, relatively few schools enjoy a robust and problem-free system. Technical support remains the most problematic area, whether you are the co-ordinator picking up the pieces each time something stops working, or the teacher earnestly trying to incorporate ICT into your lessons despite being frustrated by equipment that does not work as expected, or indeed the pupil who can not access the software they need, or their workspace, or can not save or print their work. Technical support of your network will potentially cause you more sleepless nights than anything else. It pays, therefore, to be clear from the outset what you are looking to achieve.

First let us be clear about the parameters. Your school will effectively have two networks – administration and curriculum. Your jurisdiction is the curriculum network. Your administration network, that is the headteacher's and office computers that host and transfer pupil data between yourself and the local authority, will almost certainly be maintained by the local authority as they have to ensure that the data is secure and that the systems are robust. They will also require certain minimum requirements to any other machines that are installed onto this network. Some of you will work in authorities that, as a result of measures to combine the curriculum and administration networks, are providing service level agreements for the curriculum machines also. Most likely, however, the school will be responsible for maintaining the curriculum network including teacher laptops etc. If this is the case in your school, now is the time to review how this will be accomplished. Your options will be:

1 Do it yourself, that is, staff employed by the school will be responsible for the running of the network.
2 Receive technical support from your link secondary school; possibly as part of that school's specialist status they may have committed to supporting cluster primary school links.
3 Employ a private commercial company via an annual contract to fulfil this function for you.
4 Employ an external contractor to firefight on an hourly rate as and when needed.
5 A combination of any of the above.

If you are not sure which system you presently employ, clarify this now. Maintaining a primary school network requires a balanced combination of specialized knowledge and time. I believe that the amount of time invested in the network is the critical factor in creating a robust system so that maintenance becomes proactive rather than reactive, developmental rather than firefighting. Invariably schools feel that they need to buy into specialized 'expert' managed services. This is fine if you can afford them. Costs for a fortnightly half-day visit from a commercial contractor will start at around £1,500 per annum, but that afternoon visit very rarely satisfies the school's requirements. If you have such a visit, you should consolidate this by employing a teaching assistant to cover part of the timetable to look after the day-to-day maintenance requirements, leaving your contractor to focus on the server and so on.

In an ideal world each school would employ its own expert technical staff, however, unless you are an extremely large primary school then this is not going to be possible, although you may be able to work with a cluster of schools to 'share' a qualified technician. Alternatively, you may have within your community a parent or student who can take on this work part time. As you complete your hardware audit try to form an understanding of your school's technical needs. A typical primary school will today have between 30 and 70 machines, probably running on a client server network. It is the inclusion of the server that places the demands of this network outside the lay person's ability to maintain and repair it. If advertising for a part-time technician be clear as to what is required of the post. In effect you need someone to:

● Monitor network use to ensure E-safety
● Maintain your network security and integrity via anti virus software and adequate back-up procedures
● Maintain a secure Internet and intranet connection
● Maintain and upgrade the network operating system as necessary
● Manage the Dynamic Host Configuration Protocol (DHCP) server (assign IP addresses to each personal computer [PC] accessing the Internet)
● Add and manage machines' access to the local area network
● Fault find and repair equipment as necessary
● Add software to the server and other machines on the network
● Manage print servers and so on.

This is not a definitive list but may help to demystify this area.

Your technical support audit should result in you feeding back to the ICT group a short annual report that addresses the following questions.

● Who is supporting your network? Try to move towards a sustainable mixed economy of support that is not overly reliant upon expensive commercial contracts.
● What service is being provided? Review the areas highlighted above. If you have a technical support contract in which technicians are constantly reinstalling printers and so on then it's probably not running efficiently.
● What is it costing?

Table 2.2 provides a crude but illuminating overview of the true cost of supporting a network. A half day of support per week is likely to cost between £1,500 and £3,500 which has to be provided from the school budget. If a qualified teacher (you) is providing this support, then spending an afternoon per week with the server is adding a hidden cost of £3,000 a year including on costs, more if you are higher up the pay scale. Apologies again to those co-ordinators who like to dabble, but to be effective you have to focus upon teaching and learning. Put the screwdriver away!

Table 2.2 Technical support comparative costs

	School technician TA	ICT co-ordinator	Commercial technician
1 day a week	£2,912 per annum*	£4,800 per annum#	£6,000 per annum
$\frac{1}{2}$ day a week	£1,456 per annum*	£2,400 per annum#	£3,500 per annum
$\frac{1}{2}$ day a fortnight	£728 per annum*	£1,200 per annum#	£2,000 per annum

Notes:
* Paid at £8 per hour (plus on costs, National Insurance contribution and so on).
# Based upon salary of £24,000 per annum (plus on costs).

Do contact the local authority and other cluster schools to get a sense of what is available in your area. This is something you can do immediately and there may already be support out there that your school has failed to tap into. If the local authority offers a service level agreement that is robust then it is probably wise to tap into this, as it is likely to be quite cost-effective. Above all, make sure that funding for the support is written into the budget and that it does not fall upon you to provide support without proper consideration of cost.

10th October

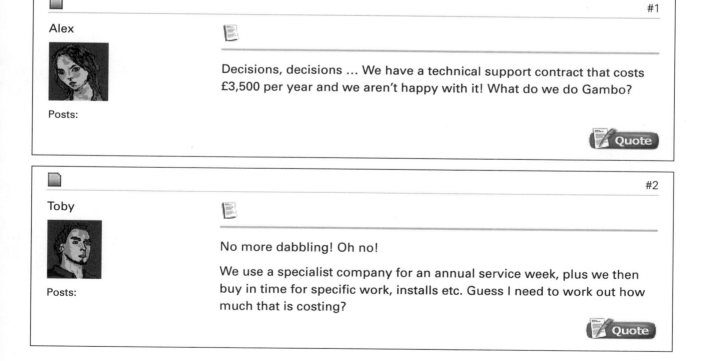

#1

Alex

Posts:

Decisions, decisions … We have a technical support contract that costs £3,500 per year and we aren't happy with it! What do we do Gambo?

Quote

#2

Toby

Posts:

No more dabbling! Oh no!

We use a specialist company for an annual service week, plus we then buy in time for specific work, installs etc. Guess I need to work out how much that is costing?

Quote

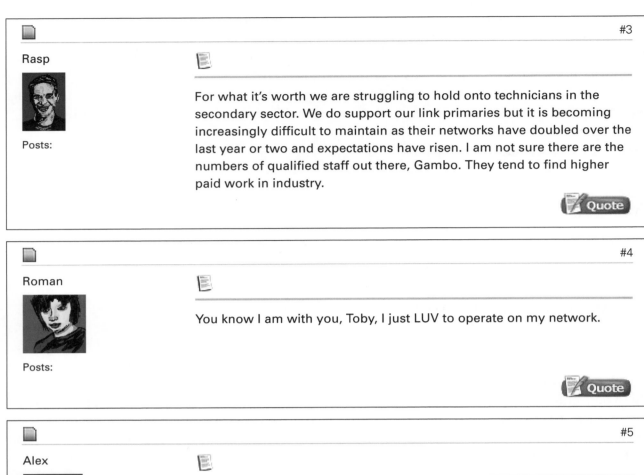

#3

Rasp

Posts:

For what it's worth we are struggling to hold onto technicians in the secondary sector. We do support our link primaries but it is becoming increasingly difficult to maintain as their networks have doubled over the last year or two and expectations have risen. I am not sure there are the numbers of qualified staff out there, Gambo. They tend to find higher paid work in industry.

Quote

#4

Roman

Posts:

You know I am with you, Toby, I just LUV to operate on my network.

Quote

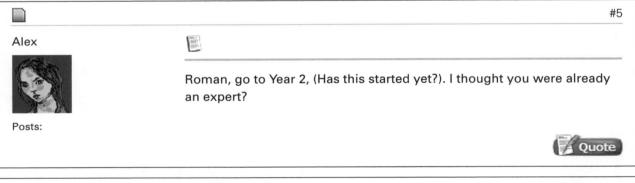

#5

Alex

Posts:

Roman, go to Year 2, (Has this started yet?). I thought you were already an expert?

Quote

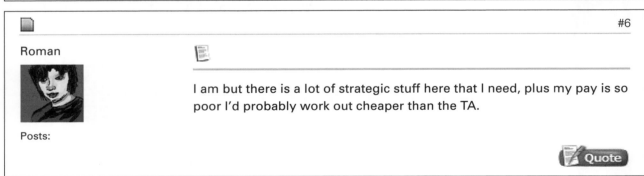

#6

Roman

Posts:

I am but there is a lot of strategic stuff here that I need, plus my pay is so poor I'd probably work out cheaper than the TA.

Quote

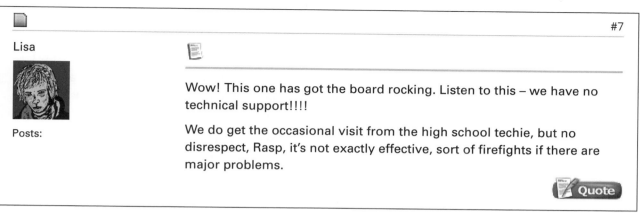

Lisa

Posts:

Wow! This one has got the board rocking. Listen to this – we have no technical support!!!!

We do get the occasional visit from the high school techie, but no disrespect, Rasp, it's not exactly effective, sort of firefights if there are major problems.

#7

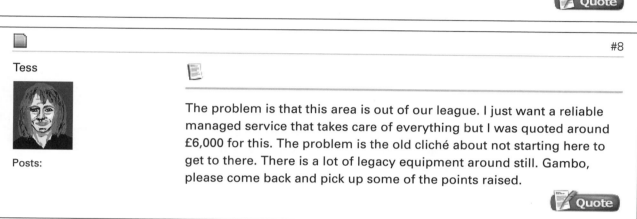

Tess

Posts:

The problem is that this area is out of our league. I just want a reliable managed service that takes care of everything but I was quoted around £6,000 for this. The problem is the old cliché about not starting here to get to there. There is a lot of legacy equipment around still. Gambo, please come back and pick up some of the points raised.

#8

11th October

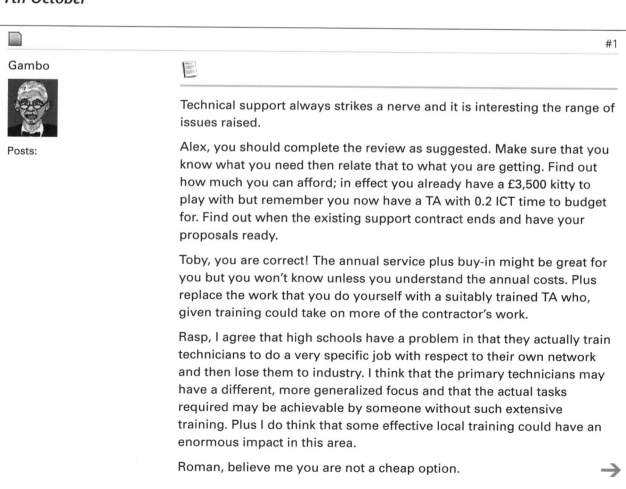

Gambo

Posts:

Technical support always strikes a nerve and it is interesting the range of issues raised.

Alex, you should complete the review as suggested. Make sure that you know what you need then relate that to what you are getting. Find out how much you can afford; in effect you already have a £3,500 kitty to play with but remember you now have a TA with 0.2 ICT time to budget for. Find out when the existing support contract ends and have your proposals ready.

Toby, you are correct! The annual service plus buy-in might be great for you but you won't know unless you understand the annual costs. Plus replace the work that you do yourself with a suitably trained TA who, given training could take on more of the contractor's work.

Rasp, I agree that high schools have a problem in that they actually train technicians to do a very specific job with respect to their own network and then lose them to industry. I think that the primary technicians may have a different, more generalized focus and that the actual tasks required may be achievable by someone without such extensive training. Plus I do think that some effective local training could have an enormous impact in this area.

Roman, believe me you are not a cheap option.

#1

Lisa, Your situation has to be corrected immediately; you simply cannot exist without some form of network management. Complete the review as suggested and liaise immediately via your E-learning co-ordinator for a £2,000 to £3,000 budget for technical support. Either you are already spending this invisibly through teacher downtime or your network won't be working properly and you are not delivering the curriculum.

Tess, I agree but the cost of the managed service on offer is only a problem if you can't afford it. School's have to understand the real cost of running their networks efficiently. Do look into the possibility of providing a second tier of support in-house. Remember my point about the knowledge–time balance. It is the time-consuming low-level maintenance that becomes disabling. With regard to the legacy equipment this again can be a poisoned chalice in terms of hidden costs. Ideally all of your equipment will be less than 3 years old and under warranty. Once you shine a light upon the true cost of maintaining that old stand-alone machine in Year 1 etc. it may not be cost-effective to keep.

For a more detailed guide to technical support take a look at the FITS (Framework for ICT Technical Support) materials that BECTA have produced (www.becta.org.uk/tsas).

Okay, I'll post again on the 23rd October when we will start the strategic review using the BECTA self-review framework. That gives you another ten days or so to formulate and deliver to your team your technical support strategy as well as completing the initial hardware audit. Have fun!

23rd October

Week 8, Task 6 – Strategic Audit and Self-Review 1

I earlier set the target of commencing the self-review framework from BECTA for this week. Let us just back pedal a little and establish the rationale for this. Successful E-enabled schools do not appear at random or by accident. They require clear subject leadership that involves vision (which we have already established) and careful planning in order for that vision to be realized. In order to be effective you have to be able to plan strategically. You need to oversee a wide range of areas that collectively form the ICT co-ordinators brief and at this early stage in your time as ICT co-ordinator you should audit and self-evaluate where the school is up to strategically against national criteria. In so doing you may benchmark your school and identify what needs to be done both in the short- and medium-term to progress to the next stage of development. Done effectively this strategic review will formulate activities that can go directly into a development or action plan. As with the hardware audit there are several models that may be adopted, however, I think that you would need to be on very secure ground to choose to ignore the national self-review model that BECTA introduced in April 2006. Until 2005 Naace (the National Association Advisors for Computing in Education) led in this field and nationally (UK) promoted the Naace Mark as a means to self-review. Now the UK government has actively promoted the idea of a universal 'model of maturity' that all schools should pursue. BECTA was commissioned to work with partners such as Naace (National Association of Advisers for Computers Education), Ofsted, NCSL (National College for School Leadership), TDA (Training and Development Agency) and the national strategies to provide an online matrix for this review that covered the eight core strategic elements that will now align with those used when setting up your subject leader file. Ultimately schools that score highly during self-review may go on to apply for the ICT Mark award.

The online framework details the areas that you need to reflect upon and provides a lot of materials to support self-evaluation using the eight key elements. The evaluation can be done online at http://matrix.becta.org.uk.

You should discuss the school's participation within the ICT team that has been established and ultimately agree who completes which part of the review, however in the first instance ensure that the school is registered and browse the matrix to get an overview of what is involved. Familiarize yourself with its layout and the sort of questions that may involve input from the wider team. Do not feel rushed to fill anything in although there is no harm in trying it out as you can always review each judgement at a later date. Next month we will actually aim to complete the audit and in December we can tackle the action planning elements. If you have not already done so, use your E-Learning co-ordinator to access staff meeting time next month to deliver the framework to staff, ideally a whole meeting at the start of the month or regular ten-minute slots to put the review clearly upon the school's agenda. Let us try to get under the surface of this a little more. As strategic leader, the maturity model upon which the matrix is based is worth examining a little more closely. It will be helpful to understand what each of the five levels represents within each strand. They are:

Level 5 – Localized use, typically at this stage a school's use of ICT will rely upon individual teacher innovation. Good practice is not disseminated nor embedded across the school.

Level 4 – Internal co-ordination, ICT develops in a bottom-up manner. Where resources are developed that are judged to be effective then they may be shared. There will be an overall school plan that oversees individual use of ICT.

Level 3 – Process redesign, typically the school's ICT strategy is developed to an extent where the systems operate in a more top-down manner. Processes are redesigned as ICT impacts upon school practice.

Level 2 – Network redesigns and embedding, when school systems have been redesigned as a result of ICT these are now secure and embedded. Note that this is generally, although not always, the threshold indicative of the national ICT Mark standard.

Level 1 – Redefinition and innovative use when ICT will provide new add-on services to learners, new learning experiences that innovate and redefine the learning environment.

Our two-year challenge is to become ICT Mark accredited, that is, to broadly reach Level 2 categorization against most of the elements, strands and aspects of the framework.

We will be looking at this review throughout the rest of the term but I suggest that this week you focus upon registering your school and establishing access rights before familiarizing yourself with the overall content of the framework. In the first instance register the school using the DfES (Department for Education and Skills) number and register yourself as administrator – this enables you to allocate different users password access to different areas of the site using tokens. If you are not the E-learning co-ordinator it may be that this manager registers the school and themselves as administrator, providing you with authorized access. I suspect that you are probably the best person to administer the system and should take a look at it now before I go on. Post your feedback via the blog.
Good Luck!

24th October

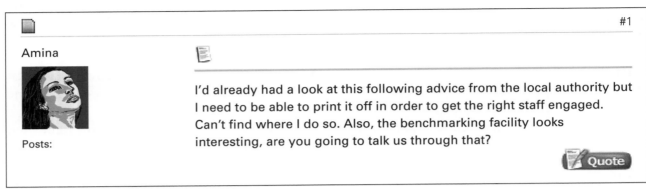

Amina

Posts:

#1

I'd already had a look at this following advice from the local authority but I need to be able to print it off in order to get the right staff engaged. Can't find where I do so. Also, the benchmarking facility looks interesting, are you going to talk us through that?

Quote

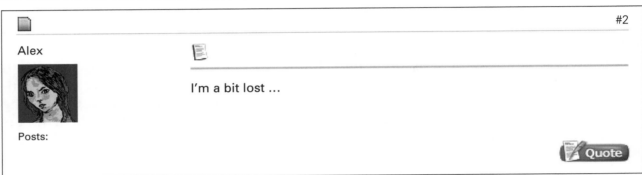

Alex

Posts:

#2

I'm a bit lost ...

Quote

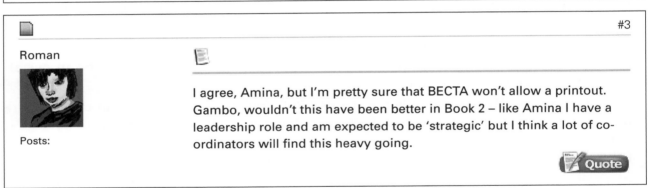

Roman

Posts:

#3

I agree, Amina, but I'm pretty sure that BECTA won't allow a printout. Gambo, wouldn't this have been better in Book 2 – like Amina I have a leadership role and am expected to be 'strategic' but I think a lot of co-ordinators will find this heavy going.

Quote

25th October

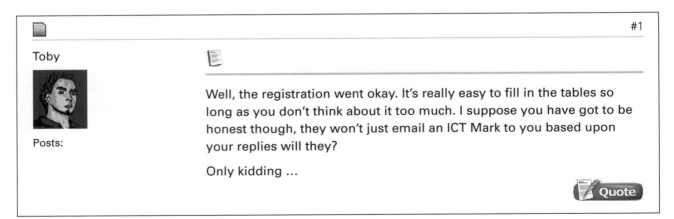

Toby

Posts:

#1

Well, the registration went okay. It's really easy to fill in the tables so long as you don't think about it too much. I suppose you have got to be honest though, they won't just email an ICT Mark to you based upon your replies will they?

Only kidding ...

Quote

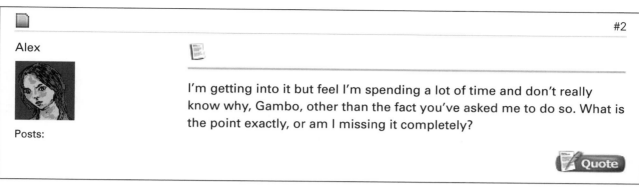

Alex

Posts:

#2

I'm getting into it but feel I'm spending a lot of time and don't really know why, Gambo, other than the fact you've asked me to do so. What is the point exactly, or am I missing it completely?

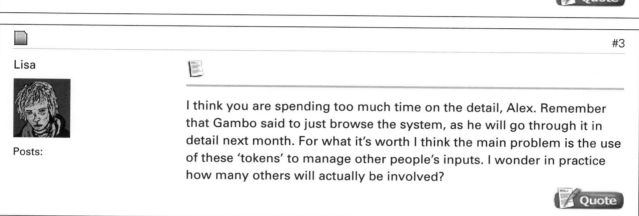

Lisa

Posts:

#3

I think you are spending too much time on the detail, Alex. Remember that Gambo said to just browse the system, as he will go through it in detail next month. For what it's worth I think the main problem is the use of these 'tokens' to manage other people's inputs. I wonder in practice how many others will actually be involved?

26th October

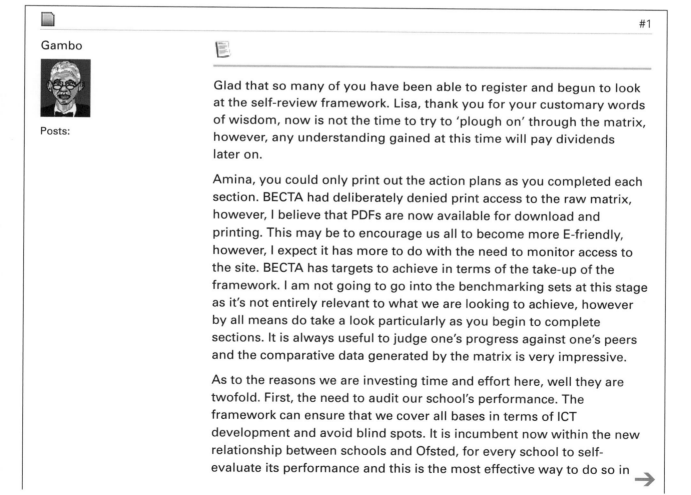

Gambo

Posts:

#1

Glad that so many of you have been able to register and begun to look at the self-review framework. Lisa, thank you for your customary words of wisdom, now is not the time to try to 'plough on' through the matrix, however, any understanding gained at this time will pay dividends later on.

Amina, you could only print out the action plans as you completed each section. BECTA had deliberately denied print access to the raw matrix, however, I believe that PDFs are now available for download and printing. This may be to encourage us all to become more E-friendly, however, I expect it has more to do with the need to monitor access to the site. BECTA has targets to achieve in terms of the take-up of the framework. I am not going to go into the benchmarking sets at this stage as it's not entirely relevant to what we are looking to achieve, however by all means do take a look particularly as you begin to complete sections. It is always useful to judge one's progress against one's peers and the comparative data generated by the matrix is very impressive.

As to the reasons we are investing time and effort here, well they are twofold. First, the need to audit our school's performance. The framework can ensure that we cover all bases in terms of ICT development and avoid blind spots. It is incumbent now within the new relationship between schools and Ofsted, for every school to self-evaluate its performance and this is the most effective way to do so in terms of ICT. If you choose another system you need to be on very secure ground as to why you rejected the national model and chose a different one that was more appropriate for your school. Secondly, in order to be effective you need to plan and to execute actions that will address the school's ICT needs. This again is the most effective means of doing so. In the third part of the review (December) we will directly tackle the framework's action planning functions. Trust me on this, by Christmas you will have gained a thorough command of the strategic direction in which the school is heading and will have clear actions to achieve your goals. Finally, yes Toby, honesty is essential. To create an artificial picture of the school's position would help no one and would ultimately mean that no suitable actions were generated to take the school forward. Furthermore, an external assessor awards the ICT Mark. This again, along with the benchmarking aspect, we can pick up at a later date.

Quote

Chapter 3 • *November*

1st November

We are midway through your first term as ICT co-ordinator, or possibly as the E-learning co-ordinator and the team structure that was arranged in September will be very important with regard to the self-review audit that we will be discussing this month. If you are not clear about specific roles, now might be a good time to hold that conversation within the team. During November we shall build upon October's audits as follows:

1 Complete the BECTA self-review framework and in so doing enlist the commitment of all staff towards the school's E-learning strategy
2 Undertake a software audit to confirm the status of existing licences, the capacity and suitability of your curriculum software and capacity to sustain E-Learning once the direct funding of E-learning credits has ceased
3 Begin a review of provision for the discrete ICT curriculum to establish how core skills have traditionally been taught and their impact upon pupils' learning.

Week 9, Task 7 – Strategic Audit and Self-Review 2

Table 3.1 provides an overview of the eight key elements of the self-review matrix and incorporates the main strands for each element. In addition I have indicated which person from within the ICT team I believe should lead on this section (emboldened) and also which colleagues might support that evaluation. The key point being that it is not the sole responsibility of the ICT co-ordinator to complete the matrix in isolation simply to produce another document for relevant senior colleagues; indeed, if you were to do so you would certainly miss an excellent opportunity to activate the support of key colleagues. Clearly the key responsibility for completing and co-ordinating the form lies with the E-learning co-ordinator given that their brief is specifically cross-curricular and carries senior management status in order to engage colleagues, access staff meeting time and impact swiftly and directly upon the school's self-evaluation and improvement planning processes. Clarify whether this person is you, if not be sure to revisit the section relating to developing the ICT team to ensure it is coherent.

Strategically you need to ensure that the self-review audit becomes a whole-school issue, that is probably your main success criterion.

Has the whole staff, or at least have key staff, engaged with the self-review process and in so doing gained insight into the issues facing the school on its journey towards E-confidence?

Launch the 'event' at a staff meeting, negotiate ten minutes for updates throughout the month if you are spreading the task throughout November, or take the whole meeting and divide it between a collective launch and then split up to actually allow time for completion. Remember the administration, access passwords and so on were completed last month. If you are the 'administrator' you will already have identified key staff who will have been provided with 'tokens' to access their respective elements. Staff may work upon their element during PPA (planning, preparation and assessment) time or in small groups during team meetings or in place of staff meetings before coming together as a whole staff to discuss the outcomes. Be aware that the review will raise issues for staff and that this is good. Over the next few pages I shall explore each element in turn before addressing any issues that arise via the blog.

Table 3.1 Self-review framework element: leadership

Element	Strand	Responsible officer
1 – Leadership and Management	1a. Vision 1b. Strategy 1c. Use of management information systems 1d. 1 Monitoring and evaluation	**E-learning co-ordinator**
		ICT co-ordinator
		ICT governor
2 – Curriculum	2a. The planned ICT curriculum 2b. Pupils' actual ICT experiences 2c. Curriculum leadership and review	**ICT co-ordinator**
		E-Learning co-ordinator
		Other subject leaders/SENCO
3 – Learning and teaching	3a. Teachers' planning, use and evaluation 3b. Learning with ICT 3c. Leadership of learning and teaching	**Other subject leaders/SENCO**
		E-Learning co-ordinator
		ICT co-ordinator
4 – Assessment	4a. Assessment of, and with, ICT	**ICT co-ordinator**
		E-Learning co-ordinator
		Other subject leaders/SENCO
5 – Professional Development	5a. Planning 5b. Implementation 5c. Review	**E-learning co-ordinator**
		ICT co-ordinator
		ICT governor
6 – Extended Opportunities for Learning	6a. Awareness and understanding 6b. Planning and implementation	**E-learning co-ordinator**
		Other subject leaders/SENCO
		ICT governor
7 – Resources	7a. Provision 7b. Access 7c. Management	**E-learning co-ordinator**
		Technical support/TA
		ICT co-ordinator
8 – Impact on Pupil Outcomes	8a. Pupils' progress in ICT capability 8b. Pupils' progress more widely 8c. Attitudes and behaviour	**E-learning co-ordinator**
		ICT co-ordinator
		Other subject leaders/SENCO

Available on the net at http://www.sagepub.co.uk/wrightbk1

2nd November

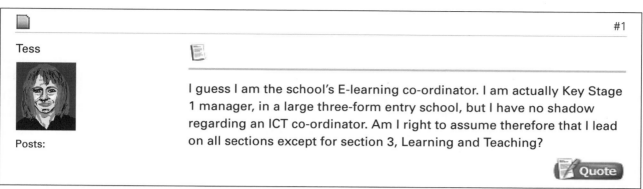

Tess

Posts:

#1

I guess I am the school's E-learning co-ordinator. I am actually Key Stage 1 manager, in a large three-form entry school, but I have no shadow regarding an ICT co-ordinator. Am I right to assume therefore that I lead on all sections except for section 3, Learning and Teaching?

Quote

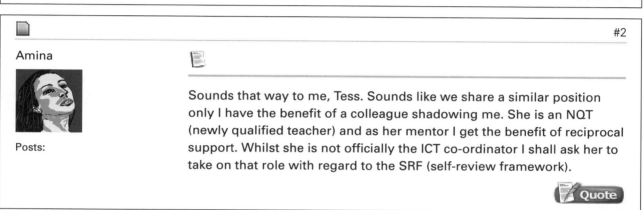

Amina

Posts:

#2

Sounds that way to me, Tess. Sounds like we share a similar position only I have the benefit of a colleague shadowing me. She is an NQT (newly qualified teacher) and as her mentor I get the benefit of reciprocal support. Whilst she is not officially the ICT co-ordinator I shall ask her to take on that role with regard to the SRF (self-review framework).

Quote

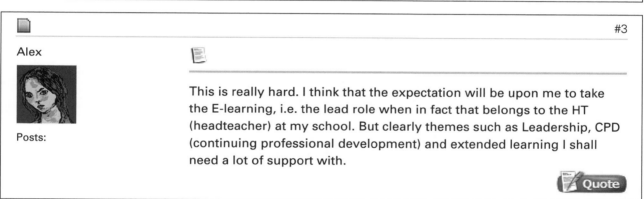

Alex

Posts:

#3

This is really hard. I think that the expectation will be upon me to take the E-learning, i.e. the lead role when in fact that belongs to the HT (headteacher) at my school. But clearly themes such as Leadership, CPD (continuing professional development) and extended learning I shall need a lot of support with.

Quote

3rd November

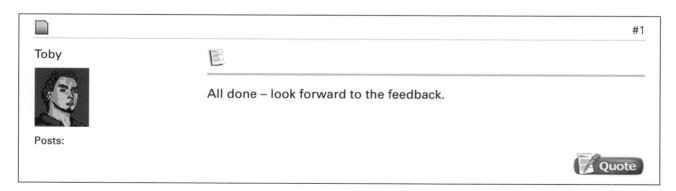

Toby

Posts:

#1

All done – look forward to the feedback.

Quote

6th November

Element 1 – Leadership and Management

This first element is strategic and will help to reconcile a lot of the work you have already completed in terms of vision, and the action plan will provide you with 'next steps' to move the school on. A senior manager should complete this element. This person may be the E-learning co-ordinator but for many schools will be the headteacher or deputy headteacher supported by the ICT co-ordinator. The ICT governor will also need to have sight of this portion of the review. They may choose to access it from home once a token has been provided and the co-ordinator has initially completed it. This will provide governors with an opportunity to question and to challenge the school's ICT strategy as well as providing a clear strategic brief to feed back to the broader governing body. Alternatively there is no reason why a governor should not come into school and work alongside staff as the form is completed. Governors may take a particular interest in strand 1b-5 that relates to budgetary effectiveness. Strands that relate to the use of management information systems (for example, Schools Information Management System (SIMS)) will require further senior manager engagement; it might also be an idea to involve your assessment co-ordinator if they have not already been engaged. Likewise security and safety elements are critical for the headteacher (who may delegate to a senior manager (E-learning co-ordinator) and to the governor).

At the risk of repeating myself, I cannot overstate that an ICT co-ordinator who is not a senior manager at the school should not be completing this element in isolation.

Element 2 – Curriculum

This element will most directly relate to the operational work of the ICT co-ordinator and/or the E-learning co-ordinator, however, all other subject leaders will need to engage with a number of the strands as they relate to the development of ICT across each curriculum area. This is another powerful way of transmitting this message regarding the development of the school's curriculum. Section 2c relates directly to curriculum leadership, development and review with regard to ICT. I think that it would be ideal for subject leaders to work in pairs to complete these strands and to gain ownership of the action points that are likely to be generated.

Element 3 – Learning and Teaching

The third element follows on directly from that of curriculum and needs to feature your subject leaders. Logically this can be completed at the same time as Element 2. The emphasis placed upon inclusion requires input from your special needs co-ordinator (SENCO), and once again I feel that this provides a strong awareness-raising opportunity and creates a common reference point for your future work with colleagues. You may already be seeing the benefit of the SRF as a process that schools can work through as a team.

It also brings ICT to the heart of learning and challenges schools where the use of technology remains peripheral. The E-learning co-ordinator will need to bring together colleagues' responses and produce a planned strategy for developing ICT as a learning and teaching tool.

I shall post again in a couple of days time regarding the next three elements of the framework. It would be helpful if comments added to the blog in the meantime focus upon Elements 1, 2 and 3.

7th November

#1

Alex

Posts:

Gambo, your review of the matrix has been very helpful in the absence of a printout to show to colleagues. We shall be completing it at the end of the month when ICT is on action and I have the full backing of the headteacher to host a staff meeting and team meetings. That means that the school is heavily investing in the project so I trust you that I shall get a return on this. Julie, the HT, is the administrator and will complete Element 1 at home (she says) this week. Will post any early feedback that I get.

Quote

#2

Guest

Posts:

I have registered as a guest, hope colleagues (Alex) don't mind my posting upon your blog. I am actually a headteacher at a Wiltshire primary school as well as being the school's ICT co-ordinator; I guess I am the classic E-learning co-ordinator. The school has NAACE-Mark accreditation. I followed the adviser's comments regarding using the SRF as a means of getting staff engaged with the whole-school E-learning strategy and have found that it has acted like a search light illuminating myself and colleagues to a multitude of areas, strategic issues, that hadn't appeared upon our radar. I wanted to particularly comment about the MIS (management information system) aspects of Element 1. It quickly became apparent that the school lacked a strategy for data management to sit alongside the curriculum plan. Traditionally the two elements had always been kept apart. I think many schools will struggle to score highly on these criteria that place great store in teacher access to data and data sharing in general. That said, the project has provided clear targets for my school team to address. I look forward to logging in and following the debate on a regular basis.

Quote

#3

Roman

Posts:

I think this has gone okay for me. I've got a lot out of working with the other subject leaders who've now got a better idea what is involved in my role. The SENCO may be problematic though! ... Anyone else spend a lot of time on 3a-2?

'Planning for ICT as a means of developing inclusion.' We scored Level 4 on that one!

Quote

Tess

Posts:

It's where we go from here that interests me now. As an audit this has been very useful, but now that the pig has been weighed as they say, its time to fatten it up a bit.

Quote

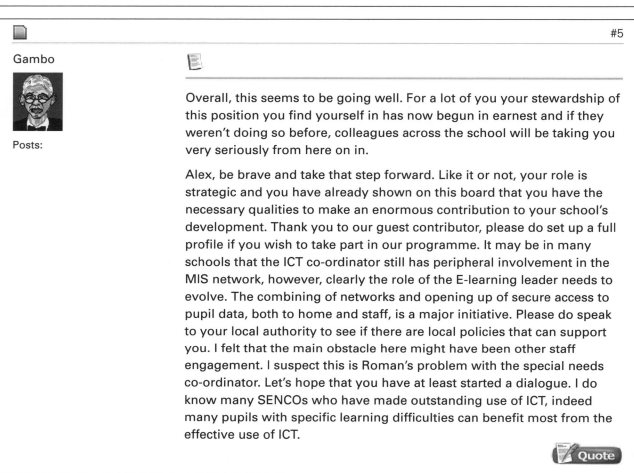

Gambo

Posts:

Overall, this seems to be going well. For a lot of you your stewardship of this position you find yourself in has now begun in earnest and if they weren't doing so before, colleagues across the school will be taking you very seriously from here on in.

Alex, be brave and take that step forward. Like it or not, your role is strategic and you have already shown on this board that you have the necessary qualities to make an enormous contribution to your school's development. Thank you to our guest contributor, please do set up a full profile if you wish to take part in our programme. It may be in many schools that the ICT co-ordinator still has peripheral involvement in the MIS network, however, clearly the role of the E-learning leader needs to evolve. The combining of networks and opening up of secure access to pupil data, both to home and staff, is a major initiative. Please do speak to your local authority to see if there are local policies that can support you. I felt that the main obstacle here might have been other staff engagement. I suspect this is Roman's problem with the special needs co-ordinator. Let's hope that you have at least started a dialogue. I do know many SENCOs who have made outstanding use of ICT, indeed many pupils with specific learning difficulties can benefit most from the effective use of ICT.

Quote

8th November

Element 4 – Assessment

I think that this element is relatively straightforward. The ICT co-ordinator should lead because of the central place given here to the assessment of ICT as a core subject. This in my experience remains the weakest area of ICT for a variety of reasons that we shall discuss in detail at a later date. For now you will have a chance to reflect upon the range of assessments and record-keeping systems for ICT that are employed at your school. Clearly there is a role here for the assessment co-ordinator, who will not only have an opinion regarding the initial strands but will need a significant involvement relating to the use of ICT as a tool to assist assessment, possibly incorporating online systems that automate marking tasks and generate analyses for teachers. There is also a senior management focus here, hence the involvement of the E-learning co-ordinator, who will also support your response to the target-setting section.

Element 5 – Professional Development

When planning staff CPD for ICT it is essential that you have an understanding of the whole-school context, hence the need for the E-learning co-ordinator to lead this element. Successful schools will operate a top-down approach which demonstrates a mature ongoing commitment to staff development based upon an understanding of what is needed to sustain quality teaching and learning opportunities that keep pace with ever-increasing change. Contrast this with fire-fighting ad hoc systems in which training is reactive and often a last resort. Links with monitoring and development make it desirable for the ICT governor to engage with this element also, and they will value the opportunity to work alongside staff whilst gaining real insight into how the school strategy evolves in order to match the needs of the learner.

Element 6 – Extending Opportunities for Learning

Once again the E-learning co-ordinator will lead the completion of this element. It is challenging for many schools as it deals with the whole 'Extended Schools' agenda, which is new and far from being embedded within schools. Governor involvement will again be beneficial. Do not be too concerned at this stage if a lot of progress has yet to be made against some of the strands. The benchmarking data should reassure your headteacher that you are not alone in needing to develop strategy in this area. Your school may have personalization standards funding that could be used to address many of the issues and targets raised by the self-assessment. Ultimately it is what the school does as a result of the appraisal that is most important, not the appraisal itself.

9th November

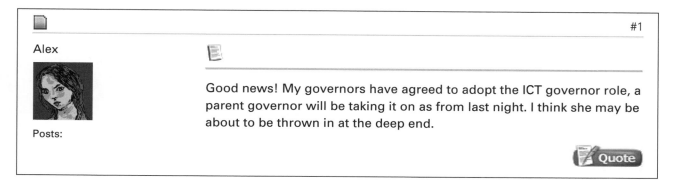

Alex

Posts:

#1

Good news! My governors have agreed to adopt the ICT governor role, a parent governor will be taking it on as from last night. I think she may be about to be thrown in at the deep end.

Quote

10th November

Element 7 – Resources

The lead officer is the E-learning co-ordinator supported by the ICT co-ordinator and either the in-house TA who supports the upkeep of the network resources or, possibly, external ICT support through discussion with the ICT co-ordinator. The first few pages deal with general resource issues and are relatively straightforward, however, subsequent strands, which address issues of access to management systems, will again prove challenging to a lot of schools. Finally, section 7c deals with procurement procedures with regard to total cost of ownership and will certainly require some senior management input.

Element 8 – Impact on Pupil Outcomes

The final element to be reviewed will be led by the E-learning co-ordinator supported by the ICT co-ordinator and other subject leaders. This element which deals with impact is a significant addition to the Naace-Mark framework and standards that preceded the self-review framework. Created in partnership with Ofsted it sets out to indicate what impact the investment in ICT has had upon learning. Its three strands deal, first, with respect to the discrete ICT subject area and then as a cross-curricular tool including its use to promote thinking skills and creativity. The final strand within this section asks colleagues to judge the manner in which attitudes, behaviour and motivation have been affected by ICT. Decisions made here will need to be quantified and broad-ranging discussions regarding the adoption of ICT within your school may need to be completed prior to, during and following the completion of this section of the matrix.

11th November

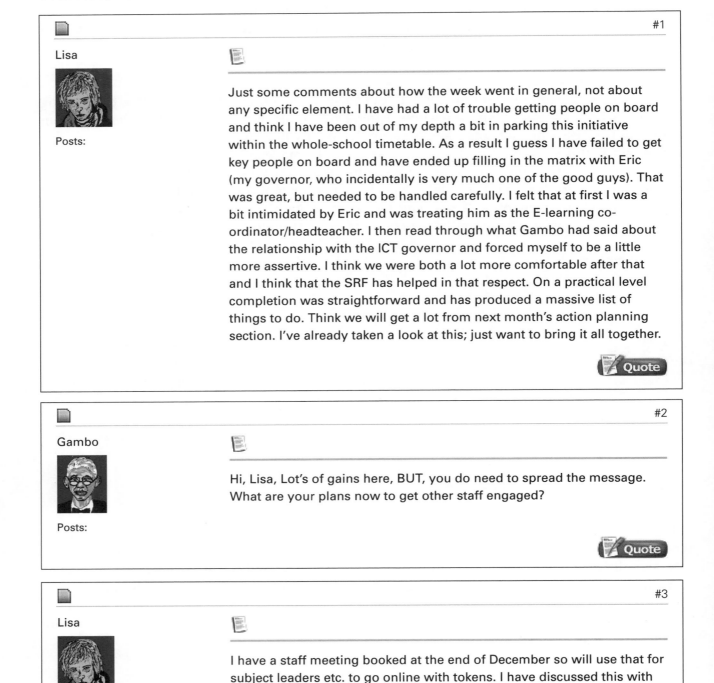

#1

Lisa

Posts:

Just some comments about how the week went in general, not about any specific element. I have had a lot of trouble getting people on board and think I have been out of my depth a bit in parking this initiative within the whole-school timetable. As a result I guess I have failed to get key people on board and have ended up filling in the matrix with Eric (my governor, who incidentally is very much one of the good guys). That was great, but needed to be handled carefully. I felt that at first I was a bit intimidated by Eric and was treating him as the E-learning co-ordinator/headteacher. I then read through what Gambo had said about the relationship with the ICT governor and forced myself to be a little more assertive. I think we were both a lot more comfortable after that and I think that the SRF has helped in that respect. On a practical level completion was straightforward and has produced a massive list of things to do. Think we will get a lot from next month's action planning section. I've already taken a look at this; just want to bring it all together.

Quote

#2

Gambo

Posts:

Hi, Lisa, Lot's of gains here, BUT, you do need to spread the message. What are your plans now to get other staff engaged?

Quote

#3

Lisa

Posts:

I have a staff meeting booked at the end of December so will use that for subject leaders etc. to go online with tokens. I have discussed this with the HT who is really onboard for shared ownership etc.

Quote

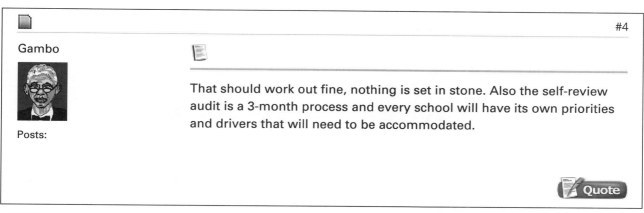

Gambo

Posts:

That should work out fine, nothing is set in stone. Also the self-review audit is a 3-month process and every school will have its own priorities and drivers that will need to be accommodated.

#4

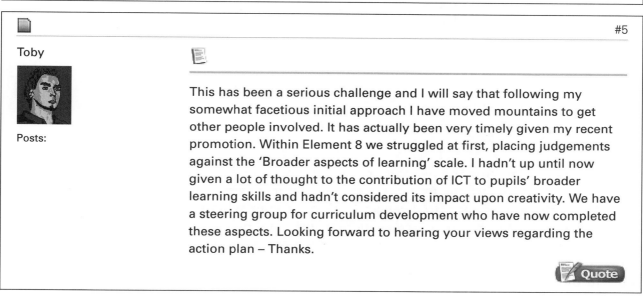

Toby

Posts:

This has been a serious challenge and I will say that following my somewhat facetious initial approach I have moved mountains to get other people involved. It has actually been very timely given my recent promotion. Within Element 8 we struggled at first, placing judgements against the 'Broader aspects of learning' scale. I hadn't up until now given a lot of thought to the contribution of ICT to pupils' broader learning skills and hadn't considered its impact upon creativity. We have a steering group for curriculum development who have now completed these aspects. Looking forward to hearing your views regarding the action plan – Thanks.

#5

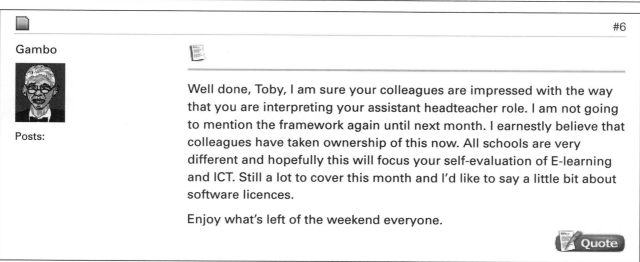

Gambo

Posts:

Well done, Toby, I am sure your colleagues are impressed with the way that you are interpreting your assistant headteacher role. I am not going to mention the framework again until next month. I earnestly believe that colleagues have taken ownership of this now. All schools are very different and hopefully this will focus your self-evaluation of E-learning and ICT. Still a lot to cover this month and I'd like to say a little bit about software licences.

Enjoy what's left of the weekend everyone.

#6

13th November

Week 11, Task 8 – Completing a Network Software Audit

The software review follows on from last month's hardware audit and shares its objective from your standpoint of providing you with an overview of resources available within the school and the degree to which they are well matched to the school needs both now and in the medium-term future. However, principally you will be assessing the school's position with relation to Figure 3.1

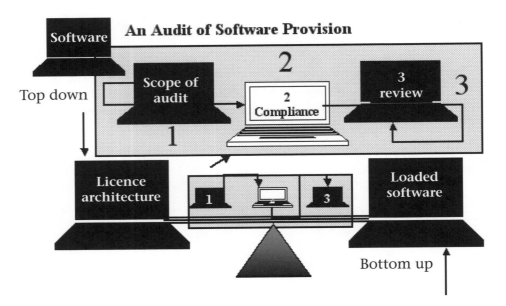

Figure 3.1 Software audit template

Available on the net at http://www.sagepub.co.uk/wrightbk1

The diagram represents the two core tasks that you should complete this week and demonstrates the need to balance the two with reference to three overriding considerations. You have to identify all the existing software licences in place at your school and reconcile these with the actual software loaded and used across the network. The two approaches to the review should balance. However, if this activity has not been undertaken for some time it is unlikely they will do so, in which case you will need to resolve any imbalance. In assessing the order of the balance, you will incorporate the key themes set across Figure 3.1 in order to complete a review next month to identify future issues that may need immediate action.

You will clarify your understanding of the audit's scope of enquiry, that is what to include and what to leave out. Gain an understanding of national and international copyright compliance legislation and review licence agreements to ensure that best value is in place.

Scope of review

Virtually all software products will require licences to cover their use, which may be in the form of a one-off document or even CD (compact disc) key or may require an annual subscription payment. Schools must be able to account for all software used upon its equipment. This includes both curriculum and administration software and should incorporate peripheral use such as teachers' laptops and so on. As with the hardware audit, it is likely that your administration machines are provided by the local authority and supported by their technical team. If so, the software on these machines may also have separate licence arrangements. You should confirm that this is so, otherwise incorporate them within the review.

From a top-down perspective you will need to ensure that you have licence agreements in place for the network's operating systems, including any client licences required to access the curriculum server. You will then need to check that any 'Office' type software is fully licensed both for staff and student usage. Licences will be required for each piece of specialized curriculum software. You need to check that teachers' laptops are properly licensed for any software application loaded upon them.

Compliance

Any software that you use will have to comply with the EULA or End User Licence Agreement. This dictates your legal rights to use the software under specific instances and you have to ensure that you are not using it inappropriately. For example, if your original suite installation was for a server and 15 client machines but this network has since doubled, you need to ensure that each new machine is covered with the appropriate server client software licence. The EULA states how many computers the software may legally be installed and used upon. Microsoft is used throughout UK schools as a core tool and there are a range of licensing options open to you, latest details are best obtained from the Microsoft website: http://www.microsoft.com/uk/education/how-to-buy/compliance/.

Do remember that you have a legal responsibility to respect the copyright owner's conditions of use.

Review

Having completed your survey so that you are confident you are complying with all licence conditions, you should now review the current position in terms of whether you have the software that you need, whether you are paying for software that you do not use and whether or not the software that you have could be licensed more efficiently. This will be covered in depth next month. So this week first check the licence agreements are in place, then use the audit form (Table 3.2) to revisit your network machines and to detail software currently installed whilst identifying any discrepancies.

You have about two weeks to complete the audit and may choose to run it concurrent with the self-review framework.

15th November

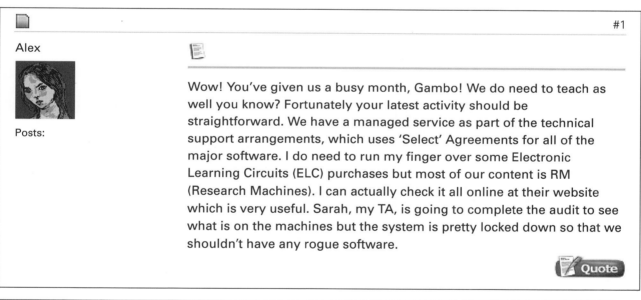

#1

Alex

Posts:

Wow! You've given us a busy month, Gambo! We do need to teach as well you know? Fortunately your latest activity should be straightforward. We have a managed service as part of the technical support arrangements, which uses 'Select' Agreements for all of the major software. I do need to run my finger over some Electronic Learning Circuits (ELC) purchases but most of our content is RM (Research Machines). I can actually check it all online at their website which is very useful. Sarah, my TA, is going to complete the audit to see what is on the machines but the system is pretty locked down so that we shouldn't have any rogue software.

Quote

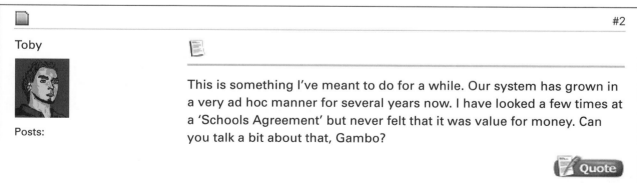

#2

Toby

Posts:

This is something I've meant to do for a while. Our system has grown in a very ad hoc manner for several years now. I have looked a few times at a 'Schools Agreement' but never felt that it was value for money. Can you talk a bit about that, Gambo?

Quote

Table 3.2 Software audit template

Location:	Make S/N	Operating system	Client licence	Office apps	Curriculum apps	License checked /notes
Computer 1						
Computer 2						
Computer 3						
Computer 4						
Computer 5						
Computer 6						

Available on the net at http://www.sagepub.co.uk/wrightbk1

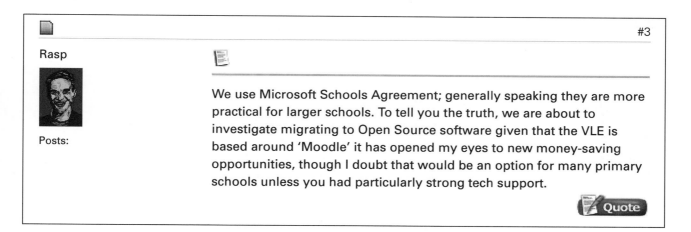

Rasp

Posts:

#3

We use Microsoft Schools Agreement; generally speaking they are more practical for larger schools. To tell you the truth, we are about to investigate migrating to Open Source software given that the VLE is based around 'Moodle' it has opened my eyes to new money-saving opportunities, though I doubt that would be an option for many primary schools unless you had particularly strong tech support.

Quote

17th November

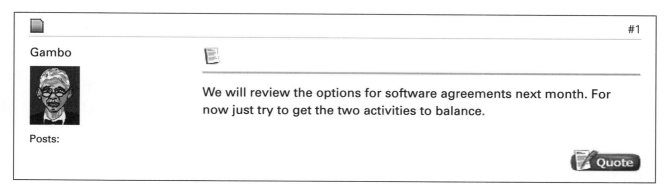

Gambo

Posts:

#1

We will review the options for software agreements next month. For now just try to get the two activities to balance.

Quote

21st November

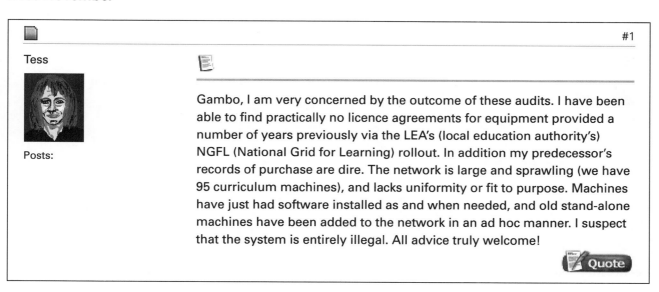

Tess

Posts:

#1

Gambo, I am very concerned by the outcome of these audits. I have been able to find practically no licence agreements for equipment provided a number of years previously via the LEA's (local education authority's) NGFL (National Grid for Learning) rollout. In addition my predecessor's records of purchase are dire. The network is large and sprawling (we have 95 curriculum machines), and lacks uniformity or fit to purpose. Machines have just had software installed as and when needed, and old stand-alone machines have been added to the network in an ad hoc manner. I suspect that the system is entirely illegal. All advice truly welcome!

Quote

22nd November

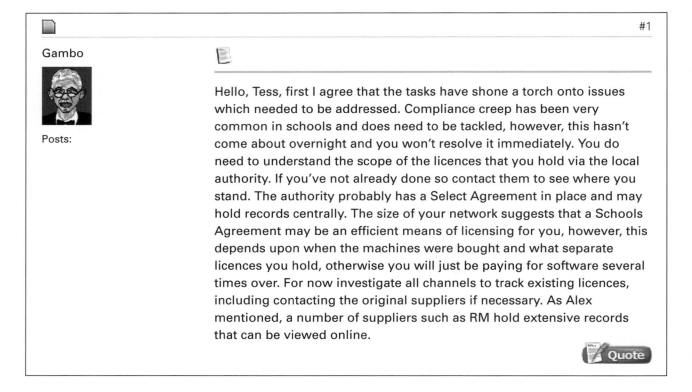

Gambo

Posts:

Hello, Tess, first I agree that the tasks have shone a torch onto issues which needed to be addressed. Compliance creep has been very common in schools and does need to be tackled, however, this hasn't come about overnight and you won't resolve it immediately. You do need to understand the scope of the licences that you hold via the local authority. If you've not already done so contact them to see where you stand. The authority probably has a Select Agreement in place and may hold records centrally. The size of your network suggests that a Schools Agreement may be an efficient means of licensing for you, however, this depends upon when the machines were bought and what separate licences you hold, otherwise you will just be paying for software several times over. For now investigate all channels to track existing licences, including contacting the original suppliers if necessary. As Alex mentioned, a number of suppliers such as RM hold extensive records that can be viewed online.

23rd November

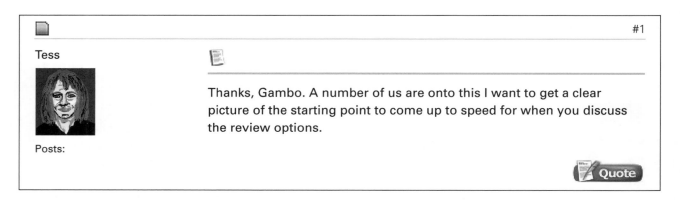

Tess

Posts:

Thanks, Gambo. A number of us are onto this I want to get a clear picture of the starting point to come up to speed for when you discuss the review options.

26th November

Week 12, Task 9 – Review Provision for the Discrete ICT Curriculum

I echo Alex's sentiments regarding the amount that you have achieved this month, therefore your third task will be one that involves personal study. The activities that have been advocated so far have been aimed at providing you with a substantial audit of the systems and strategies in place within your school, which will ultimately determine your success in embedding ICT and E-learning across the school. The next set of actions relate more directly to the traditional curriculum subject leader role. It is time to reflect upon your curriculum subject of ICT, and to decide how well it has been and is being taught within your school.

As subject leader your core responsibility is to ensure that the national curriculum for ICT is delivered fully within your school. Your ability to do so rests upon your own professional understanding of your subject area. This will also raise questions about your own curriculum expertise that may need to be addressed, particularly if you are a new co-ordinator. If you are not already confident then you need to get to know the national curriculum for ICT for each phase of your school. Spend some time over the next week or so extending your knowledge and understanding. There are a number of core documents that you need to be familiar with: the National Curriculum Programme of Study can be downloaded from the Internet at http://www.nc.uk.net/nc/contents/ICT--pos.html.

You need to be clear about the four core strands that make up each pupil's knowledge, skills and understanding. These are:

1 Finding Things Out
2 Developing Ideas and Making Things Happen
3 Exchanging and Sharing Information
4 Reviewing, Modifying and Evaluating Work as it Progresses.

In addition, be familiar with the breadth of study through which the knowledge skills and understanding will be taught. Think of this as a fifth strand.

5 Breadth of Study.

Finland Develops Extremely Revolting Bread

This is a simple mnemonic that I have used to quickly remember the strands. These will not relate directly to the Units of Work that you are probably familiar with. They are generic skills that cut across the subject, so do take time to familiarize yourself with them. They have great significance when one reflects upon how the subject is assessed.

Tables 3.3 and 3.4 provide a succinct overview of each strand. Spend some time improving your overall familiarity with them. Of course, if you already have them mapped out that is fine. As you do so begin to ask yourself how this curriculum is actually taught at your school. Get a feel for the strengths and weaknesses and how you interpret the Programme of Study via your scheme of work. Next month we will take a closer look at the Attainment Targets, located online at http://www.nc.uk.net/nc/contents/ICT---ATT.html; The National Curriculum in Action, at http://www.ncaction.org.uk/subjects/ict/levels.htm; and the QCA Scheme of Work for ICT that shows how the ICT Programme of Study for Key Stages 1 and 2 can be translated into manageable units of work, http://www.standards.dfes.gov.uk/schemes2/it/?view=get.

Plenty for you to be going on with. I'll be back in December to complete each of the ongoing reviews for this term and I shall try to leave the season of goodwill relatively clear.

Table 3.3 The ICT Programmes of Study for Key Stage 1

<table>
<tr>
<td colspan="2" align="center">KS1</td>
<td colspan="2">During Key Stage 1 pupils explore ICT and learn to use it confidently and with purpose to achieve specific outcomes. They start to use ICT to develop their ideas and record their creative work. They become familiar with hardware and software.</td>
</tr>
<tr>
<td rowspan="4">5. Breadth of Study

Pupils should be taught the knowledge, skills and understanding through:

a) Working with a range of information to investigate the different ways it can be presented.

b) Exploring a variety of ICT tools.

c) Talking about the uses of ICT inside and outside school.</td>
<td></td>
<td>1. Finding Things Out</td>
<td>2. Developing Ideas and Making Things Happen</td>
</tr>
<tr>
<td></td>
<td>Pupils should be taught how to:

a) Gather information from a variety of sources.

b) Enter and store information in a variety of forms.

c) Retrieve information that has been stored.</td>
<td>Pupils should be taught:

a) To use text, tables, images and sound to develop their ideas.

b) How to select from and add to information they have retrieved for particular purposes.

c) How to plan and give instructions to make things happen.

d) To try things out and explore what happens in real and imaginary situations.</td>
</tr>
<tr>
<td></td>
<td>3. Exchanging and Sharing Information</td>
<td>4. Reviewing Modifying and Evaluating Work as it Progresses</td>
</tr>
<tr>
<td></td>
<td>Pupils should be taught:

a) How to share their ideas by presenting information in a variety of forms.

b) To present their completed work effectively.

Reviewing, modifying and evaluating work as it progresses.</td>
<td>Pupils should be taught to:

a) Review what they have done to help them develop their ideas.

b) Describe the effects of their actions.

c) Talk about what they might change in future work.</td>
</tr>
</table>

Available on the net at http://www.sagepub.co.uk/wrightbk1

Table 3.4 The ICT Programmes of Study for Key Stage 2

<table>
<tr><td rowspan="2"><h2>KS2</h2></td><td colspan="2">During Key Stage 2 pupils use a wider range of ICT tools and information sources to support their work in other subjects. They develop their research skills and decide what information is appropriate for their work. They begin to question the plausibility and quality of information. They learn how to amend their work and present it in a way that suits its audience.</td></tr>
<tr><td>

1. Finding Things Out

</td><td>

2. Developing Ideas and Making Things Happen

</td></tr>
</table>

<table>
<tr><td>

5. Breadth of Study

Pupils should be taught the knowledge, skills and understanding through:

a) Working with a range of information to consider its characteristics and purposes.

b) Working with others to explore a variety of information sources and ICT tools.

c) Investigating and comparing the uses of ICT inside and outside school.

</td><td>

Pupils should be taught:

a) To talk about what information they need and how they can find and use it.

b) How to prepare information for development using ICT, including selecting suitable sources, finding information, classifying it and checking it for accuracy.

c) To interpret information, to check it is relevant and reasonable and to think about what might happen if there were any errors or omissions.

</td><td>

Pupils should be taught:

a) How to develop and refine ideas by bringing together, organizing and reorganizing text, tables, images and sound as appropriate.

b) How to create, test, improve and refine sequences of instructions to make things happen and to monitor events and respond to them.

c) To use simulations and explore models in order to answer 'What if ... ?' questions, to investigate and evaluate the effect of changing values and to identify patterns and relationships.

</td></tr>
<tr><td></td><td>

3. Exchanging and Sharing Information

</td><td>

4. Reviewing Modifying and Evaluating Work as it Progresses

</td></tr>
<tr><td></td><td>

Pupils should be taught:

a) How to share and exchange information in a variety of forms, including email.

b) To be sensitive to the needs of the audience and think carefully about the content and quality when communicating information.

</td><td>

Pupils should be taught to:

a) Review what they and others have done to help them develop their ideas.

b) Describe and talk about the effectiveness of their work with ICT, comparing it with other methods and considering the effect it has on others.

c) Talk about how they could improve future work.

</td></tr>
</table>

Available on the net at http://www.sagepub.co.uk/wrightbk1

Chapter 4 ● *December*

3rd December

It has been a hectic term and an enormous amount has already been accomplished. During December I shall try to lighten the workload in response to the increased demands of the season but must also try to draw together each of the audits that have been featured this term. In particular you need to complete the self-review cycle by establishing how the action plan created therein will work for you. I also want to discuss your software options in the light of the audit that we completed in November and, finally, I shall recommend some light reflective holiday reading to complete your professional development with regard to your understanding of the role of ICT within the primary curriculum.

Week 13, Task 10 – Strategic Audit and Self-Review 3

Last month your school completed the BECTA self-review for ICT and E-learning, providing you with a comprehensive matrix of information referenced against eight key categories for school improvement. In addition to collating the data, the matrix will provide benchmarking information that will allow you to compare the school's current performance with that of other schools nationally and to benchmark your outcomes against similar schools.

The screenshot shown in Figure 4.1 demonstrates a sample school's performance for Element 4a of the framework, which relates to assessment. In so doing it gives a very detailed overview of practice at the school, which can be broken down into aspects. This school can be seen to be performing above the national average for aspects 1, 2 and 5 but over a level below for aspect 3

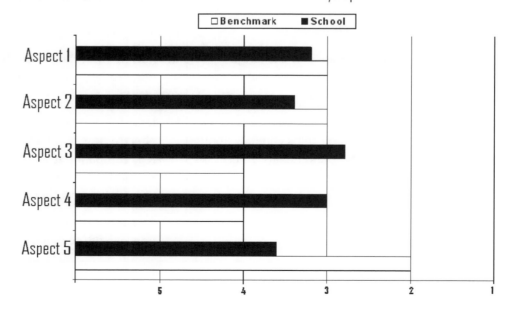

Figure 4.1 BECTA matrix benchmarking sample (reproduced with permission from BECTA)

Available on the net at http://www.sagepub.co.uk/wrightbk1

(Dialogue) and aspect 4 (Using ICT to support assessment.) The school has particular strengths in aspect 5 (ICT targets for improvement).

The matrix offers a powerful tool for planning future actions and provides a number of sophisticated tools that will allow you to customize a self-generated action plan to suit your school's individual needs. By selecting the Action Plan menu tab for this section you will be able to review your current position and access suggested next steps that can also be customized and assigned to particular staff registered with the site.

Your ICT team should now work through the action plan, completing each of these sections with the relevant status, priority, success criteria and resources required for each action to be accomplished. The matrix will guide you through this process and suggest relevant actions for each strand.

Consider two core objectives for this activity:

1 To review the action plan in order to prioritize tasks that will need to be addressed quickly.
2 To produce a report and evaluation of the exercise that signposts what the school needs to do next.

Your first task is to review the action plan generated by the matrix in order to prioritize tasks with reference to the benchmarking data and the relative position of your self-evaluation with that required for the ICT Mark (generally Level 2 or 3 as indicated.) This is going to provide you with a unique 'helicopter view' of the school's strategic position and may also identify blind spots that were not considered earlier. If the self-review has been worth anything at all, then it must now produce operations and activities at school level.

BECTA SRF All Elements

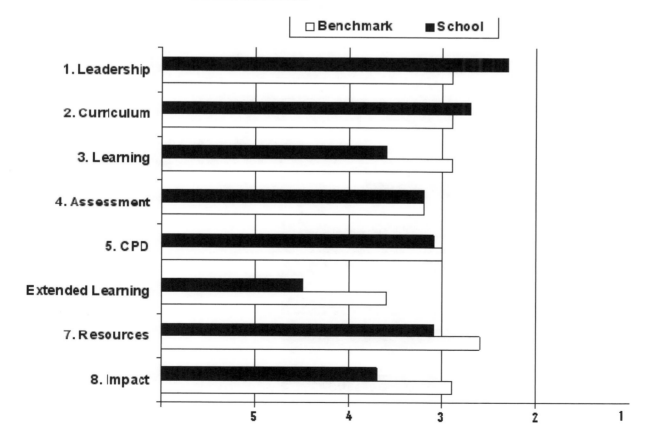

Figure 4.2 Benchmarking information for all elements (reproduced with permission from BECTA)

Available on the net at http://www.sagepub.co.uk/wrightbk1

Figure 4.2 is a second screenshot taken from the BECTA self-review framework (http://matrix. becta.org.uk) and shows collated benchmarking data for a sample school. The charts quickly highlight that the school is performing well in terms of Elements, 1, 2, 4 and 5 but performs less well with regard to the other elements, in particular Elements 6, 3 and 8. This may require prioritized action in order for the school to address any underlying problems and is an extremely useful self-analysis that should feed directly into the school's SEF.

The framework enables users to look more closely at potentially weaker areas, consequently Figure 4.3 scrutinizes progress against Element 6, 'Extending Opportunities for Learning' by strand and by aspect.

Figure 4.3 indicates that the weakest area assessed lay within strand 6a, 'Awareness and understanding' where none of the self-evaluation statements were higher than Level 5, representing only localized development. Clearly the school needs to review the manner in which it is preparing and planning for extended learning opportunities. Also within strand 6b, the first aspect needs to be examined as this too fell significantly below benchmarked schools and this school's other scores within the element.

The final figure (4.4) is taken from the action planner for strand 6a and highlights the information available within the matrix relating to the targeted strand. The matrix has highlighted a serious gap in development within this school and directed appropriate action.

Use the reports to identify your priorities and aim to produce a report and evaluation of the exercise that will be delivered to staff and governors in which priorities for the short, medium and long term are highlighted.

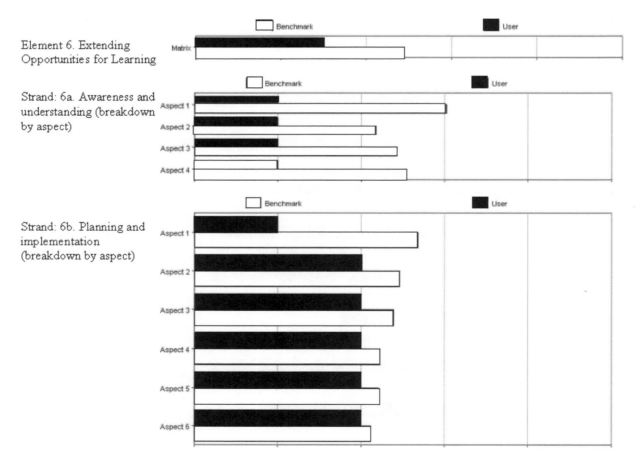

Figure 4.3 Element 6 breakdown by aspect (reproduced with permission from BECTA)

Available on the net at http://www.sagepub.co.uk/wrightbk1

Action planner for: 6a. Awareness and understanding

6a-1 Understanding

Current level: Level 5 (re-evaluate this >)

Description: Staff have no understanding of how ICT can support the extension of learning opportunities for pupils.

Comments and evidence:

Actions (customise/ignore)	Priority	Status	Date	Success	Resources
Investigate current situation in the school relating to extending opportunities for learning. Produce short term action plan to raise awareness of possibilities and develop a staff training programme.	High	Not yet started	01 Jun 06	Staff and Governors have accurate shared understanding of current position	High

Figure 4.4 Element 6a-1 Action plan (reproduced with permission from BECTA)

Available on the net at http://www.sagepub.co.uk/wrightbk1

5th December

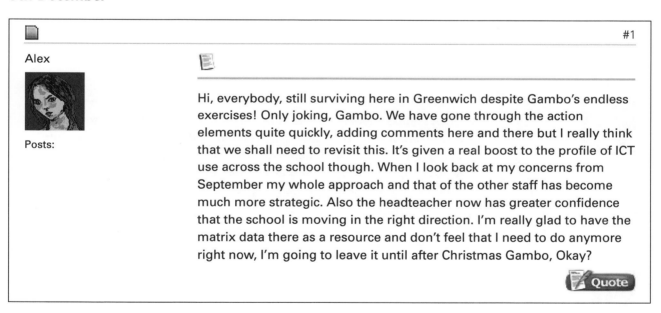

Alex

Posts:

#1

Hi, everybody, still surviving here in Greenwich despite Gambo's endless exercises! Only joking, Gambo. We have gone through the action elements quite quickly, adding comments here and there but I really think that we shall need to revisit this. It's given a real boost to the profile of ICT use across the school though. When I look back at my concerns from September my whole approach and that of the other staff has become much more strategic. Also the headteacher now has greater confidence that the school is moving in the right direction. I'm really glad to have the matrix data there as a resource and don't feel that I need to do anymore right now, I'm going to leave it until after Christmas Gambo, Okay?

Quote

7th December

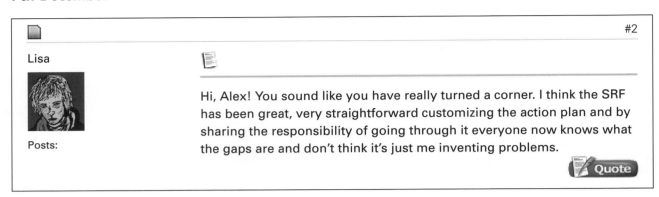

#2

Lisa

Posts:

Hi, Alex! You sound like you have really turned a corner. I think the SRF has been great, very straightforward customizing the action plan and by sharing the responsibility of going through it everyone now knows what the gaps are and don't think it's just me inventing problems.

Quote

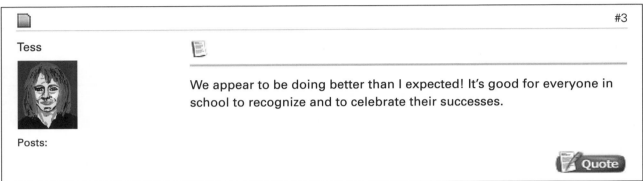

#3

Tess

Posts:

We appear to be doing better than I expected! It's good for everyone in school to recognize and to celebrate their successes.

Quote

10th December

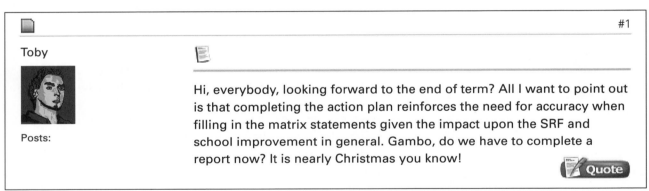

#1

Toby

Posts:

Hi, everybody, looking forward to the end of term? All I want to point out is that completing the action plan reinforces the need for accuracy when filling in the matrix statements given the impact upon the SRF and school improvement in general. Gambo, do we have to complete a report now? It is nearly Christmas you know!

Quote

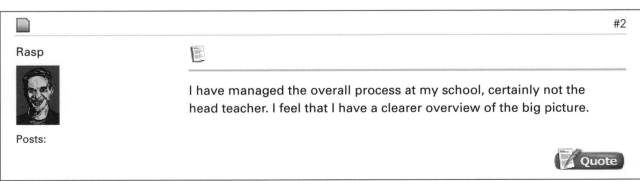

#2

Rasp

Posts:

I have managed the overall process at my school, certainly not the head teacher. I feel that I have a clearer overview of the big picture.

Quote

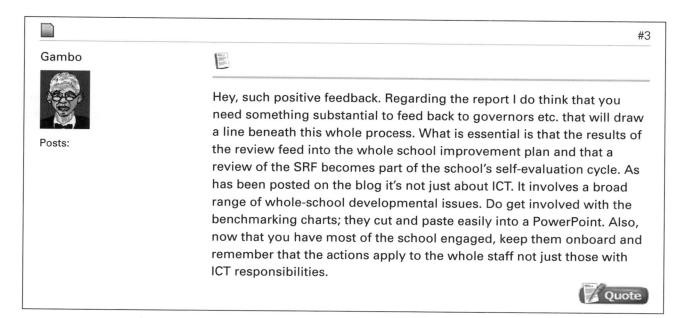

Gambo

Posts:

Hey, such positive feedback. Regarding the report I do think that you need something substantial to feed back to governors etc. that will draw a line beneath this whole process. What is essential is that the results of the review feed into the whole school improvement plan and that a review of the SRF becomes part of the school's self-evaluation cycle. As has been posted on the blog it's not just about ICT. It involves a broad range of whole-school developmental issues. Do get involved with the benchmarking charts; they cut and paste easily into a PowerPoint. Also, now that you have most of the school engaged, keep them onboard and remember that the actions apply to the whole staff not just those with ICT responsibilities.

Week 14, Task 11 – Reviewing Software Licence Agreements

This week we evaluate existing software agreements in the context of the audit that was carried out last month. You should be able to bring to this exercise both the overview of software that currently operates upon the network and an audit of the licences that you hold.

Let me begin by saying that licensing is something of a 'black art' and can be extremely complex. It is very easy to get drawn into a confused series of negotiations within which one struggles to compare like with like and loses sight of what is actually needed. It is essential therefore that we establish a few overriding principles to strategically guide our decisions.

First principle, you have to operate a legal network that is fully and appropriately licensed. You will know from last month's audits where you stand in this regard. If you have insufficient licences for the software currently installed across your school there are two clear options: either increase your licence provision or remove illegal software immediately. This is your first action point.

Aim to implement a software system that provides automatically updated software for all your core tools based upon an annual subscription charge. This removes the stresses of out-of-date software and the need to account for individual users and so on. These are the principles that rest behind the Microsoft Schools Agreement, which will be an ideal choice for many schools. However the school's agreement does not always account for the complexity and variety of journeys that schools have had so far, leaving a legacy of software that has already been bought and paid for. Schools rightly resent and resist paying again for the same software. This highlights the strategic decision now required as to whether or not it is feasible to draw a line under what has gone before and enter into a new means of securing your licences; one that is based upon the information that your audits have highlighted about the efficacy of previous systems and your actual operating needs.

A second key point to consider is that any decision regarding non-curriculum software should be made in consultation with your ICT partners. For example, with regard to your operating system (that is, the software that tells your system how to work), any sensible school will be led by its technical support partners and should not unilaterally make changes to the system. Many schools enjoy a complete managed service of support that includes management software such as RM's Community Connect and Viglen's ClassLink; however, the chances are that your school runs a Microsoft operating system on its network.

Supporting Microsoft networks is relatively straightforward, given that most commercial technicians are familiar with the software, and your core decision is how to acquire licenses. Do you buy piecemeal, adding new licences as machines are added to the network or software is upgraded, or join an annual subscription which guarantees that all the school's assets are covered and up to date but runs the danger of paying for software many times over? The Microsoft Schools Agreement also includes its Office applications and as a crude rule of thumb if you use Microsoft Office on your curriculum machines (although it is not strictly curriculum software and certainly is not eligible for ELC purchase), then a Schools Agreement may well prove cost-effective.

If you choose to license individual applications, then most of the complexity and issues traditionally come from the server and access to it. Each additional application is likely to land you with extra licensing costs. In order to legally access the server for file or print sharing, a client access licence or CAL will be required, providing permission to access the services of the server. This is worth bearing in mind when you decide that you want 50 machines to access that laser printer in the ICT suite. The Schools Agreement takes care of this by incorporating it within the basic agreement.

Invariably, therefore, you may end up paying for services that not all the machines are using and such arrangements should not be entered into lightly. Make no mistake, not withstanding the recent renegotiations of price, full Schools Agreements are expensive so make sure you are only paying for the applications that you need. There is a useful licensing comparison table available from Microsoft at http://www.microsoft.com/uk/education/how-to-buy/licensing-comparison/.

In order to qualify for the Schools Agreement you must reach a minimum level of 50 units that are based upon the total number of eligible machines on the network multiplied by the number of products you wish to use on these machines. All eligible machines must be counted. This total figure is your unit count and dictates the cost for one year or multiplied by three for the three-year agreement option.

Individual prices are available from registered Microsoft resellers. The US equivalent arrangement have a handy cost calculator on the US Microsoft website: http://www.microsoft.com/education/sacalculator.aspx. This provides estimates in dollars but is a useful ballpark guide. Expect to pay around £1,500 per year for a 50-station suite with basic client access, office upgrades and so on.

If you decide to remain outside such an overarching agreement, then look again at your own supplier to check that there is not an existing Select Agreement available from the local authority that would make individual software purchases more efficient. In either case, schools should be aware of the new relationship that now exists between Microsoft and UK schools and ensure that the significant savings achieved in 2004 via the Microsoft Agreement for Schools (not to be confused with the Microsoft Schools Agreement) have been reflected within their own agreements.

BECTA has now produced a software framework agreement that includes the facility for you to, in effect, order quotations from all accredited suppliers for your non-curriculum software needs, producing a mini competition amongst suppliers. This is available from the procurement section of the BECTA website: http://procurementtools.becta.org.uk/.

Finally, consider also the life span of each product. The schools agreement works out at around a third of the cost of an equivalent outright purchase. So whilst it is entirely viable over a three-year period, from the fourth year onwards the agreement becomes expensive.

15th December

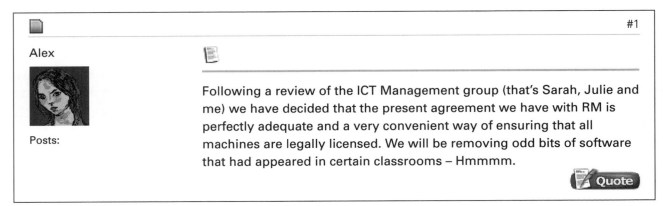

#1

Alex

Posts:

Following a review of the ICT Management group (that's Sarah, Julie and me) we have decided that the present agreement we have with RM is perfectly adequate and a very convenient way of ensuring that all machines are legally licensed. We will be removing odd bits of software that had appeared in certain classrooms – Hmmmm.

Quote

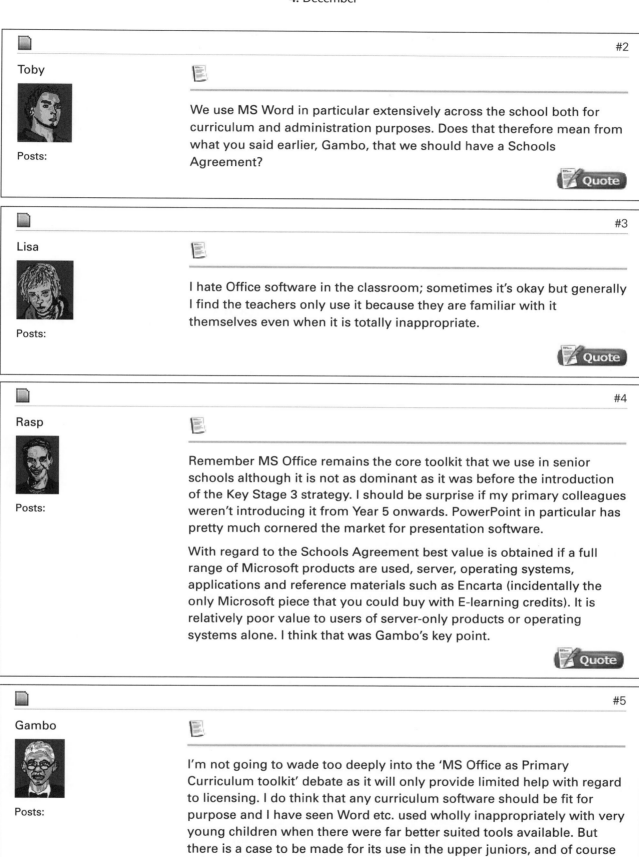

#2

Toby

Posts:

We use MS Word in particular extensively across the school both for curriculum and administration purposes. Does that therefore mean from what you said earlier, Gambo, that we should have a Schools Agreement?

Quote

#3

Lisa

Posts:

I hate Office software in the classroom; sometimes it's okay but generally I find the teachers only use it because they are familiar with it themselves even when it is totally inappropriate.

Quote

#4

Rasp

Posts:

Remember MS Office remains the core toolkit that we use in senior schools although it is not as dominant as it was before the introduction of the Key Stage 3 strategy. I should be surprise if my primary colleagues weren't introducing it from Year 5 onwards. PowerPoint in particular has pretty much cornered the market for presentation software.

With regard to the Schools Agreement best value is obtained if a full range of Microsoft products are used, server, operating systems, applications and reference materials such as Encarta (incidentally the only Microsoft piece that you could buy with E-learning credits). It is relatively poor value to users of server-only products or operating systems alone. I think that was Gambo's key point.

Quote

#5

Gambo

Posts:

I'm not going to wade too deeply into the 'MS Office as Primary Curriculum toolkit' debate as it will only provide limited help with regard to licensing. I do think that any curriculum software should be fit for purpose and I have seen Word etc. used wholly inappropriately with very young children when there were far better suited tools available. But there is a case to be made for its use in the upper juniors, and of course staff invariably prefer it to any of the open office alternatives. Two points to consider are: is the present software properly licensed and installed via OEM agreement (i.e. bought with the equipment) and are there plans in place for the wholesale replacement or upgrade of equipment?

Quote

16th December

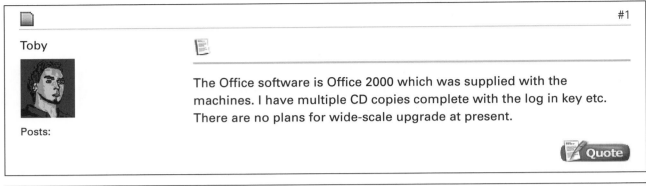

Toby

Posts:

> The Office software is Office 2000 which was supplied with the machines. I have multiple CD copies complete with the log in key etc. There are no plans for wide-scale upgrade at present.

#1

Quote

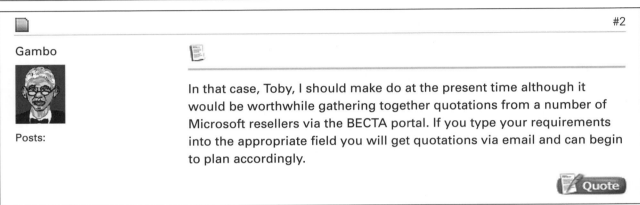

Gambo

Posts:

> In that case, Toby, I should make do at the present time although it would be worthwhile gathering together quotations from a number of Microsoft resellers via the BECTA portal. If you type your requirements into the appropriate field you will get quotations via email and can begin to plan accordingly.

#2

Quote

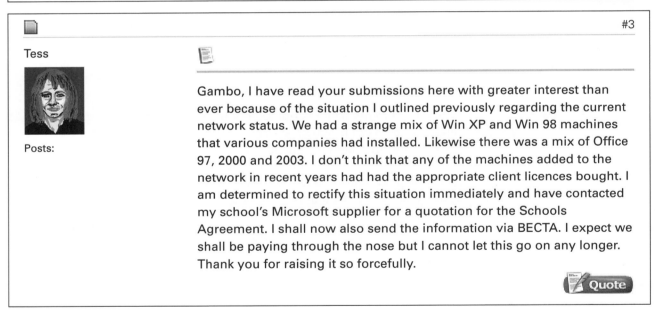

Tess

Posts:

> Gambo, I have read your submissions here with greater interest than ever because of the situation I outlined previously regarding the current network status. We had a strange mix of Win XP and Win 98 machines that various companies had installed. Likewise there was a mix of Office 97, 2000 and 2003. I don't think that any of the machines added to the network in recent years had had the appropriate client licences bought. I am determined to rectify this situation immediately and have contacted my school's Microsoft supplier for a quotation for the Schools Agreement. I shall now also send the information via BECTA. I expect we shall be paying through the nose but I cannot let this go on any longer. Thank you for raising it so forcefully.

#3

Quote

20th December

Week 15, Task 12 – Understanding Attainment in ICT

To finish the term I am going to return to the discrete curriculum subject of ICT and the manner in which the national curriculum for ICT is being taught. Last month we looked at the core strands of the Programme of Study in order to focus your understanding of what the subject of ICT is really all about. Very often I speak to co-ordinators who will fluently describe the QCA (Qualifications and Curriculum Authority) Scheme of Work for ICT but do not relate these units back to the actual skills, knowledge and understanding that each child needs to acquire. This month you should continue developing your understanding with reference to the ICT Attainment Targets.

An Attainment Target sets out the skills, knowledge and understanding which pupils of different abilities and maturities are expected to have by the end of each key stage, as defined by the Education Act 1996, section 353a. Each subject has its own targets that comprise level descriptions of increasing difficulty: http://www.nc.uk.net/nc/contents/ICT---ATT.html.

Our core interest relates to the level descriptors from Level 1 to Level 5. It is possible that you may encounter children operating at Level 6, although our secondary colleagues would hotly contest this. That is a debate, which will resurface when we discuss assessment in greater detail. For now, let us focus on the five main levels of primary attainment. Each description describes the types and range of performance that pupils working at that level should characteristically demonstrate, and provides the basis for making judgements about pupils' performance.

Try to familiarize yourself with the overall progression across the levels.

In Table 4.1 I have divided the level descriptors between the individual aspects of the Programme of Study. As with any moderation exercise it is important to understand the manner in which the language develops as one moves through the levels. Note within the 'Finding Things Out' aspect how simple exploration and awareness of information evolves into use of appropriate stored information, then interrogation of data and accuracy and organization which feature at Level 5.

Your final activity of the year is therefore to examine Table 4.1 and to begin to get some sense of the progression of skills, knowledge and understanding within each aspect.

Table 4.1 Level descriptors by attainment strand

	Finding Things Out
L1	Pupils explore information from various sources, showing they know that information exists in different forms.
L2	They enter, save and retrieve work.
L3	Pupils use ICT to save information and to find and use appropriate stored information, following straightforward lines of enquiry.
L4	Pupils understand the need for care in framing questions when collecting, finding and interrogating information.
L5	Pupils select the information they need for different purposes, check its accuracy and organize it in a form suitable for processing.

	Developing Ideas and Making Things Happen
L1	They recognize that many everyday devices respond to signals and instructions. They make choices when using such devices to produce different outcomes.
L2	Pupils use ICT to organize and classify information and to present their findings. They use ICT to help them generate, amend and record their work and share their ideas in different forms, including text, tables, images and sound. They plan and give instructions to make things happen and describe the effects. They use ICT to explore what happens in real and imaginary situations.
L3	They use ICT to generate, develop, organize and present their work. They use sequences of instructions to control devices and achieve specific outcomes. They make appropriate choices when using ICT-based models or simulations to help them find things out and solve problems.
L4	They add to, amend and combine different forms of information from a variety of sources. They use ICT systems to control events in a predetermined manner and to sense physical data. They use ICT-based models and simulations to explore patterns and relationships, and make predictions about the consequences of their decisions.
L5	Pupils select the information they need for different purposes, check its accuracy and organize it in a form suitable for processing. They use ICT to structure, refine and present information in different forms and styles for specific purposes and audiences. They create sequences of instructions to control events, and understand the need to be precise when framing and sequencing instructions. They understand how ICT devices with sensors can be used to monitor and measure external events. They explore the effects of changing the variables in an ICT-based model.

Table 4.1 continued

	Exchanging and Sharing Information
L1	They use ICT to work with text, images and sound to help them share their ideas. They talk about their use of ICT.
L2	Pupils use ICT to organize and classify information and to present their findings. They use ICT to help them generate, amend and record their work and share their ideas in different forms, including text, tables, images and sound. They talk about their experiences of ICT both inside and outside school.
L3	They use ICT to generate, develop, organize and present their work. They share and exchange their ideas with others. They describe their use of ICT and its use outside school.
L4	They use ICT to present information in different forms and show they are aware of the intended audience and the need for quality in their presentations. They exchange information and ideas with others in a variety of ways, including using email.
L5	They use ICT to structure, refine and present information in different forms and styles for specific purposes and audiences. They exchange information and ideas with others in a variety of ways, including using email. They discuss their knowledge and experience of using ICT and their observations of its use outside school.
	Reviewing Modifying and Evaluating Work as it Progresses
L1	They talk about their use of ICT.
L2	They use ICT to help them generate, amend and record their work and share their ideas in different forms, including text, tables, images and sound. They talk about their experiences of ICT both inside and outside school.
L3	They use ICT to generate, develop, organize and present their work. They describe their use of ICT and its use outside school.
L4	They interpret their findings, question plausibility and recognize that poor-quality information leads to unreliable results. They add to, amend and combine different forms of information from a variety of sources. They use ICT to present information in different forms and show they are aware of the intended audience and the need for quality in their presentations. They compare their use of ICT with other methods and with its use outside school.
L5	They use ICT to structure, refine and present information in different forms and styles for specific purposes and audiences. They discuss their knowledge and experience of using ICT and their observations of its use outside school. They assess the use of ICT in their work and are able to reflect critically in order to make improvements in subsequent work.
	Breadth of Study
L1	Pupils explore information from various sources, showing they know that information exists in different forms.
L2	They talk about their experiences of ICT both inside and outside school.
L3	They describe their use of ICT and its use outside school.
L4	They compare their use of ICT with other methods and with its use outside school.
L5	They exchange information and ideas with others in a variety of ways, including using email. They discuss their knowledge and experience of using ICT and their observations of its use outside school.

Available on the net at http://www.sagepub.co.uk/wrightbk1

Here is how progression is defined within the National Curriculum (http://www.ncaction.org.uk/subjects/ict/progress.htm):

Level 1 is characterized by the use of ICT to explore options and make choices to communicate meaning. Pupils develop familiarity with simple ICT tools.

Level 2 is characterized by purposeful use of ICT to achieve specific outcomes.

Level 3 is characterized by the use of ICT to develop ideas and solve problems.

Level 4 is characterized by the ability to combine and refine information from various sources.

Level 5 is characterized by combining the use of ICT tools within the overall structure of an ICT solution. Pupils critically evaluate the fitness for purpose of work as it progresses.

Have a look at the National Curriculum in Action website, http://www.ncaction.org.uk/subjects/ict/progress.htm for examples of what these levels mean in practice. This is not a moderation or assessment exercise, so do not worry about being able to assign levels at this stage. We shall be covering that later. The objective is to improve your familiarity with the strands and the progression through them.

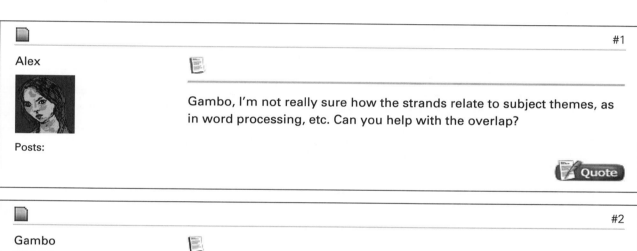

#1

Alex

Posts:

Gambo, I'm not really sure how the strands relate to subject themes, as in word processing, etc. Can you help with the overlap?

Quote

#2

Gambo

Posts:

There is no direct overlap I am afraid, Alex. You have to remember that the National Curriculum refers to the core strands of the Programmes of Study. These will be taught through a range and variety of activities. Also remember that ultimately any pupil's level of attainment for the subject ICT needs to be achieved across all of these strands. I do have a similar chart with the levels cross-referenced to the 4 core curriculum areas plus use of ICT in the real world (Table 4.2) that I shall post.

Quote

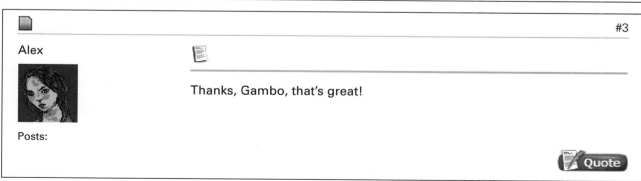

#3

Alex

Posts:

Thanks, Gambo, that's great!

Quote

Table 4.2 Level descriptors by theme

	Word Processing, Multimedia and Internet
L1	Pupils should explore information from different sources, showing they know that information exists in different forms. Pupils will use ICT to work with text, images and sound.
L2	Pupils will enter, save and retrieve their work. They will use ICT to help them generate, amend and record their work and share their ideas in different forms, including text, tables, images and sound.
L3	Pupils use ICT to generate, develop, organize and present their work.
L4	They can add to, amend and combine different forms of information from a variety of sources. Pupils use ICT to present information in different forms and show they are aware of intended audience and the need for quality in their presentations. They exchange information and ideas with others in a variety of ways, including email.
L5	Pupils use ICT to structure, refine and present information in different forms and styles for specific purposes and audiences. They exchange information and ideas with other in a variety of ways, including email. They assess the use of ICT in their work and are able to reflect critically in order to make improvements in subsequent work.
	Data Handling
L1	
L2	Pupils use ICT to organize and classify information and to present their findings
L3	They use ICT to save information and to find and use appropriate stored information, following straightforward lines of enquiry.
L4	Pupils understand the need for care in framing questions when collecting, finding and interrogating information. Pupils interpret their findings, question plausibility and recognize that poor-quality information leads to unreliable results.
L5	Pupils select the information they need for different purposes, check its accuracy and organize it in a form suitable for processing.
	Simulation and Modelling
L1	
L2	Pupils use ICT to explore what happens in real and imaginary situations
L3	They make appropriate choices when using ICT-based models or simulations to help them find things out and solve problems.
L4	Pupils use ICT-based models and simulations to explore patterns and relationships, and make predictions about the consequences of their decisions.
L5	They explore the effect of changing the variables in an ICT-based model.
	Control and Monitoring
L1	Pupils recognize that many everyday devices respond to signals and instructions … make choices when using such devices to produce different outcomes.
L2	They plan and give instructions to make things happen and describe the effects
L3	Pupils use sequences of instructions to control devices and achieve specific outcomes.
L4	They use ICT systems to control events in a predetermined manner and to sense physical data.
L5	They create sequences of instructions to control events, and understand the need to be precise when framing and sequencing instructions. Pupils understand how ICT devices with sensors can be used to monitor and measure external events.

Table 4.2 continued

Using ICT in the Real World	
L1	Pupils talk about their use of ICT.
L2	Pupils talk about their experiences of ICT both inside and outside school.
L3	They describe their use of ICT and its use outside school
L4	They compare their use of ICT with other methods and with its use outside school.
L5	Pupils discuss their knowledge and experience of using ICT and their observations of its use outside school.

Available on the net at http://www.sagepub.co.uk/wrightbk1

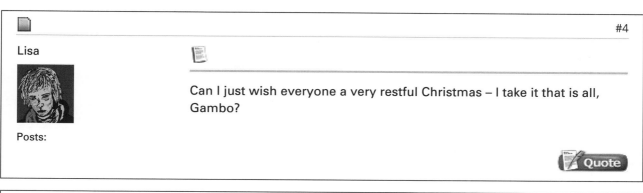

#4

Lisa

Posts:

Can I just wish everyone a very restful Christmas – I take it that is all, Gambo?

Quote

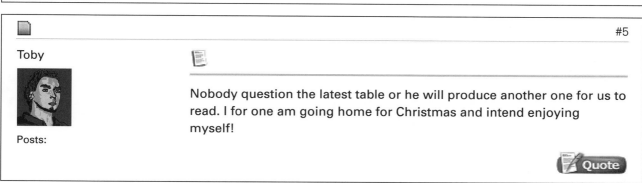

#5

Toby

Posts:

Nobody question the latest table or he will produce another one for us to read. I for one am going home for Christmas and intend enjoying myself!

Quote

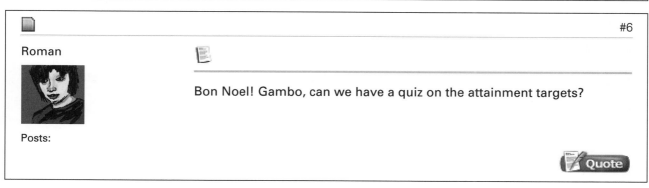

#6

Roman

Posts:

Bon Noel! Gambo, can we have a quiz on the attainment targets?

Quote

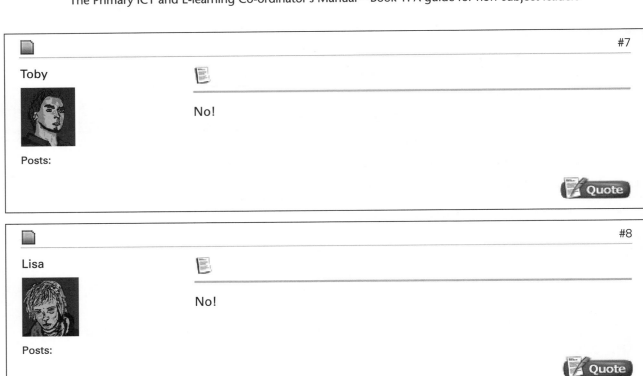

#7

Toby

Posts:

No!

Quote

#8

Lisa

Posts:

No!

Quote

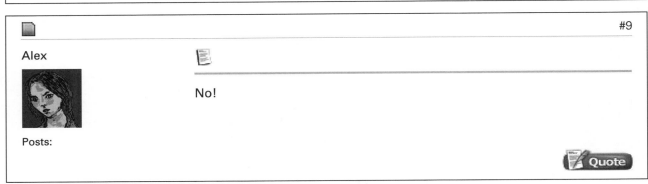

#9

Alex

Posts:

No!

Quote

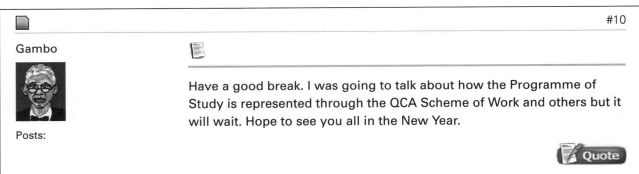

#10

Gambo

Posts:

Have a good break. I was going to talk about how the Programme of Study is represented through the QCA Scheme of Work and others but it will wait. Hope to see you all in the New Year.

Quote

Chapter 5 • *January*

1st January

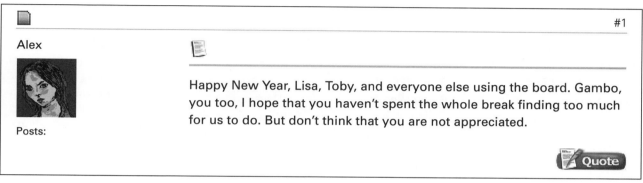

Alex

Posts:

> #1

Happy New Year, Lisa, Toby, and everyone else using the board. Gambo, you too, I hope that you haven't spent the whole break finding too much for us to do. But don't think that you are not appreciated.

Quote

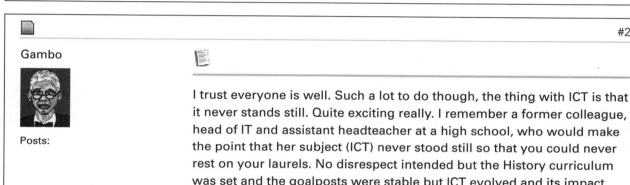

Gambo

Posts:

> #2

I trust everyone is well. Such a lot to do though, the thing with ICT is that it never stands still. Quite exciting really. I remember a former colleague, head of IT and assistant headteacher at a high school, who would make the point that her subject (ICT) never stood still so that you could never rest on your laurels. No disrespect intended but the History curriculum was set and the goalposts were stable but ICT evolved and its impact was immediate. That's why I am trying to get you up to speed quickly and I hope to a large extent that has been achieved.

This term I should like to complete two major reviews that will run through the next 4 months. First, I want you to revise the school's policy for ICT. This is a major undertaking and I intend to look at different areas each month to be considered by your ICT group and customized for your own school. Secondly, I want to develop the way in which your own role at school interrelates with other subject leader colleagues in order to form a definitive overview of cross-curricular ICT within your own school. These are the two themes that we shall return to throughout the coming months. In addition, as you now know, I like to vary your tasks to keep your leadership sharp, so we shall look at a series of shorter focused tasks throughout this period as well.

I have prepared a plan for the term, indicated in Table 5.1

Table 5.1 Spring term plan

SPRING TERM			
JANUARY	FEBRUARY	MARCH	APRIL
REVISING THE ICT POLICY In which co-ordinators will review and revise the school policy. We shall complete a fundamental review of existing policies to ensure that they have kept pace with technological and pedagogical change within schools. This significant document will be rewritten over the course of the term using templates developed in line with ICT Mark criteria.			
Part 1 Introduction, Vision, Aims and Objectives. Roles and Responsibilities. Planning and Delivery Of Content. Teaching and Learning.	**Part 2** Assessment, Recording and Reporting. Progression and Differentiation. Equal Opportunities and Inclusion. Community Access and Extended Learning.	**Part 3** Resources. Professional Development. Management of Information, Transfer and Transition. Legislation. Staff Laptop Computers.	**Part 4** Child Protection and Internet Access. Health and Safety. Anti-Virus Procedures. Monitoring, Evaluation and Review.
E-SAFETY – Monitoring the Internet With the advent of the Every Child Matters bill E-safety is a priority for all schools. I shall be discussing this in detail in the second year of this programme but feel it essential to look at monitoring arrangements before then hence this unit.	**PRINTING** Causes more headaches than anything else related to the school network. So what is your print strategy? Why have printers at all? Are we working in the same way as we did 5 years ago? If so it may be time to change.	**Managing Technical Support** In the first term we looked strategically at the existing technical support arrangements and the sort of support we wanted for the future. This week we will spend a little bit of time discussing how that support is managed on a practical level.	
CROSS-CURRICULAR REVIEW A complete review of the manner in which ICT is used as a teaching and learning tool across other subject areas. Both in terms of developments within the Primary Strategy and statutory requirements from the National Curriculum for each subject area.			
A Statutory Framework To begin with it is of value to understand exactly what ICT should be used in each curriculum area. We begin by examining QCA guidelines as well as Primary Strategy resources. How have these been used within your school?	**Planned Access Autumn – Spring – Summer Terms** Following on from January's overview we will prepare a detailed cross-curricular map beginning for each school term in order to ensure that minimal requirements are being met. We shall discuss means of implementing such a strategy without constraining our more competent teachers. Are you providing each pupil with their entitlement to ICT within a variety of subject areas?		**Primary Strategy** Theoretical review and re-focus for the cross-curricular application of English and mathematics with reference to the emergence of the Primary Strategy as the key driver of ICT initiatives.

Available on the net at http://www.sagepub.co.uk/wrightbk1

3rd January

Week 17, Task 13 – Writing a Policy for ICT, Part 1

Your policy for ICT is an essential document that you must have in place and which will be agreed and referred to by all staff and stakeholders. It sets out how you use ICT in teaching, learning and the wider context of the school and, furthermore, articulates the school's aims and vision for ICT. It provides guidelines for new staff on how and what should be taught and provides the school with support should things go wrong. Hopefully, schools have a policy already in place that has been agreed by staff and governors. The key questions likely to arise are:

1 When was it written or last updated?
2 What is the quality and validity of the content particularly if it is out of date?
3 Do all staff have ownership of the policy, that is, are they aware of key commitments that may be included?

Depending upon your degree of satisfaction with your existing document (hopefully discovered when we did the subject leader file review in September) you should track it against the guidance I shall provide throughout the spring term and amend or rewrite it accordingly. The policy you will then have will meet all ICT Mark criteria. You can find a number of examples of ICT policies from a quick Google search of the Internet.

This week and next we shall be looking at the first five components of the policy. Please take a look at your current policy and I shall be online midweek to go through the first part of it.

4th January

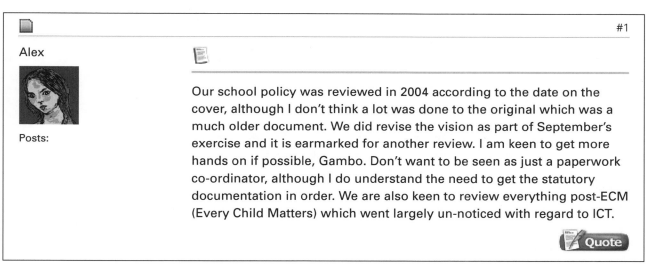

Alex

Posts:

Our school policy was reviewed in 2004 according to the date on the cover, although I don't think a lot was done to the original which was a much older document. We did revise the vision as part of September's exercise and it is earmarked for another review. I am keen to get more hands on if possible, Gambo. Don't want to be seen as just a paperwork co-ordinator, although I do understand the need to get the statutory documentation in order. We are also keen to review everything post-ECM (Every Child Matters) which went largely un-noticed with regard to ICT.

#1

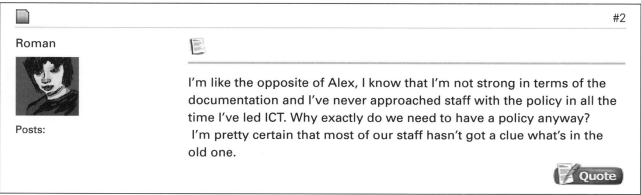

Roman

Posts:

I'm like the opposite of Alex, I know that I'm not strong in terms of the documentation and I've never approached staff with the policy in all the time I've led ICT. Why exactly do we need to have a policy anyway? I'm pretty certain that most of our staff hasn't got a clue what's in the old one.

#2

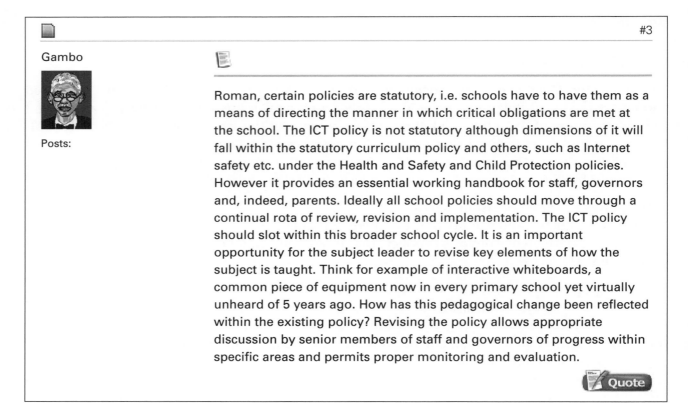

Gambo

Posts:

Roman, certain policies are statutory, i.e. schools have to have them as a means of directing the manner in which critical obligations are met at the school. The ICT policy is not statutory although dimensions of it will fall within the statutory curriculum policy and others, such as Internet safety etc. under the Health and Safety and Child Protection policies. However it provides an essential working handbook for staff, governors and, indeed, parents. Ideally all school policies should move through a continual rota of review, revision and implementation. The ICT policy should slot within this broader school cycle. It is an important opportunity for the subject leader to revise key elements of how the subject is taught. Think for example of interactive whiteboards, a common piece of equipment now in every primary school yet virtually unheard of 5 years ago. How has this pedagogical change been reflected within the existing policy? Revising the policy allows appropriate discussion by senior members of staff and governors of progress within specific areas and permits proper monitoring and evaluation.

Quote

5th January

Remember that the policy needs to go to staff and governors, and should provide opportunity for genuine discussion and revision. This should not simply be a rubber-stamping exercise. The policy document cover should clearly thereafter document dates of agreement by staff, governors and should include proposed date of the next revision.

Principles, vision and aims for the use of ICT

Here first include the vision that you agreed back in September before identifying your specific aims that have derived from this vision, examples below.

Our specific Aims for ICT are:

- *To provide pupils with opportunities to develop their ICT capabilities in all areas specified by the National Curriculum.*
- *To develop pupils' awareness of the use of computers not only in the classroom, but also in everyday life.*
- *To allow pupils to evaluate the potential of computers and also their limitations.*
- *To develop logical thinking and problem solving.*
- *To provide opportunities for pupils to gain knowledge about ICT tools.*

Decide in discussion with your colleagues, which are the core aims for ICT at your school.

Roles and responsibilities

Being mindful of the work that we did on team-building at the beginning of the year, this is a formative moment to consolidate the new ICT structure and to embed those roles and responsibilities within school policy. Each member of your ICT team needs to be incorporated here.

All teaching staff will support the delivery of the ICT curriculum in the following ways.

The class teacher will:

- *Ensure the safe use of equipment, manage computer access for pupils and actively teach required ICT skills.*
- *Inform the ICT co-ordinator of any issues or faults arising with respect to ICT equipment.*
- *Use ICT effectively to promote learning whenever it is appropriate to do so.*
- *Make use of the ICT room, and ensure pupils are aware of the protocols of its use.*
- *Ensure that the school's E-safety procedures are known and implemented within their classroom.*
- *Ensure that pupils do not import ICT objects either via the Internet, disk or other device onto school computers that pose a risk to the school network.*
- *Promote a positive image of ICT and ensure pupils' work is purposeful and appropriate and conducted with confidence and enjoyment.*
- *Be aware of specific issues where notified, for example, shutdown procedures, recharging of laptops, file management, local area network (LAN) monitoring, use of digital cameras.*

In order to achieve our declared aims with respect to ICT, the following additional roles and responsibilities should also be observed.

The E-learning co-ordinator will:

- *Formulate plans for the use of ICT across the curriculum to enhance teaching and learning in all subject areas.*
- *Develop use of ICT for planning, record-keeping and tracking pupil progress.*
- *Monitor all work in ICT including assessment and recording. This will involve overseeing the development of a portfolio of exemplar work and assessments.*
- *Highlight areas for the development of IT within the school development plan.*
- *Take the lead in policy development and the integration of ICT into schemes of work designed to ensure progression and continuity in pupils' experience of ICT throughout the school.*
- *Fulfil the role of E-safety co-ordinator as described within the E-safety policy.*
- *Manage the school network and links with the local authority schools intranet.*
- *Maintain an up-to-date inventory of ICT resources and ensure that all staff are aware of how to use the resources which are available.*
- *Monitor the use of resources and the budget accordingly, including the co-ordination and the purchase and maintenance of equipment.*
- *Be line manager for the ICT technician.*
- *Ensure that all ICT hardware and software is in good working order for use by children and staff.*
- *Encourage and lead systematic development of knowledge and skills of teachers, support staff and adult help, to enable them to fully support, access and use ICT.*
- *Induct new staff to the ICT systems used for teaching and learning.*
- *Develop use of ICT for school administration.*
- *Develop and manage the school website.*
- *Maximize the use of home–school links and develop extended use of ICT facilities by parents and the wider community.*
- *Keep abreast of current thinking by reading and attendance at courses.*

In addition, a member of the teaching staff may take on some responsibility as ICT co-ordinator to support the E-learning co-ordinator with regard to curriculum development.

The ICT co-ordinator will:

- *Work with the E-learning co-ordinator to periodically review and monitor the work in ICT including assessment and recording.*
- *Support colleagues in their efforts to include ICT in their development of detailed work plans, in their implementation of those schemes of work and in assessment and record-keeping activities*

- *Monitor progress in the discrete subject of ICT and advise the E-learning co-ordinator on action needed.*
- *Highlight areas for the development of ICT within the school development plan.*
- *Encourage and lead systematic development of knowledge and skills of teachers, support staff and adult help, to enable them fully to support, access and use ICT.*

These descriptions are based upon the extended model of ICT management structure headed by a senior manager who is the E-learning co-ordinator and supported by an ICT co-ordinator. Alternatively, colleagues may need to combine most of the above within the remit of the ICT co-ordinator with an additional inclusion of the headteacher who will partially fulfil the role of E-learning co-ordinator.

Here is an alternative text for ICT co-ordinator in such a school where there is no E-learning co-ordinator.

ICT co-ordinator will:

- *Formulate plans for the use of ICT across the curriculum to enhance teaching and learning in all subject areas.*
- *Develop use of ICT for planning, record-keeping and tracking pupil progress.*
- *Monitor the work in ICT including assessment and recording. This will involve overseeing the development of a portfolio of exemplar work and assessments.*
- *Highlight areas for the development of IT within the school development plan.*
- *Take the lead in policy development and the integration of IT into schemes of work designed to ensure progression and continuity in pupils' experience of IT throughout the school.*
- *Manage the school network and links with regional WAN (wide area network).*
- *Maintain an up-to-date inventory of ICT resources and ensure that all staff are aware of how to use the resources which are available.*
- *Monitor the use of resources and the budget accordingly.*
- *Co-ordinate the purchase and maintenance of equipment.*
- *Be line manager for the ICT technician.*
- *Ensure that all ICT hardware and software is in good working order for use of children and staff.*
- *Encourage and lead systematic development of knowledge and skills of teachers, support staff and adult help, to enable them fully to support, access and use ICT.*
- *Induct new staff to the ICT systems used for teaching and learning.*
- *Develop use of ICT for school administration.*
- *Develop and manage the school website.*
- *Maximize the use of home–school links and develop extended use of ICT facilities by parents and the wider community.*
- *Keep abreast of current thinking by reading and attendance at courses.*

If you have not already grasped the nettle regarding the team's job descriptions, here is the opportunity to do so.

The ICT technician will:

- *Install and build new computer systems as directed by the ICT co-ordinator.*
- *Evaluate the nature of any technical failures and, following discussion with ICT co-ordinator, undertake necessary repairs.*
- *Support teaching staff in the setting up and organization of ICT equipment.*
- *Maintain anti-virus software updates ensuring that all equipment is protected from known virus attack.*
- *Monitor the backing up of files onto server data tapes and periodically run checks to ensure this process is running correctly.*
- *Routinely check desktop set-ups to ensure that PC performance is maximized.*
- *Add and remove programmes to and from computers as necessary.*

- *Maintain the computer-based register for all machines and use this to log ongoing changes.*
- *Routinely check the school's printers to ensure efficient use of resources and to minimize downtime.*
- *Evaluate the efficacy of classroom computer performance and to rebuild and reformat as directed by the ICT co-ordinator.*
- *Monitor computer-cabling systems within classrooms and inform ICT co-ordinator of any Health and Safety concerns.*

Clearly this again depends upon the nature of the technical support available within the school. Next week I shall cover the two remaining elements for the policy. I am happy to follow up any matters arising over the weekend.

7th January

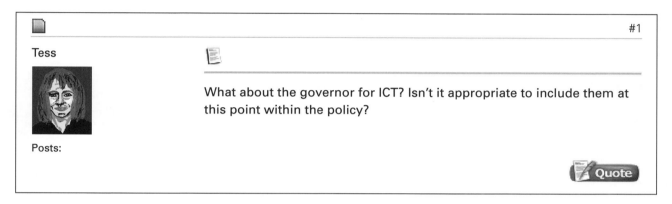

8th January

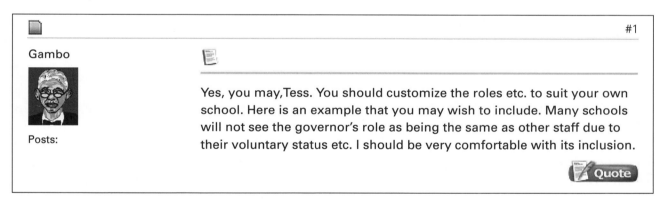

The E-learning (ICT) governor will:

- *Ensure that the governing body meets its responsibilities in helping the school resource, plan and deliver a coherent and effective ICT strategy.*
- *Support the school's strategic ICT development and contribute to the school's vision for the future use of ICT.*
- *Raise awareness within the governing body of the use of ICT within the school.*
- *Report developments in ICT annually to parents.*
- *Contribute to the formulation of the school ICT policy.*
- *Ensure that the level of skill amongst teaching and support staff in the application of ICT to learning is prioritized within the governing body.*
- *Ensure that the governing body has agreed an Internet safe use policy and that responsibility for E-safety has been appropriately allocated to a member of staff.*
- *Consider how the school can develop as a focus for E-learning and how the school's ICT facilities can be made available out of school hours for use by pupils and the wider community.*

9th January

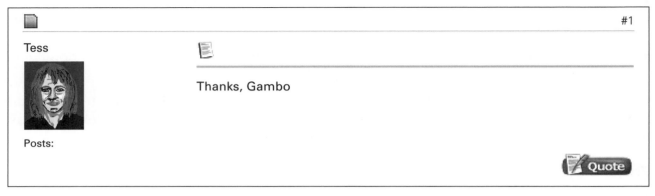

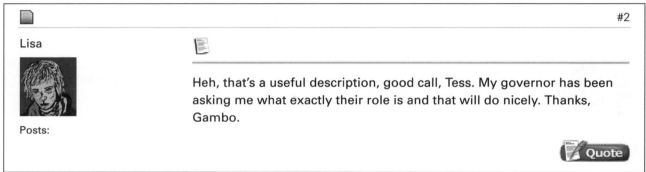

10th January

Planning and delivery of content
*At ********** (name of school) a pupil's entitlement to ICT will consist of two separate though clearly interrelated and overlapping components.*

As a discrete subject
The teaching of a specific skill based programme of study for ICT based upon the Programme of Study as outlined in the National Curriculum (NC) and articulated within the school's ICT planning matrix. The school follows the QCA Scheme of Work for ICT (amend as appropriate). All children between Years 1 and 6 spend one hour per week fulfilling the relevant task for that week. In order to ensure delivery of this entitlement, each Key Stage 1 (KS1) and Key Stage 2 (KS2) class has timetabled access to the ICT suite. Foundation stage classes will receive timetabled access for one term (again, customize). Medium-term planning will be produced across the year groups based upon the appropriate Unit of Study highlighted within the Scheme of Work. These plans will identify both learning objectives and assessment opportunities linked to specific activities.

Supporting the broad curriculum
The use of ICT skills and resources is a statutory requirement of all NC subjects with the exception of physical education (PE) and a National Curriculum skill. Information and communication technology therefore should be a key factor in all areas of the curriculum, from research using CD-ROMs and web browsers to the use of word-processing to produce quality original text. Staff should carefully consider opportunities in which ICT facilities may complement learning objectives in other subjects, and plan for their use accordingly. In order to ensure delivery of this entitlement, each classroom has access to an interactive whiteboard and multimedia projector connected to a networked laptop computer (customize). Staff may also reserve the ICT suite for support activities for literacy and numeracy when not scheduled for core ICT activities.

The ICT cross-curricular support matrix (we will cover this shortly) will act as a medium-term planning framework and identifies specific activities and software which year teams should use to address learning objectives in other subjects. Each class has networked access to web-based resources and each pupil will be assigned moderated access to virtual learning resources using the ***** virtual learning environment (customize).

Some very important practical messages of how the two areas – discrete ICT and cross-curricular – will be realized within your school. Be specific; imagine you are an NQT who is not sure about the difference between the two spheres. Let the policy be a handbook that makes it explicit. Individual colleagues may also want to stretch or squeeze areas relating to interactive whiteboards and virtual learning environments (VLEs) depending upon your individual circumstances.

Learning and teaching

In order to promote high standards of learning and good progress, staff should prepare lessons in line with the learning and teaching policy. Teaching of ICT will focus upon the teaching of objectives in sufficient breadth and depth, structuring them in a way that ensures good progression. Planning should take account of the need of all pupils to use ICT in appropriate contexts throughout both key stages, and will provide opportunities for pupils to experience a variety of learning strategies including: collaborative group work, investigative work, problem-solving, and enquiry-based learning. The use of ICT will be planned carefully and differentiated to match the needs of individuals and groups of children. Interactive technologies such as the classroom interactive whiteboards may enhance opportunities for learning when planned effectively.

14th January

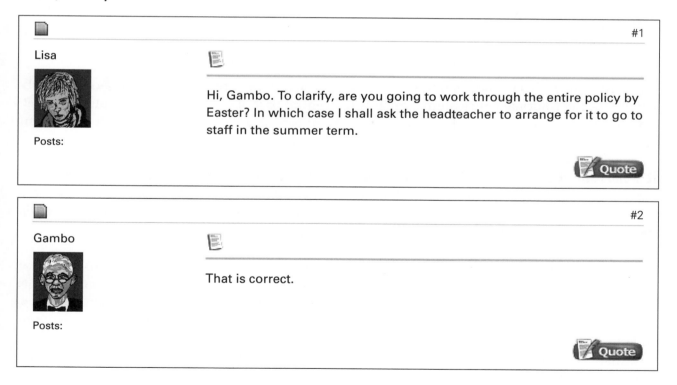

#1

Lisa

Posts:

Hi, Gambo. To clarify, are you going to work through the entire policy by Easter? In which case I shall ask the headteacher to arrange for it to go to staff in the summer term.

Quote

#2

Gambo

Posts:

That is correct.

Quote

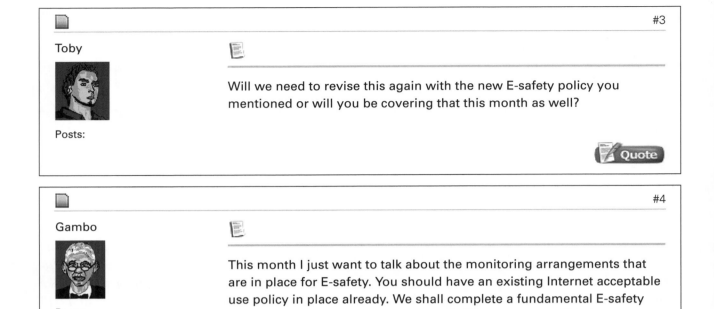

Toby

Posts:

Will we need to revise this again with the new E-safety policy you mentioned or will you be covering that this month as well?

Quote

Gambo

Posts:

This month I just want to talk about the monitoring arrangements that are in place for E-safety. You should have an existing Internet acceptable use policy in place already. We shall complete a fundamental E-safety review next year in the second part of this programme. This is a very important review that will involve the commitment of all staff. For now, the ICT policy review will not include that. However, the policy needs to be revisited annually anyway and, so, in 12 months' time the next minor review will incorporate the new E-safety documents.

Quote

18th January

Week 19, Task 14 – Using ICT across the Curriculum, Statutory Requirements

We spent some time last month developing our understanding of the role of ICT as a discrete subject within the National Curriculum, which is the central part of the co-ordinator's role. However, more and more emphasis is placed upon the use of ICT as a tool that may have a significant impact upon learning right across the curriculum in each individual subject area.

'ICT made an indirect impact on standards through improved opportunities for collaboration, creativity and to problem solving. Pupils were interested, enthusiastic and curious about ICT and this contributed to their engagement and motivation. This drove them to explore the potential of ICT, helped them to sustain their concentration and promoted their independent learning.' (Ofsted, 2005: 2)

This shift in focus in recent years lies more than anything else behind my emphasis upon the role of the E-learning co-ordinator, which we have discussed previously at length. Your task this week is to orchestrate with colleagues a system that will audit this usage to ensure that school systems and practices are sufficient to allow all learners to make the best use of new technologies in order to access the curriculum.

In many schools cross-curricular use of ICT is becoming a strength. The BECTA Review 2005 reported that skills and confidence of staff in using ICT in teaching had shown a marked improvement over the five years to 2003; a trend supported by a study of the educational impact of broadband that found that the reliability offered by broadband gave practitioners the confidence to use technology 'live' in class (Underwood et al., 2005). This increase in teachers' willingness to utilize E-learning resources alongside enormous national investment, both in infrastructure and content, means that the task of auditing use in school and local impact is now essential.

Invariably the development of cross-curricular ICT has often been ad hoc as resources have become available and innovative teachers have applied them creatively. You need to ensure that within your school the whole is at least equal to the sum of these individual parts and implement a top-down audit that references usage against the National Curriculum for each subject area. A useful starting point is the QCA document, *ICT in Other Subjects*, which is a reference guide to indicate ICT provision in the Programmes of Study for other subjects in the National Curriculum.

Table 5.2 is an extract showing the National Curriculum requirements for science during Key Stage 1. It stipulates the minimum use of ICT within science during the key stage in order for that subject's order to be delivered. The E-learning co-ordinator's role is to match this against current existing practice in school and to identify any areas that may not be met. There are three main ways to achieve this:

1 Ask other subject leaders to highlight any or all use of ICT within their area of the curriculum, cross-referenced to the subject matrix and the National Curriculum from which it derives. The advantage of this approach is that for E-learning to become embedded, a key factor is the support and expertise of other subject leaders. Having each co-ordinator as an ICT champion with oversight of their own area is an enormous benefit and so their engagement at this stage is welcomed. One disadvantage is that they may not be as well informed as individual class teachers as to what is happening in terms of ICT in any particular cohort.

Table 5.2 Cross-curricular ICT opportunities in science for Key Stage 1

Subject	Statutory requirement	ICT opportunity
Science	**Scientific enquiry**	**Scientific enquiry**
	2g – pupils should be taught to communicate what happened in a variety of ways, including using ICT	**2g** – ICT link: this requirement builds on ICT/3
	Breadth of study **1c** – pupils should be taught the knowledge, skills and understanding through using a range of sources of information and data, including ICT- based sources	
	Life processes and living things **2a** – pupils should be taught to recognize and compare the main external parts of the bodies of humans and other animals	**Life processes and living things** **2a** – pupils could use multimedia sources to make comparisons **4** – Variation and classification – pupils could use data collected to compile a class database
	Materials and their processes **1b** – pupils should be taught to sort objects into groups on the basis of simple material properties	**Materials and their processes** **1b** – pupils could use a software package to combine words and pictures about materials and objects
	Physical processes **3c** – pupils should be taught that there are many kinds of sound and sources of sound	**Physical processes** **3c** – pupils could use sensors to detect and compare sounds

Available on the net at http://www.sagepub.co.uk/wrightbk1

2   The second option is to ask individual class teachers to highlight use within their class of ICT across the range of subject areas. This will produce the opposite outcomes in so much that the actual intelligence of what is being implemented within that classroom will be strong although the activity itself is not going to have the same impact in terms of subject leader CPD.

3   A third alternative is to complete a paper audit yourself, based upon a trawl of medium-term plans. Whilst not sounding an attractive proposition, it does mean that you can get on with it without the need to mobilize support from colleagues and probably use up limited goodwill at the same time. The obvious disadvantage is that colleagues will not have ownership of the initiative.

If possible, go for the first option. This will need forward planning, however, you may be fortunate and subject leaders may already have this information available, particularly in the core subjects. Next month we shall examine ways in which to map the core requirements across the curriculum.

19th January

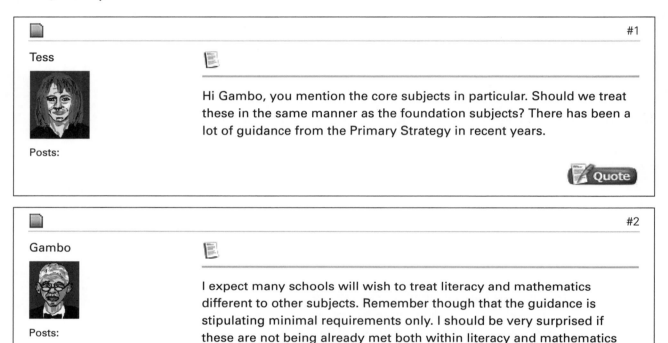

Tess

Posts:

#1

Hi Gambo, you mention the core subjects in particular. Should we treat these in the same manner as the foundation subjects? There has been a lot of guidance from the Primary Strategy in recent years.

Quote

Gambo

Posts:

#2

I expect many schools will wish to treat literacy and mathematics different to other subjects. Remember though that the guidance is stipulating minimal requirements only. I should be very surprised if these are not being already met both within literacy and mathematics due to the volume of Primary Strategy materials that are available.

Quote

20th January

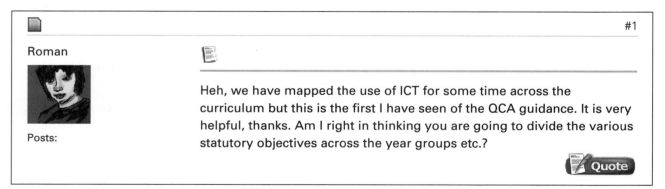

Roman

Posts:

#1

Heh, we have mapped the use of ICT for some time across the curriculum but this is the first I have seen of the QCA guidance. It is very helpful, thanks. Am I right in thinking you are going to divide the various statutory objectives across the year groups etc.?

Quote

Gambo

Posts:

#2

Yes, throughout this term we will aim to produce a cross-curricular plan, which maps against each of the targets. That is for all accept the core subjects. I do think that these are best treated slightly differently to other subjects. Tables 5.3 and 5.4 are derived directly from the QCA documentation and provide a complete overview of what needs to be completed.

Table 5.3 Cross-curricular ICT opportunities for Key Stage 1

Subject	Statutory requirement	ICT opportunity
Maths	**Breadth of study** **1f** – pupils should be taught the knowledge, skills and understanding through exploring and using a variety of resources and materials, including **ICT**	
	Number **1f** – pupils should be taught to communicate in spoken, pictorial and written form, at first using informal language and recording, then mathematical language and symbols	**Number** **1f** – pupils could use ICT to communicate results using appropriate mathematical symbols
	Shape, space and measures **1b** – pupils should be taught to select and use appropriate mathematical equipment when solving problems involving measures or measurement **4b** – pupils should be taught to understand angle as a measure of turn using whole turns, half-turns and quarter-turns	**Shape, space and measures** **1b** – pupils could use both digital and analogue devices to measure weight or time **4b** – pupils could programme a toy to follow a path involving half- and quarter-turns
English	**Reading – Non-fiction and non-literary texts** **7a** – the range should include print and **ICT-based** information texts, including those with continuous text and illustrations	**Reading – Non-fiction and non-literary texts** **2a** – pupils should be taught to use the organizational features of non-fiction texts, including captions, illustrations, contents, index and chapters to find information **ICT note**: organizational features in CD-ROMs and web pages include icons, hot-links and menus
	Writing – Planning and drafting **2b** – working with the teacher, in order to be able to develop their writing, pupils should be taught to assemble and develop ideas on **screen** and on paper	**Writing – Planning and drafting** **2c** – pupils should be taught to plan and review their writing, discussing the quality of what is written **ICT opportunity**: pupils could compare print-outs from two different drafts of their own writing to check revisions and improvements

Table 5.3 Continued

Subject	Statutory requirement	ICT opportunity
Science	**Scientific enquiry** **2g** – pupils should be taught to communicate what happened in a variety of ways, including using ICT	**Scientific enquiry** **2g** – ICT link: this requirement builds on ICT/3
	Breadth of study **1c** – pupils should be taught the knowledge, skills and understanding through using a range of sources of information and data, including ICT-based sources	
	Life processes and living things **2a** – pupils should be taught to recognize and compare the main external parts of the bodies of humans and other animals	**Life processes and living things** **2a** – pupils could use multimedia sources to make comparisons **4** – variation and classification – pupils could use data collected to compile a class database
	Materials and their processes **1b** – pupils should be taught to sort objects into groups on the basis of simple material properties	**Materials and their processes** **1b** – pupils could use a software package to combine words and pictures about materials and objects
	Physical processes **3c** – pupils should be taught that there are many kinds of sound and sources of sound	**Physical processes** **3c** – pupils could use sensors to detect and compare sounds
History	**4a** – pupils should be taught how to find out about the past from a range of sources of information **5** – pupils should be taught to select from their knowledge of history and communicate it in a variety of ways	**4a** – pupils could use information from a CD-ROM to find out about the life of a significant person, or the way of life in the past **5** – pupils could order important events in a story on an onscreen time line
Geography	**2c** – in developing geographical skills, pupils should be taught to use globes, maps and plans at a range of scales **2d** – in developing geographical skills, pupils should be taught to use secondary sources of information [*for example, CD-ROM*] **4a** – pupils should be taught to make observations about where things are located and about other features in the environment **6b** – pupils should be taught the knowledge, skills and understanding through the study of two localities, a locality either in the UK or overseas that has physical and/or human features that contrast with the locality of the school	**2c** – pupils could use a programmable toy to develop instructions for following a route **2d** – ICT link: this requirement builds on ICT/1a **4a** – pupils could use a digital camera to record people, places and events observed outside the classroom **6b** – pupils could use CD-ROMs or the Internet to investigate a contrasting locality

Table 5.3 Continued

Subject	Statutory requirement	ICT opportunity
Art and Design	**4a** – pupils should be taught about visual and tactile elements, including colour, pattern and texture, line and tone, shape, form and space	**4a** – pupils could use 'paint' software to explore shape, colour and pattern
Music	**2b** – pupils should be taught how to explore, choose and organize sounds and musical ideas **3b** – pupils should be taught how to make improvements to their own work	**2b** – pupils could use software designed to enable exploration of sounds **3b** – pupils could use recording equipment to recall sounds and identify and make improvements
DT	**1a** – pupils should be taught to generate ideas by drawing on their own and others' experiences **1e** – pupils should be taught to communicate their ideas using a variety of methods, including drawing and using models **2e** – pupils should be taught to use simple finishing techniques to improve the appearance of their product, using a range of equipment	**1a** – pupils could use word-processing or desktop publishing (DTP) software and a printer to plan and display their ideas **1e** – pupils could use word-processing or desktop publishing (DTP) software and a printer to plan and display their ideas **2e** – pupils could use 'paint' software and a colour printer to produce a pattern for finishing a product
PE		**Dance activities** **6** – pupils could use videos of movements and actions to develop their ideas
		Gymnastic activities **8** – pupils could use videos of movements and actions to develop their ideas Pupils could use a concept keyboard to record the order of specific actions in their sequences

Available on the net at http://www.sagepub.co.uk/wrightbk1

Table 5.4 Cross-curricular ICT opportunities for Key Stage 2

Subject	Statutory requirement	ICT opportunity
Maths	**Breadth of study** **1f** – pupils should be taught the knowledge, skills and understanding through exploring and using a variety of resources and materials, including **ICT**	
	Number **1c** – pupils should be taught to select and use appropriate mathematical equipment, including ICT	**Number** **4d** – pupils should be taught to recognize, represent and interpret simple number relationships, constructing and using formulae in words then symbols **ICT opportunity**: pupils could construct and use a formula to transform one list of data to another

Table 5.4 Continued

Subject	Statutory requirement	ICT opportunity
Maths	**Shape, space and measures** **3b** – pupils should be taught to transform objects in practical situations; transform images using **ICT**	**Shape, space and measures** **1c** – pupils should be taught to approach spatial problems flexibly, including trying alternative approaches to overcome difficulties **ICT opportunity**: pupils could use software to create repeating patterns, such as tessellations **2c** – pupils should be taught to make and draw with increasing accuracy 2-D and 3-D shapes and patterns; recognize reflective symmetry in regular polygons, recognize their geometrical features and properties including angles, faces, pairs of parallel lines and symmetry, and use these to classify shapes and solve problems **ICT opportunity**: pupils could use object drawing software to plan alternative layouts for a room
	Processing, representing and handling data **2c** – pupils should be taught to represent and interpret discrete data using graphs and diagrams, including pictograms, bar charts and line graphs, then interpret a wider range of graphs and diagrams, using **ICT** where appropriate	
English	**Reading – Non-fiction and non-literary texts** **7a** – print and **ICT-based** information texts, including those with continuous text and illustrations	**Reading –- Non-fiction and non-literary texts** **2a** – pupils should be taught to use the organisational features of non-fiction texts, including captions, illustrations, contents, index and chapters to find information **ICT note**: organizational features in CD-ROMs and web pages include icons, hot-links and menus
	Reading – non-fiction and non-literary texts **9b** –- the range should include print and **ICT-based** reference and information materials (for example, textbooks, reports, encyclopaedias, handbooks, dictionaries, thesauruses, glossaries, CD-ROM, Internet)	**Reading – Literature** **8** – pupils could use moving image text (for example, television, film, multimedia) to support their study of literary texts and to study how words, images and sounds are combined to convey meaning and emotion

Table 5.4 Continued

Subject	Statutory requirement	ICT opportunity
English	**Writing – Planning and drafting** **2** – to develop their writing on paper and on **screen**, pupils should be taught to: a) plan – note and develop initial ideas; d) proofread – check the draft for spelling and punctuation errors, omissions and repetitions **ICT note**: on screen includes using the planning and proofing tools in a word processor (for example, thesaurus, grammar checker)	**Writing – Composition** **1 – ICT opportunity**: pupils could compose on **screen** and on paper Planning and drafting **Breadth of study** **11** – The range of readers for writing should include teachers, the class, other children, adults, the wider community and imagined readers **ICT note**: readers could include those contacted through post, fax or email
Science	**Scientific enquiry** **2f** – pupils should be taught to make systematic observations and measurements, including the use of **ICT** for data logging **2h** – pupils should be taught to use a wide range of methods, including diagrams, drawings, ... and **ICT**, to communicate data in an appropriate and systematic manner	**Scientific enquiry** **2f – ICT link**: this requirement builds upon ICT/2b **2h – ICT link**: requirement builds on ICT/3
	Breadth of study **1c** – pupils should be taught the knowledge, skills and understanding through using a range of sources of information and data, including **ICT-based** sources **2h – Statutory**: pupils should be taught to use a wide range of methods, including diagrams, drawings, ... and **ICT**, to communicate data in an appropriate and systematic manner	**2h – ICT link**: this requirement builds on ICT/3
	Life processes and living things **2b** – pupils should be taught about the need for food for activity and growth, and about the importance of an adequate and varied diet for health **2c** – pupils should be taught that the heart acts as a pump to circulate the blood through vessels around the body, including through the lungs **2e** – pupils should be taught that humans and some other animals have skeletons and muscles to support and protect their bodies and to help them move	**Life processes and living things** **2b** – pupils could use a database or spreadsheet to analyse data about types of food in school lunches **2c** – pupils could use video or CD-ROM to see things that cannot be directly observed **2e** – pupils could use video or CD-ROM to see things that cannot be directly observed

Table 5.4 Continued

Subject	Statutory requirement	ICT opportunity
Science	**2f** – pupils should be taught about the main stages of the human life cycle **4a** – pupils should be taught to make and use keys **5b** – pupils should be taught about the different plants and animals found in different habitats **5f** – pupils should be taught that micro-organisms are living organisms that are often too small to be seen, and that they may be beneficial or harmful	**2f** – pupils could use video or CD-ROM to see things that cannot be directly observed **4a** – pupils could use a branching database to develop and use keys **5b** – pupils could use video or CD-ROM to compare non-local habitats **5f** – pupils could use simulation software to show changes in the populations of micro-organisms in different conditions
	Materials and their processes **2b** – pupils should be taught to describe changes that occur when materials are heated or cooled **2e** – pupils should be taught the part played by evaporation and condensation in the water cycle	**Materials and their processes** **2b** – pupils could use sensors to record temperature changes **2e** – pupils could use CD-ROM or the Internet to research water supplies in a range of localities
	Physical processes **1a** – pupils should be taught to construct circuits, incorporating a battery or power supply and a range of switches, to make electrical devices work **3f** – pupils should be taught how to change the pitch and loudness of sounds produced by some vibrating objects **4b** – pupils should be taught how the sun appears to change during the day and how shadows change as this happens **4c** – pupils should be taught how day and night are related to the spin of the Earth on its own axis **4d** – pupils should be taught that the Earth orbits the Sun once each year and that the Moon take approximately 28 days to orbit the Earth	**Physical processes** **1a** – pupils could use simulation software to extend an investigation of components in a series circuit **3f** – pupils could use sensors to detect and compare sounds made under different conditions **4b** – pupils could use video or CD-ROM to study models of the Sun, Earth and Moon system **4c** – pupils could use video or CD-ROM to study models of the Sun, Earth and Moon system **4d** – pupils could use video or CD-ROM to study models of the Sun, Earth and Moon system
History	**4a** – pupils should be taught to find out about the events, people and changes studied from an appropriate range of sources of information, including **ICT-based** sources **4b** – pupils should be taught to ask and answer questions and to select and record information relevant to the focus of the enquiry **5c** – pupils should be taught to communicate their knowledge and understanding of history in a variety of ways	**4b** – pupils could use a census database to search for information and identify and explain patterns of change **5c** – pupils could use digitised maps to identify and colour-code features important to local study

Table 5.4 Continued

Subject	Statutory requirement	ICT opportunity
Geography	**1e** – in undertaking geographical enquiry, pupils should be taught to communicate in ways appropriate to the task and audience, for example, by writing to a newspaper about a local issue, using email to exchange information about the locality with another school **2d** – in developing geographical skills, pupils should be taught to use secondary sources of information, including aerial photographs [for example, stories, information texts, the Internet …] **2f** – in developing geographical enquiry, pupils should be taught to use **ICT** to help in geographical investigations [for example, by creating a data file to analyse fieldwork data] **3d** – pupils should be taught to explain why places are like they are **3f** – pupils should be taught to describe and explain how and why places are similar to and different from places in the same country and elsewhere in the world	**1e – ICT link:** this requirement builds on ICT/3a, 3b **2d** – pupils could use a database to sort, question, and present information about different countries **3d** – pupils could use the internet to access comparative weather information about different locations **3f** – pupils could use the internet to access comparative information about different locations
Art and Design	**1c** – pupils should be taught to collect visual and other information to help them develop their ideas, including using a sketchbook **2b** – pupils should be taught to apply their experience of materials and processes, including drawing, developing their control of tools and techniques **3a** – pupils should be taught to compare ideas, methods and approaches in their own and other's work and say what they think and feel about them **5c** – pupils should be taught the knowledge, skills and understanding through using a range of materials and processes, including **ICT** [for example … digital media]	**1c** – pupils could use digital and video cameras to record observations **2b** – pupils could use digital images as a starting point for creative textile work **3a** – pupils could develop their own class art gallery on the school website **5d** – pupils should be taught the knowledge, skills and understanding through investigating art, craft and design in the locality and in a variety of genres, styles and traditions [for example, … on the Internet]
Music	**5d** – pupils should be taught the knowledge, skills and understanding through using **ICT** to capture, change and combine sounds	**4c** – pupils should be taught how music is produced in different ways [for example, through the use of different resources, including ICT] and described through relevant established and invented notations **ICT link:** this requirement builds on ICT/1b

Table 5.4 Continued

Subject	Statutory requirement	ICT opportunity
PSHE / Citizenship	2k – guideline: pupils should be taught to explore how the media present information	2k – pupils could use the Internet to look at different reports about the same issue
DT	1a – pupils should be taught to generate ideas for products after thinking about who will use them and what they will be used for, using information from a variety of sources, including **ICT-based** sources 1b – pupils should be taught to develop ideas and explain them clearly, putting together a list of what they want their design to achieve 1c – pupils should be taught to plan what they have to do, suggesting a sequence of actions and alternatives if needed 1d – pupils should be taught to communicate design ideas in different ways as these develop, bearing in mind aesthetic qualities and the uses and purposes for which the product is intended 2e – pupils should be taught to use finishing techniques to strengthen and improve the appearance of their product, using a range of equipment including **ICT** [for example, 'drawing' software or computer-aided design (CAD) software and a printer] 4c – pupils should be taught how mechanisms can be used to make things move in different ways, using a range of equipment including an **ICT** control program	1b – pupils could use desktop publishing (DTP) software and a colour printer to develop and communicate their design ideas 1c – pupils could use desktop publishing (DTP) software and a colour printer to develop and communicate their design ideas 1d – pupils could use desktop publishing (DTP) software and a colour printer to develop and communicate their design ideas 4c – **ICT link**: this requirement builds on ICT/2b
PE		**Dance activities** 6 – pupils could use video recordings of their sequences and dances to compare ideas and quality Pupils could use video and CD-ROMs of actions, balances and body shapes to improve performance
		Gymnastic activities 8 – pupils could use video recordings of their sequences and dances to compare ideas and quality Pupils could use video and CD-ROMs of actions, balances and body shapes to improve performance
		Athletic activities 10 – pupils could use video and CD-ROMs of actions, balances and body shapes to improve performance

Table 5.4 Continued

Subject	Statutory requirement	ICT opportunity
MFL		**2a** – pupils can be taught about other countries and cultures by working with authentic materials including some from ICT-based sources **Links with other subjects** Learning another language presents opportunities for the reinforcement of knowledge, skills and understanding developed in other curriculum areas. These opportunities can be exploited through using ICT, for example email with schools abroad, materials from the Internet and satellite television

Available on the net at http://www.sagepub.co.uk/wrightbk1

25th January

Week 20, Task 15 – An Initial Review of Internet Safety Arrangements

For the remainder of this month I want you to spend a little time considering what arrangements are in place within your school with regard to Internet safety. In many ways this is now a *nom de guerre*, as we really need to be talking about E-safety in a much broader sense. This will be a core focus for next year when we shall complete a root and branch review of all procedures in line with BECTA's 2005 guidance (BECTA, 2005). For now I just want to raise your level of awareness with regard to the many issues that surround a school's duty of care with regard to child protection and safe use of the Internet. Under the Children's Act, Every Child Matters which became law late in 2004, every school was required to refocus its provision with regard to the five core outcomes for children. Once again we shall complete a thorough review of procedures against these outcomes next year, however for now Outcome 2, 'Staying Safe', places specific requirements upon schools to ensure that children are provided with a safe environment. From an ICT perspective, this means that the security of the school network is one of its highest priorities and that self-evaluation of school systems must be robust and their outcome visible within the school's SEF. This week you should consider your strategies with regard to this whole area. Be mindful of the forthcoming major review next year that will require staff training and, potentially, curriculum interventions. Speak to your ICT governor now as this will be an issue that governors, and indeed parents, are rightfully alert to. Ultimately, all staff who work in schools have a duty of care to ensure that the children are able appropriately and safely to use the Internet and other technologies. It pays to be mindful of the fact that children are vulnerable when using the Internet and may either knowingly or unknowingly expose themselves to danger.

As a minimum measure, schools must have an Internet acceptable use policy in place. A lead member of staff, that is, part of the senior management team (ideally the E-learning co-ordinator) should be identified and should act as the central point of contact for all safety issues within the school. In developing your E-safety strategy, consider some of the following questions raised within the national guidelines:

Have you got in place a clear policy on acceptable use of the Internet and email for staff and pupils?
Do staff sign the policy as acceptance of its terms?
Have you got in place procedures for reporting accidental access to inappropriate materials?

Do staff and pupils know about these procedures?
Have you got in place sanctions for deliberate access to inappropriate materials?
Are pupils aware of these sanctions?
Are pupils and their parents provided with a copy of the acceptable use policy/rules for ICT use when the pupil joins the school?
Have you got in place a system that reminds pupils of Internet safety rules each time they log onto the network? (BECTA, 2005: 47–50)

Finally, schools have a responsibility to monitor Internet usage. How is this being done at your school? Are staff aware that their use may be monitored and does it state so on the acceptable use policy that they sign? If not there may be additional data protection issues to be considered.

All schools need to plan for a thorough E-safety review. Here are some things that you may want to enact immediately.

Action needed

1 Identify the Internet Safety Coordinator.
2 Decide when your Internet Acceptable Use Policy will be reviewed and updated.
3 Plan to raise staff awareness of the E–Safety agenda.
4 Identify how Internet safety is taught to pupils at your school and decide whether this provision is adequate.
5 Be clear about what monitoring arrangements are in place and judge whether these are adequate.

26th January

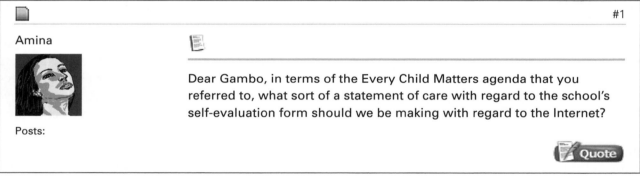

Amina

Posts:

#1

Dear Gambo, in terms of the Every Child Matters agenda that you referred to, what sort of a statement of care with regard to the school's self-evaluation form should we be making with regard to the Internet?

Quote

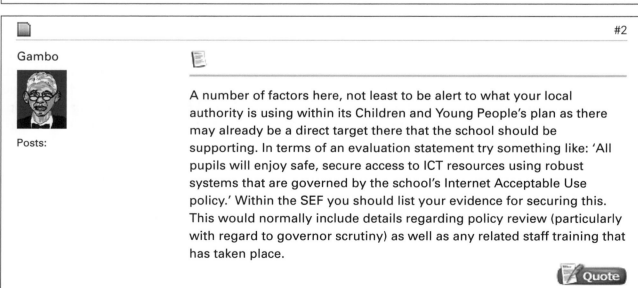

Gambo

Posts:

#2

A number of factors here, not least to be alert to what your local authority is using within its Children and Young People's plan as there may already be a direct target there that the school should be supporting. In terms of an evaluation statement try something like: 'All pupils will enjoy safe, secure access to ICT resources using robust systems that are governed by the school's Internet Acceptable Use policy.' Within the SEF you should list your evidence for securing this. This would normally include details regarding policy review (particularly with regard to governor scrutiny) as well as any related staff training that has taken place.

Quote

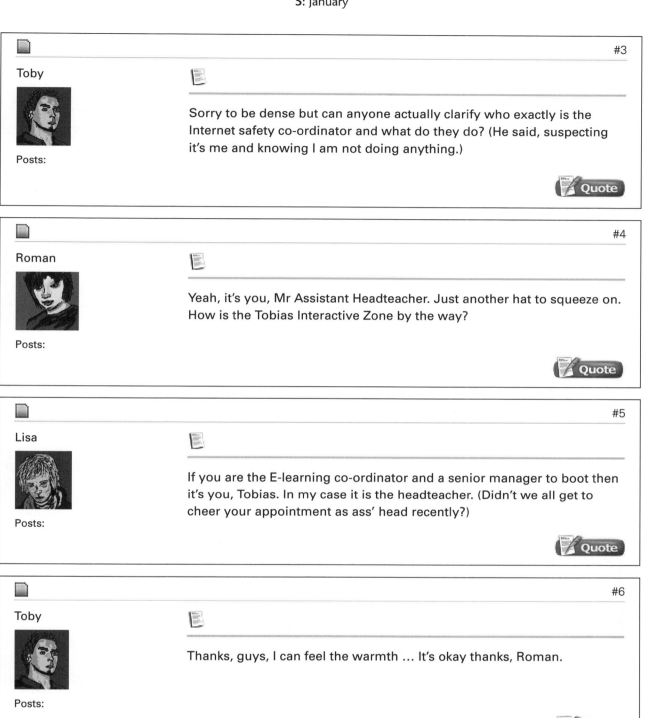

| | #3 |

Toby

Posts:

Sorry to be dense but can anyone actually clarify who exactly is the Internet safety co-ordinator and what do they do? (He said, suspecting it's me and knowing I am not doing anything.)

Quote

| | #4 |

Roman

Posts:

Yeah, it's you, Mr Assistant Headteacher. Just another hat to squeeze on. How is the Tobias Interactive Zone by the way?

Quote

| | #5 |

Lisa

Posts:

If you are the E-learning co-ordinator and a senior manager to boot then it's you, Tobias. In my case it is the headteacher. (Didn't we all get to cheer your appointment as ass' head recently?)

Quote

| | #6 |

Toby

Posts:

Thanks, guys, I can feel the warmth ... It's okay thanks, Roman.

Quote

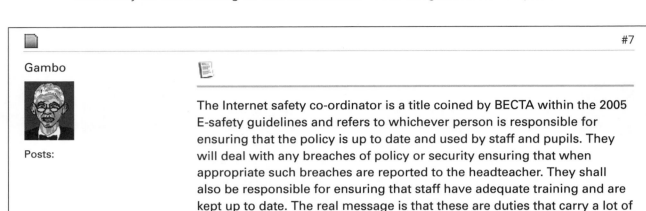

#7

Gambo

Posts:

The Internet safety co-ordinator is a title coined by BECTA within the 2005 E-safety guidelines and refers to whichever person is responsible for ensuring that the policy is up to date and used by staff and pupils. They will deal with any breaches of policy or security ensuring that when appropriate such breaches are reported to the headteacher. They shall also be responsible for ensuring that staff have adequate training and are kept up to date. The real message is that these are duties that carry a lot of responsibility and if there isn't an obvious candidate then it will fall upon the headteacher who may delegate duties to the ICT co-ordinator. This lies at the heart of the discussion we had about the make up of the ICT team.

Quote

27th January

#1

Alex

Posts:

Hi, everyone, I've not posted so much lately but everyone else seems to have taken up the slack. What I want to know is with regard to reminding the children about safe Internet use every time they use the computers. How is it practical to do so? What are other guys doing?

Quote

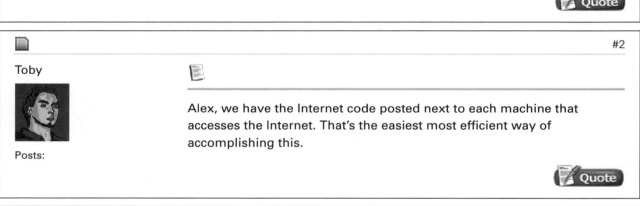

#2

Toby

Posts:

Alex, we have the Internet code posted next to each machine that accesses the Internet. That's the easiest most efficient way of accomplishing this.

Quote

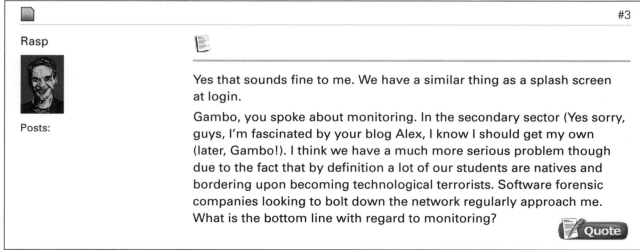

#3

Rasp

Posts:

Yes that sounds fine to me. We have a similar thing as a splash screen at login.

Gambo, you spoke about monitoring. In the secondary sector (Yes sorry, guys, I'm fascinated by your blog Alex, I know I should get my own (later, Gambo!). I think we have a much more serious problem though due to the fact that by definition a lot of our students are natives and bordering upon becoming technological terrorists. Software forensic companies looking to bolt down the network regularly approach me. What is the bottom line with regard to monitoring?

Quote

28th January

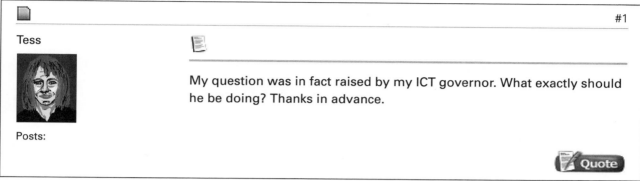

Tess

Posts:

#1

My question was in fact raised by my ICT governor. What exactly should he be doing? Thanks in advance.

Quote

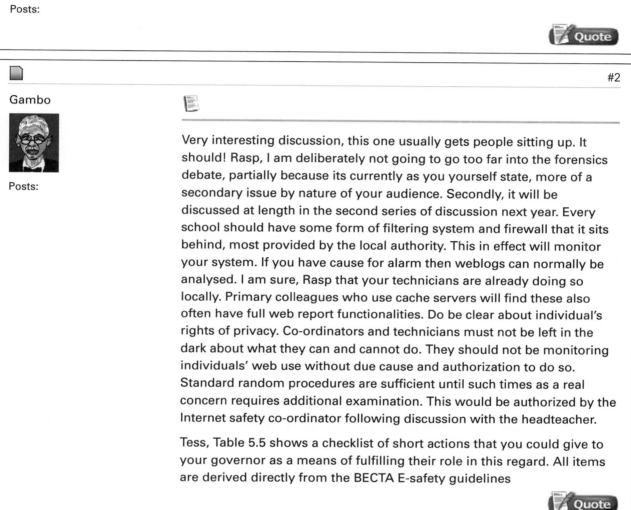

Gambo

Posts:

#2

Very interesting discussion, this one usually gets people sitting up. It should! Rasp, I am deliberately not going to go too far into the forensics debate, partially because its currently as you yourself state, more of a secondary issue by nature of your audience. Secondly, it will be discussed at length in the second series of discussion next year. Every school should have some form of filtering system and firewall that it sits behind, most provided by the local authority. This in effect will monitor your system. If you have cause for alarm then weblogs can normally be analysed. I am sure, Rasp that your technicians are already doing so locally. Primary colleagues who use cache servers will find these also often have full web report functionalities. Do be clear about individual's rights of privacy. Co-ordinators and technicians must not be left in the dark about what they can and cannot do. They should not be monitoring individuals' web use without due cause and authorization to do so. Standard random procedures are sufficient until such times as a real concern requires additional examination. This would be authorized by the Internet safety co-ordinator following discussion with the headteacher.

Tess, Table 5.5 shows a checklist of short actions that you could give to your governor as a means of fulfilling their role in this regard. All items are derived directly from the BECTA E-safety guidelines

Quote

Table 5.5 Governor's Internet checklist

1. Does the school currently have an 'Acceptable Use Internet Policy'?

2. Is there a nominated person in charge of coordinating Internet safety issues?

3. Is the policy up to date and relevant?

4. Is the policy supported by clear procedures should an incident occur?

5. Are incidents logged?

6. Is this policy one of a suite of documents that cover a range of technology usage, that is, pupil access to Internet ready mobile phones?

7. Are staff aware of their responsibilities with regard to their own use of the Internet?

8. How is the school network monitored?

9. Has the school considered adding additional filtering capability using an Internet cache?

10. Are pupils and their parents provided with a copy of the acceptable use policy/rules for ICT use when the pupil joins the school?

11. Are pupils reminded of Internet safety rules each time they use the technology? (Posted guide by each machine?)

12. Do school browsers default to an appropriate homepage?

13. Do pupils use a child-friendly search engine?

14. Are pupils able to access unrestricted messenger and chat services?

15. Is pupil use of email monitored?

16. Is Internet use adequately supervised?

17. Are pupils taught how to use the Internet safely and effectively?

18. Are pupils taught about copyright issues and plagiarism?

19. Are official guidelines adhered to with regard to children not being identifiable from photographs on the Internet?

20. Does the person in charge of Internet safety carry out risk analysis on a regular basis?

Available on the net at http://www.sagepub.co.uk/wrightbk1

Chapter 6 • February

Week 21, Task 16 – Writing a Policy for ICT, Part 2

Once again you should aim to engage the whole ICT team in discussing how these areas fit within your school in order to realize a really effective and valid policy to take to staff in the summer term. We begin with Section 5 of the document, which relates to assessment, record-keeping and reporting pupil progress.

Assessment, recording and reporting

Teacher assessments of ICT capability will be recorded throughout the year and reported to parents at the end of each academic year. Judgements of attainment should be completed against each Unit of Study using the stated learning outcomes. Formative assessment is used to guide the progress of individual pupils in their use of ICT. It involves identifying each child's progress, determining what each child has learned and what therefore should be the next stage in their learning. Teachers in the course of our teaching mostly carry out formative assessment informally. Suitable tasks for assessment of ICT work include: small group discussions; specific ICT assignments for individual pupils and individual discussions in which children are encouraged to appraise their own work and progress.

Staff should keep examples of pupils' work using the pupil folders that are set up on individual computer drives and principally those stored upon the school file server and available across the school network. A record of each pupil's progress can also be kept incorporating the pupil disks, alternatively, samples of work may be printed out and included in profile folders. Sufficiently detailed records should be accumulated to form and support a judgement on each pupil's level of attainment.

Where ICT is used across the curriculum, class records will demonstrate individuals' use of ICT and ensure equal access to resources in line with the school's equal opportunities policy.

Most important here is the recognition of what the school procedures are in terms of both assessment and record-keeping. Many schools confuse the two and in reality maintain a lot of records but do very little assessment. The assessment of ICT is a core focus for next term when I shall encourage you to conduct a root-and-branch review of what is happening and what it tells you about the standard of ICT at your school. For now match the sample policy text to your own current practice and enshrine in policy the practical procedures that enable all staff to maintain a professional view of the standards achieved.

2nd February

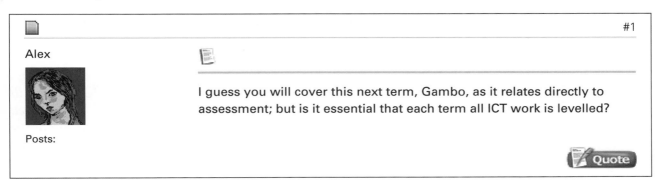

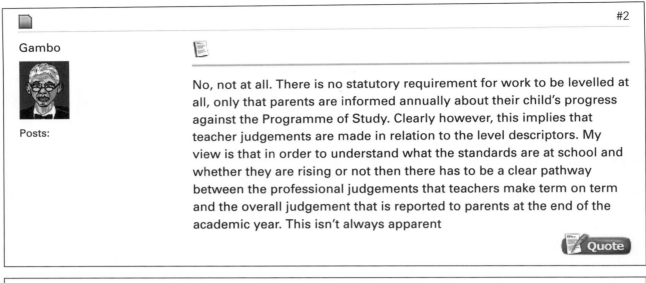

#2

Gambo

Posts:

No, not at all. There is no statutory requirement for work to be levelled at all, only that parents are informed annually about their child's progress against the Programme of Study. Clearly however, this implies that teacher judgements are made in relation to the level descriptors. My view is that in order to understand what the standards are at school and whether they are rising or not then there has to be a clear pathway between the professional judgements that teachers make term on term and the overall judgement that is reported to parents at the end of the academic year. This isn't always apparent

Quote

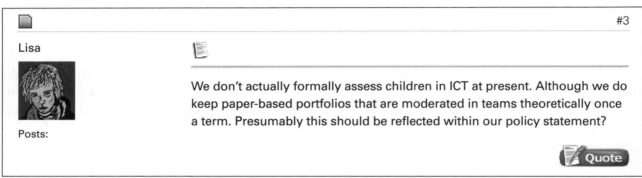

#3

Lisa

Posts:

We don't actually formally assess children in ICT at present. Although we do keep paper-based portfolios that are moderated in teams theoretically once a term. Presumably this should be reflected within our policy statement?

Quote

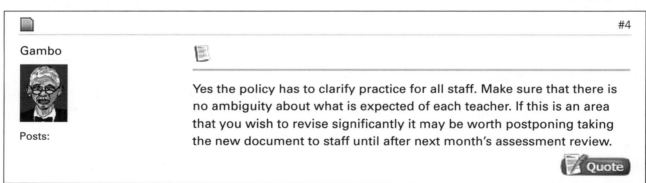

#4

Gambo

Posts:

Yes the policy has to clarify practice for all staff. Make sure that there is no ambiguity about what is expected of each teacher. If this is an area that you wish to revise significantly it may be worth postponing taking the new document to staff until after next month's assessment review.

Quote

3rd February

Progression and differentiation

As in all subjects curriculum planning should ensure continuity and progression. The school recognizes that progression in ICT involves four main aspects:

- *The progressive development of pupils' skills, knowledge and understanding*
- *Breadth of ICT applications*
- *Increased complexity of contexts in which ICT is applied*
- *The growing autonomy of the pupil in their learning.*

Adherence to the QCA Scheme of Work and its emphasis upon the acquisition of specific ICT skills will establish an appropriately planned progression of skills and activities across both Key Stages. At each level, the children are required to use progressively more complex ICT skills and to make increasing use of the features and capabilities of a software package. The development of the relevant skills, knowledge and understanding requires progressive experience, preferably from an early age and across all major curriculum areas, of using a variety of software in different contexts.

Differentiation should be achieved both through differentiated activities and through differentiation of intended outcomes. For example, pupils who are progressing rapidly should be encouraged to extend their ICT experiences either through use of more challenging software, or simply an alternative software package to provide depth of experience, or by extending the set task. Children will have different aptitudes and abilities in ICT and will progress at differing rates. However, it is important that staff systematically give every pupil the opportunity to develop their skills in this curricular area.

This traditional template defines progression through four core aspects that have been around for some time, embracing both curriculum depth and breadth. Critically, progression has to be embedded within the school's planning structures and should be extremely visible. Displays and so on should emphasize the incremental developments of strands of the curriculum in order to prevent stagnation and this should be a key focus for subject monitoring, particularly within notoriously weak areas such as control and monitoring where the same key skills are too often repeated from Year 1 to Year 4.

3rd February

#1

Alex

Posts:

Gambo, should schools still be using and cross-referencing to the QCA scheme of work?

Quote

#2

Gambo

Posts:

Hi, Alex, not so, no, the QCA Scheme of Work is purely an option for schools. Many commentators now find the national scheme to be dated despite the 2003 revisions and in many ways it fails to reflect technological changes that are impacting upon us all. What it does is to provide National Curriculum coverage and progression. Therefore schools find it a useful safety net. Schools choosing alternative means of delivering the subject should ensure that these key factors are built in.

Quote

#3

Lisa

Posts:

With regard to differentiation, I often worry that I see one size fits all particularly when monitoring planning. Am I right in saying that differentiation is as important in ICT as in any other subject area? If so it's something we need to look at.

Quote

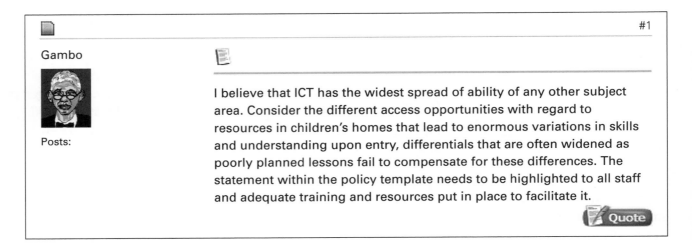

4th February

Equal opportunities and inclusion

Information and communication technology activities should be planned and recorded to ensure that all children are given the same opportunity to use and develop their skills and knowledge in accordance with the equal opportunities policy.

Pupils with special educational needs – *pupils with special educational needs benefit from using information technology as it enhances access to the curriculum, and this in turn encourages motivation and the development of skills ensuring significantly higher achievements. Therefore, the opportunities to utilize ICT should be maximized. Pupils with special needs have the same ICT entitlement as all other pupils and are offered the same curriculum.*

Able and talented – *ICT can be used to assist gifted and talented children both inside and out of school and to embed the school's aims with regard to developing excellence and enjoyment. Resources such as CD-ROMs, online information and the Internet offer a wealth of material in readily accessible form which can be matched to the needs of individual children and enable them to develop a higher level of thinking skills.*

Co-ordinators should work closely with their SENCO in defining the school's vision for ICT as a tool to support inclusion building from the work completed in relation to the self-review framework. This will enable you to produce a clear defining statement for the school's policy that the whole school can embrace and identify with. Relate the statement to practical structures that are in place for supporting inclusion, for example progress made towards ensuring out of school access to resources.

5th February

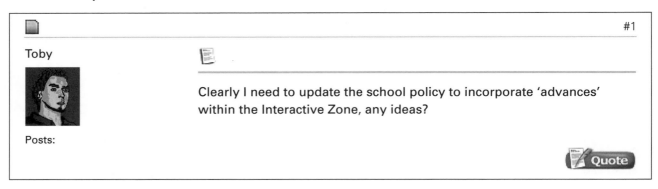

Lisa
Posts:

#2

A public health warning?

Quote

Toby
Posts:

#3

Ye of little faith! I'll send you a log-in and you will see for yourself it's having a real impact, and we are now talking to our cluster high school about linking it to their Moodle server. The transition potential is enormous.

Quote

Roman
Posts:

#4

Good for you, Toby.

Quote

Lisa
Posts:

#5

Ouch! Moodle alert!

Quote

Roman
Posts:

#6

Don't start me!

Quote

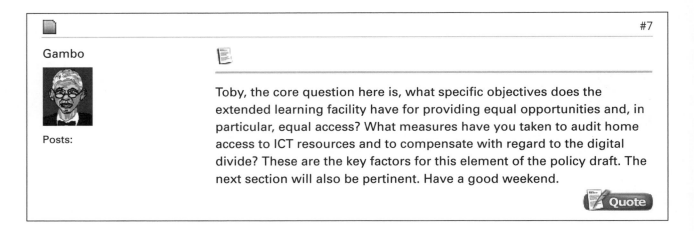

Gambo

Posts:

Toby, the core question here is, what specific objectives does the extended learning facility have for providing equal opportunities and, in particular, equal access? What measures have you taken to audit home access to ICT resources and to compensate with regard to the digital divide? These are the key factors for this element of the policy draft. The next section will also be pertinent. Have a good weekend.

Quote

8th February

Community access and extended learning

Information and communication technology can play a positive role in enabling or improving the transfer of information between pupils' homes and the school, and may be used to allow students' learning to take place in an extended home–school environment. At ……….. we have developed web-based learning resources which may be accessed via the school website in order to support the school's extended learning objectives. The E-learning co-ordinator will act as designated home school liaison officer with respect to all aspects of ICT and E-learning and will develop home–school links in line with the school's broader extended learning strategy and the school's strategy for extending learning for all pupils out of school hours.

This is an area that is developing quickly and one for which you will have defined strategies following the self-review framework activities. You may wish to list appropriate resources available via the school website and to report any specific commitment to opening access to out-of-hours learning. Schools that have now set up parent email address books for home–school communication should look to articulate the aims of such initiatives here.

Hopefully, you will be able to work through each of these sections this month within your team.

15th February

Week 23, Task 17 – Defining a Print Strategy

If you do not already have a long-term print strategy then I hope you will spend an hour or so this week reflecting upon the subject. Perhaps it is purely a technical-support issue within your school or is it simply an everyday aspect of school life? If the demands upon your print services are not well matched to your resources then you will be plagued with an inefficient system that will continually distract from your overall E-learning objectives.

Initially, let us clarify the scope of discussion. Just as your network can be divided clearly between the curriculum and administrative systems, likewise print services will replicate this. In terms of administration reprographics, this should fall outside of your remit and should be self-sufficient, not placing demands upon curriculum print resources.

So what are your curriculum needs in terms of printing and what are your current user habits? Are staff aware of the issues regarding print services or is it just a focus for complaint? Why do we print work anyway? These are fundamental questions that relate to the culture of ICT within the school. Whilst many schools do encourage children to maintain paper-based portfolios, this practice increasingly needs to be challenged and portfolios need to become electronic. It is not useful for children to stand around waiting for paper to feed from printers, and we are all familiar with the frustrations of blocked print queues. That is not to say that the paper-based systems are wrong, simply that we should not unquestioningly continue to operate in the same way as we always have. There is a strong argument, particularly with younger children, regarding the benefits of producing a paper product in terms of concrete learning, however, this can be countered by the benefits of introducing children to more abstract concepts, as they get older. I cannot understand the need or benefit of every child diligently delivering screenshots back to class after each session within the ICT suite.

With a clear principled strategy towards training you should therefore be able to minimize the amount of printing required. We do this in order to minimize the cost of consumables, hidden costs with regard to time, and the maintenance requirements that come hand in hand with heavy print systems. You need a robust solution to manage high volumes of printing in a cost-effective manner whilst avoiding downtime. Generally this will lead schools to move from a localized to a centralized shift of print traffic; a system that focuses upon efficient server-based network printers and away from consumable intensive maverick printers, ink jets, and so on.

Therefore you have two tasks. First, identify a principled position with regard to what should and should not be printed out. My personal view would be to target a movement towards pupils maintaining digital portfolios with occasional printouts for displays and so on. Secondly, consider the efficacy of your existing system in terms of maintenance and long-term total cost of ownership in comparison to a centralized printing regime.

17th February

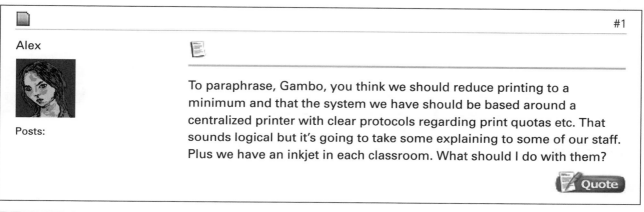

Alex

Posts:

To paraphrase, Gambo, you think we should reduce printing to a minimum and that the system we have should be based around a centralized printer with clear protocols regarding print quotas etc. That sounds logical but it's going to take some explaining to some of our staff. Plus we have an inkjet in each classroom. What should I do with them?

Quote

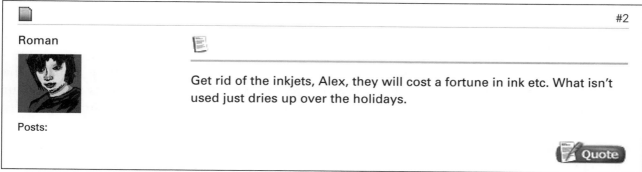

Roman

Posts:

Get rid of the inkjets, Alex, they will cost a fortune in ink etc. What isn't used just dries up over the holidays.

Quote

18th February

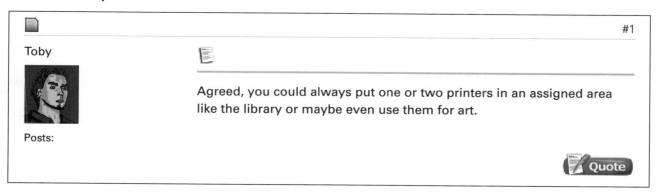

Toby

Posts:

Agreed, you could always put one or two printers in an assigned area like the library or maybe even use them for art.

Quote

19th February

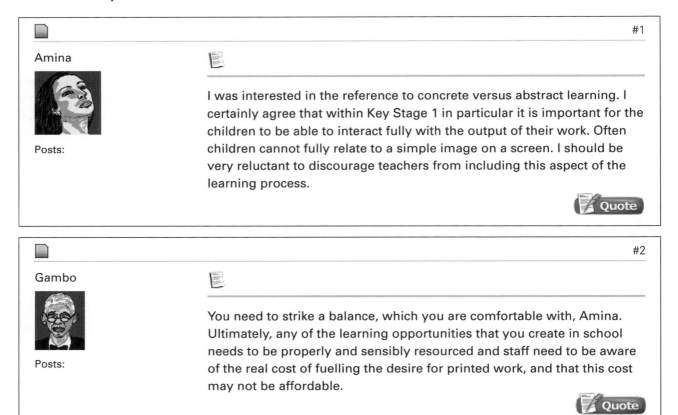

#1

Amina

Posts:

I was interested in the reference to concrete versus abstract learning. I certainly agree that within Key Stage 1 in particular it is important for the children to be able to interact fully with the output of their work. Often children cannot fully relate to a simple image on a screen. I should be very reluctant to discourage teachers from including this aspect of the learning process.

Quote

#2

Gambo

Posts:

You need to strike a balance, which you are comfortable with, Amina. Ultimately, any of the learning opportunities that you create in school needs to be properly and sensibly resourced and staff need to be aware of the real cost of fuelling the desire for printed work, and that this cost may not be affordable.

Quote

22nd February

Week 24, Task 18 – Using ICT across the Curriculum, Autumn Term Macro Plan

Last month we discussed the need for a top-down review of our provision of ICT across all subject areas that, hopefully, has created an audit of current use which you have been able to relate to the statutory National Curriculum requirements based upon the QCA guidance (Tables 5.3 and 5.4). I am now going to propose that, as co-ordinator, you need to ensure that the minimum requirements are met within your school. This can be done quite quickly having gained the comprehensive overview that you have, you just need to map out the requirements against your long-term macro plan or topic map. I am going to deal with English and mathematics separately at the end of term but will include all other subjects within a projected cross-curricular matrix for each of the three terms. Delivery of the ICT element within each subject area will only require a single activity per half-term from each cohort, however, I must stress that this is a minimum recommendation. Teachers should not be discouraged from developing ICT use whenever they feel it is appropriate; this is the minimum that you will require and should provide a focus for any moderation of cross-curricular usage. I have produced exemplar plans for each term that you could adapt to match your own topic map and resources, but if used will ensure that curriculum requirements have been met within each subject area. It should then be a simple cut and paste exercise to manoeuvre the subject-based activities to match your own long-term plans. Once completed (see exemplar in Table 6.1) the new plans may be introduced and monitored on a termly basis to ensure that the requirements are met.

I anticipate that you may complete this activity over the next few weeks and will provide templates for the spring and summer terms at the beginning of March. You may wish to see the whole picture before you allocate your own tasks but alternatively might find it easier to sort out the autumn plan first.

Table 6.1 Examplar ICT planning matrix, autumn term

Year	Subject	ICT Opportunity and Resource	Objective
1	**ART** Drawing, anatomical	Pupils could use digital and video cameras to record observations	**1c** – Collect visual and other information to help them develop their ideas
		Digital camera	
1	**HISTORY** Where I live	PowerPoint presentation in which Children could present information gathered from simple family research	**5** – Statutory: select from their knowledge of history and communicate it in a variety of ways
		PowerPoint presentation, 'My family'	
2	**MUSIC** Taking off	Pupils could use software designed to enable exploration of sounds	**2b** – Pupils should be taught how to explore, choose and organize sounds and musical ideas
		Composition software	
2	**SCIENCE** Growing up	Pupils could use multimedia sources to make comparisons **CD-ROMs** Pupils could use data collected to compile a class database **Database software**	**Life processes and living things** **2a** – Statutory: recognize and compare the main external parts of the bodies of humans and other animals **4** – Variation and classification pupils could use data collected to compile a class database
3	**HISTORY** Ancient Egypt	Pupils could use digitised maps to identify and colour-code key features. Cut & Paste additional icons	**5c** – Statutory: pupils should be taught to communicate their knowledge and understanding of history in a variety of ways
		Digital map of Ancient Egypt. Download from British Museum website	
3	**SCIENCE** Materials	Children could be introduced to a writing frame for an experimental report, which included and reinforced the preferred report format and enabled the children to use graphs to represent data findings	**Scientific enquiry** **2h** – Statutory: Pupils should be taught to use a wide range of methods, including … and ICT, to communicate data in an appropriate and systematic manner
		Word-processing software	
4	**MUSIC**	Pupils could use software designed to enable exploration of sounds	**4c** – Pupils should be taught how music is produced in different ways [through the use of different resources, including ICT]
		Composition software	
4	**DT** Textiles – bags	Pupils could use word-processing or desktop publishing **(DTP) software** and a printer to develop and communicate their design ideas	**1b** – Pupils … develop ideas and explain them clearly, putting together a list of what they want their design to achieve **1c** – Plan what they have to do, suggesting a sequence of actions and alternatives if needed **1d** – Pupils should be taught to communicate design ideas in different ways as these develop, bearing in mind aesthetic qualities and the uses and purposes for which the product is intended
		(DTP) software	
5	**SCIENCE** Earth in space	Use video or CD-ROM to study models of the Sun, Earth and Moon system	**Physical processes** **4d** – Statutory: pupils should be taught that the Earth orbits the Sun once each year and that the Moon take approximately 28 days to orbit the Earth
		Internet and CD-ROM resources	
5	**SCIENCE** Changing sounds	Pupils could use sensors and microphones to detect, record and compare sounds under different conditions. Resultant sound waves may be viewed and stored within multimedia presentations	**3f** – Pupils should be taught how to change the pitch and loudness of sounds produced by some vibrating objects **Scientific enquiry** **2f** – Make systematic observations and measurements, including the use of ICT for data logging
		WINDOWS SOUND RECORDER	
6	**PHSE and Citizenship**	Pupils could use the Internet to look at different reports about the same issue.	**2k** – Guideline: pupils should be taught to explore how the media present information
		http://www.guardiancentury.co.uk/	
6	**HISTORY** Britain since 1930	Use information from a CD-ROM and appropriate website to explore aspects of the impact of the Second World War.	**4a** – Statutory: find out about the events, people and changes studied from an appropriate range of sources of information, including ICT-based sources
		CD-ROM and Internet-based resources	

Available on the net at http://www.sagepub.co.uk/wrightbk1

23rd February

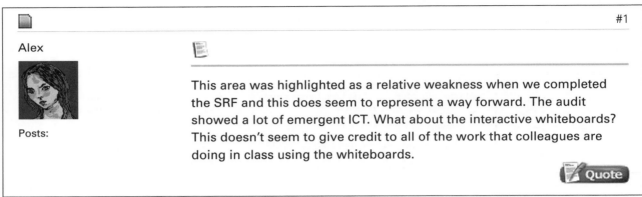

#1

Alex

Posts:

This area was highlighted as a relative weakness when we completed the SRF and this does seem to represent a way forward. The audit showed a lot of emergent ICT. What about the interactive whiteboards? This doesn't seem to give credit to all of the work that colleagues are doing in class using the whiteboards.

Quote

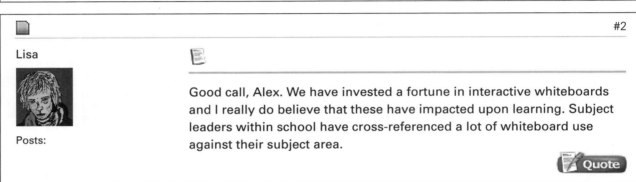

#2

Lisa

Posts:

Good call, Alex. We have invested a fortune in interactive whiteboards and I really do believe that these have impacted upon learning. Subject leaders within school have cross-referenced a lot of whiteboard use against their subject area.

Quote

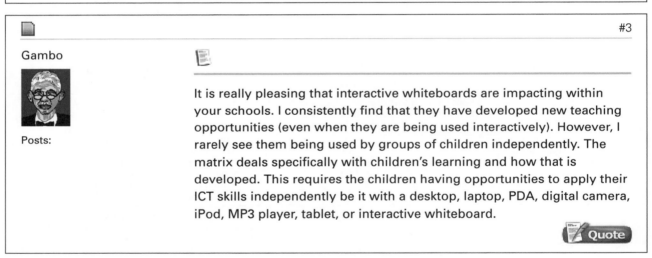

#3

Gambo

Posts:

It is really pleasing that interactive whiteboards are impacting within your schools. I consistently find that they have developed new teaching opportunities (even when they are being used interactively). However, I rarely see them being used by groups of children independently. The matrix deals specifically with children's learning and how that is developed. This requires the children having opportunities to apply their ICT skills independently be it with a desktop, laptop, PDA, digital camera, iPod, MP3 player, tablet, or interactive whiteboard.

Quote

24th February

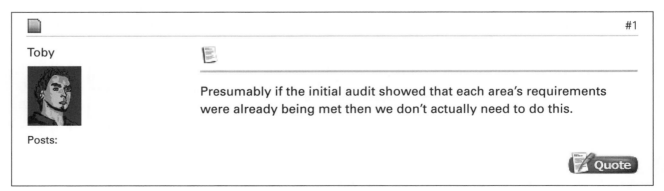

#1

Toby

Posts:

Presumably if the initial audit showed that each area's requirements were already being met then we don't actually need to do this.

Quote

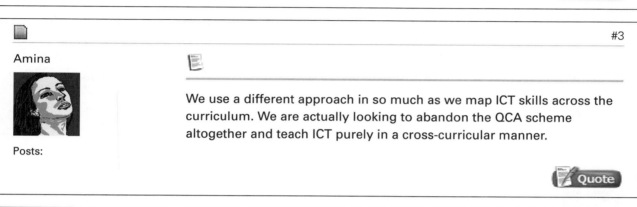

Gambo

Posts:

This provides a good opportunity to reflect upon what is being done. Your approach should be top down; if it confirms that your existing practice covers all National Curriculum requirements then great!

Quote

#2

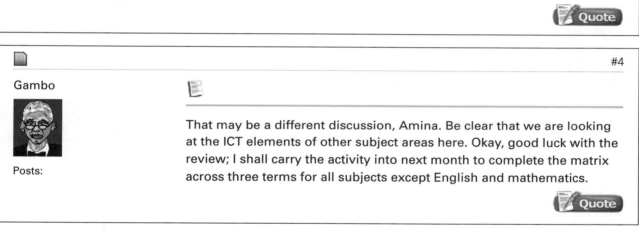

Amina

Posts:

We use a different approach in so much as we map ICT skills across the curriculum. We are actually looking to abandon the QCA scheme altogether and teach ICT purely in a cross-curricular manner.

Quote

#3

Gambo

Posts:

That may be a different discussion, Amina. Be clear that we are looking at the ICT elements of other subject areas here. Okay, good luck with the review; I shall carry the activity into next month to complete the matrix across three terms for all subjects except English and mathematics.

Quote

#4

Chapter 7 • *March*

1st March

Week 25, Task 19 – Using ICT across the Curriculum, Spring and Summer Macro Plans

Following from last month's plan for the autumn term, co-ordinators should complete their next cross-curricular plans for the foundation subjects and science using Tables 7.1 and 7.2. in order to provide a complete top-down system for implementing ICT within these areas. Structurally this is a continuation of the previous task and so I trust that everyone is confident to simply get on with it.

3rd March

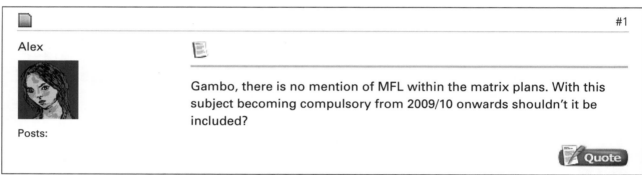

Alex

Posts:

#1

Gambo, there is no mention of MFL within the matrix plans. With this subject becoming compulsory from 2009/10 onwards shouldn't it be included?

Quote

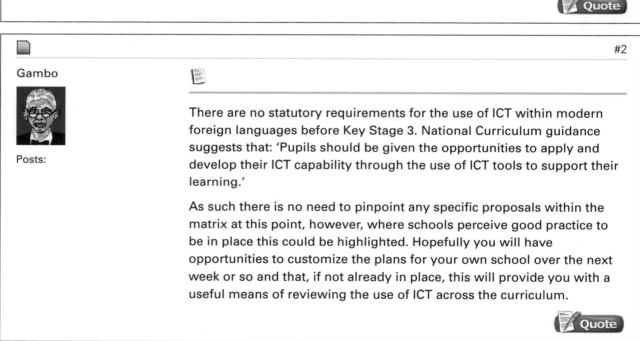

Gambo

Posts:

#2

There are no statutory requirements for the use of ICT within modern foreign languages before Key Stage 3. National Curriculum guidance suggests that: 'Pupils should be given the opportunities to apply and develop their ICT capability through the use of ICT tools to support their learning.'

As such there is no need to pinpoint any specific proposals within the matrix at this point, however, where schools perceive good practice to be in place this could be highlighted. Hopefully you will have opportunities to customize the plans for your own school over the next week or so and that, if not already in place, this will provide you with a useful means of reviewing the use of ICT across the curriculum.

Quote

Table 7.1 Examplar ICT in other subjects planning matrix, spring term

Year	Subject	ICT Opportunity/Resource	Objective
1	**MUSIC** Long and short of it	Use recording equipment to recall sounds and identify and make improvements	**3b** – Pupils should be taught how to make improvements to their own work
		Listening station. PC headset	
1	**GEOGRAPHY** Our school	Use a digital camera to record people, places and events outside the classroom	**4a** – Pupils should be taught to make observations about where things are located and about other features in the environment
		Digital camera, images for Y1 Web page	
2	**HISTORY** Victorian childhood	Use information from a CD-ROM to find out about the life of a significant person, or the way of life in the past	**4a** – Statutory: pupils should be taught how to find out about the past from a range of sources of information
		CD-ROM and BBC JAM web resource	
2	**DT** Textiles samples – puppets	Use word-processing or desktop publishing (DTP) software and a printer to plan and display their ideas	**1e** – Pupils should be taught to communicate their ideas using a variety of methods, including drawing and using models
		DTP program	
3	**GEOGRAPHY** Local study	Results of children's local study enquiry could be emailed as an attachment to partner school as a sharing of data for comparative studies	**1e** – In undertaking geographical enquiry, pupils should be taught to communicate in ways appropriate to the task and audience [for example, using email with another school]
		Email accounts, E-Pals – MS Outlook	
3	**SCIENCE** Planet Earth	Use video or CD-ROM to study models of the Sun, Earth and Moon system Teacher-prepared PowerPoint presentation	**Physical processes** **4b** – Statutory: pupils should be taught how the Sun appears to change during the day and how shadows change as this happens **4c** – Statutory: pupils should be taught how day and night are related to the spin of the Earth.
		CD-ROM or web-based resources	
4	**SCIENCE** Electricity	Pupils could use simulation software to extend an investigation of components in a series circuit	**Physical processes** **1a** – Statutory: pupils should be taught to construct circuits, incorporating a battery or power supply and a range of switches, to make electrical devices work
		CD-ROM or web-based resources – **Crocodile clips free download**	
4	**GEOGRAPHY** Region, location	Produce a database of pupils' addresses to sort, question and present information linked to field study enquiry	**2f** – Statutory: in developing geographical enquiry, pupils should be taught to use ICT to help in geographical investigations [for example, by creating a data file to analyse fieldwork data]
		Database software	
5	**HISTORY** Blackpool over 1,000 years	Use a census database to search for information and identify and explain patterns of change	**4b** – Statutory: pupils should be taught to ask and answer questions and to select and record information relevant to the focus of the enquiry
		MAPE, Greenfield Road Census database, free download	
5	**PE** Swimming	Pupils record their performance using the dig' camera, sound recording devices and laptop computers. Use spreadsheets to collect, analyse and interpret data	**11** – ICT opportunity: pupils could use a variety of electronic and digital recording, measuring, and timing devices to measure the effectiveness of performance
		Spreadsheet software, digital camera	
6	**GEOGRAPHY** India	Use the Internet to access comparative weather information	**3d** – Pupils should be taught to explain why places are like they are
		Internet, Indian metrological sites. http://www.weather.com/maps/asia	
6	**MUSIC**	Use software designed to enable exploration of sounds. Children could use software such as Music Explorer to develop their understanding of musical composition.	**5d** – Pupils should be taught the knowledge, skills and understanding through using ICT to capture, change and combine sounds
		Music composition software	

Available on the net at http://www.sagepub.co.uk/wrightbk1

Table 7.2 Examplar ICT in other subjects planning matrix, summer term

Year	Subject	ICT Opportunity/Resource	Objective
1	**SCIENCE** Sorting materials	Pupils could use software to combine words and pictures about materials and objects	**Materials and their Processes** **1b** – Pupils should be taught to sort objects into groups on the basis of simple material properties
		Branch database - online sort activities	
1	**ART** Printing	Pupils could use 'paint' software to explore shape, colour and pattern	**4a** – Pupils should be taught about visual and tactile elements, including colour, pattern and texture, line and tone, shape, form and space
		Paint program Produce digital tile and reproduce as a stamp or a repeating background design	
2	**GEOGRAPHY** Contrasting locality	Pupils could use the internet to investigate the contrasting locality – **TWINNED SCHOOL** Pupils could use a programmable toy to develop instructions for following a route	**2d** – In developing geographical skills, pupils should be taught to use secondary sources of information [for example, CD] **2C** – In developing geographical skills, pupils should be taught use globes, maps and plans at a range of scales
		Contrasting locale school website – Roamers	
2	**SCIENCE** Life in the Environment	Pupils could use multimedia software to produce a presentation in which they report the findings of their experiments	**Scientific enquiry** **2g** – Pupils should be taught to communicate what happened in a variety of ways, including using ICT
		Presentation software	
3	**DT** Snacks packaging	Pupils could use 'paint' software and a colour printer to produce a pattern for finishing a product	**2e** – Pupils should be taught to use simple finishing techniques to improve the appearance of their product, using a range of equipment
		Paint program	
3	**SCIENCE** Healthy eating	Pupils could use a database or spreadsheet to analyse data about types of food in school lunches	**Life processes and living things** **2b** – Pupils should be taught about the need for food for activity and growth, and about the importance of an adequate and varied diet for health
		Database software	
4	**SCIENCE** Plant life	ICT opportunity: pupils could use a branching database to identify different plant types. Pupils could use CD-ROM to compare non-local habitats	**4a** – Pupils should be taught to make and use keys **5b** – Pupils should be taught about the different plants and animals found in different habitats
		Branching database – CD-ROM	
4	**SCIENCE** How do we move?	Pupils could use video or CD-ROM to see things that cannot be directly observed	**2e** – Statutory: pupils should be taught that humans and some other animals have skeletons and muscles to support and protect their bodies and to help them move
		CD-ROM and web-based resources.	
5	**ART** Drawing	Pupils could use an online virtual art museum to investigate a particular aspect of art	**5d** – Pupils should be taught the knowledge, skills and understanding through investigating art, craft and design in a variety of genres, styles and traditions [for example, ... on the Internet]
		Online resource, for example The Case of Grandpa's Painting A. Pintura: Art Detective is an online game about art history and art composition	
5	**SCIENCE** Human Body	ICT opportunity: pupils could use video, CD-ROM or Internet resources to see things that cannot be directly observed	**2f** – Statutory: pupils should be taught about the main stages of the human life cycle
		CD-ROM – Internet resources	
6	**DT** Control fairgrounds	Show the children how a model can be controlled with a computer. Motor speed and direction can be controlled and a sequence of operations developed writing a program of instructions	**4c** – Statutory: pupils should be taught how mechanisms can be used to make things move in different ways, using a range of equipment including an **ICT** control program
		ROBO – Lego	
6	**ART**	Pupils could collate samples of their own work linked to the influence of local l to develop their own art gallery on the school website	**3a** – Pupils should be taught to compare ideas, methods and approaches in their own and other's work and say what they think and feel about them
		Web authoring software – VLE	

Available on the net at http://www.sagepub.co.uk/wrightbk1

15th March

Week 27, Task 20 – Writing a Policy for ICT, Part 3

Resources

The budget for ICT is reviewed annually by the headteacher, following discussion with the ICT co-ordinator based around a review of the impact of such resources upon teaching and learning. This is largely for hardware, core programmes and licences, peripherals and consumables. The purchase of software will evolve toward the individual co-ordinator's budget. Further details of resource planning are contained within the ICT development plan.

The E-learning co-ordinator will approve all software purchases. Choice of 'subject-specific' software and budget control for the purchase of such software will be the responsibility of individual subject areas. All software purchased will be licensed to the school.

Staff need to ensure that each computer and peripherals are kept in sound working order, that all wires are safely tucked away and that a safe and tidy environment exists on and around the computer trolleys. Faulty equipment should be reported to the ICT co-ordinator who will co-ordinate their referral to the manufacturer if within warranty or to the ICT technician for repair. (Future network development may include the purchase of a maintenance agreement with the supplier. This agreement will be finalized at the time of the purchase or lease.) At present there is a computer ratio of one to eight pupils, and this should be maintained or improved. The ICT co-ordinator, detailing all school hardware by location, will maintain an up-to-date resource register.

Provide a clear description of the systems operating within your school. If you have invested in web cameras, portable devices and wireless laptop suites, ensure that protocols relating to these are also incorporated within your policy. This is also a useful point at which to include Health and Safety issues relating to the use of ceiling-mounted multimedia projectors in classrooms. BECTA has issued specific guidelines relating to their use, which should be accommodated by the school's policy and may be added as an appendix to this policy.

Interactive whiteboards

Each classroom is equipped with an interactive whiteboard and associated multimedia projector. Interactive whiteboards are a tool which can assist teachers in delivering exciting and engaging lessons to learners of all ages and abilities. They enable teachers to deliver lessons interactively using a variety of methods, including video clips, use of the Internet, interactive presentations, colour visuals and traditional blackboard skills. Additionally, they allow for manipulation of text and objects, and calculations by pupils as well as teachers. All usage of the whiteboards shall comply with Health and Safety guidelines.

16th March

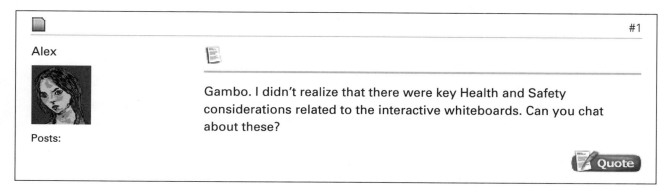

	#1
Alex Posts:	Gambo. I didn't realize that there were key Health and Safety considerations related to the interactive whiteboards. Can you chat about these? Quote

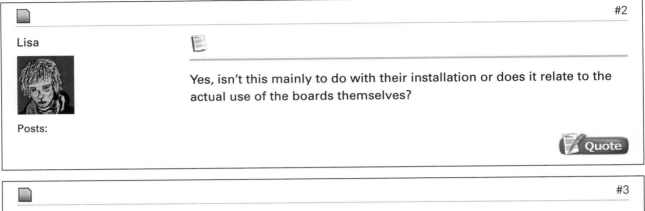

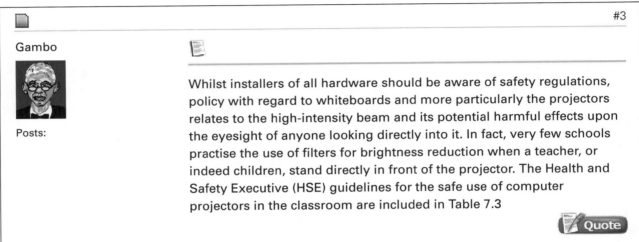

Table 7.3 Health and Safety Executive guidelines for the safe use of computer projects

The Health and Safety Executive (HSE) offers the following guidelines for the safe use of computer projectors in the classroom (reproduced under the terms of the Click-Use Licence):
Computer projectors, which are used to show presentations or to illuminate interactive whiteboards, can expose the eye to levels above one of the exposure limits by which the HSE takes its guidance. Therefore, although such exposure limits are not statutory, the HSE considers the following advice to be good practice in respect of the use of these projectors by employers in the education sector.

Guidelines

Employers should establish work procedures for teachers/lecturers and pupils/students and give instruction on their adoption so that:

- Staring directly into the projector beam is avoided at all times.
- Standing facing into the beam is minimised. Users, especially pupils and students, should try to keep their backs to the beam as much as possible.
- Pupils and students are adequately supervised when they are asked to point out something on the screen.
- Employers should also try to ensure that projectors are located out of the sight line from the screen to the audience; this ensures that, when presenters look at the audience, they do not also have to stare at the projector lamp. The best way to achieve this is by ceiling mounting rather than floor- or table-mounting the projector.
- In order to minimise the lamp power needed to project a visible presentation, employers should use room blinds to reduce ambient light levels.

Source: http://www.hse.gov.uk/radiation/nonionising/whiteboards.htm

17th March

Professional development

******* Primary School places a high priority upon staff professional development and recognizes the importance of all staff remaining abreast of developments in ICT. All eligible staff will undergo ongoing ICT training including subject based training wherever needs are identified. An annual audit will assess forthcoming training requirements for ICT in line with the school's broader CPD strategy and performance management priorities. The ICT co-ordinator offers pedagogic training internally during observable lessons and will support year teams with planning and offer technical advice when necessary.

Schools have to understand the importance of ongoing training within a subject area as dynamic as ICT. We cannot rely upon 'one-off' cure-alls such as the now notorious NOF (New Opportunities Fund) training or even the more recent Primary Strategy Hands on Support programmes. Schools have to have ownership of these initiatives. This is something I shall develop more fully in later chapters. For now, your policy should demonstrate how this is embraced within your school.

17th March

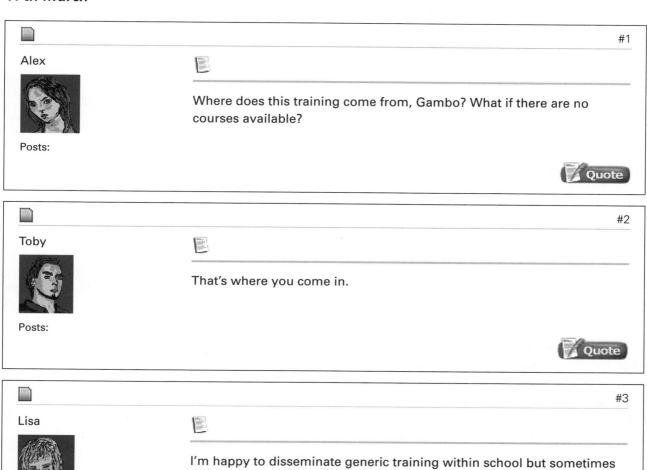

Alex — #1

Posts:

Where does this training come from, Gambo? What if there are no courses available?

Quote

Toby — #2

Posts:

That's where you come in.

Quote

Lisa — #3

Posts:

I'm happy to disseminate generic training within school but sometimes direct staff to local authority workshops.

Quote

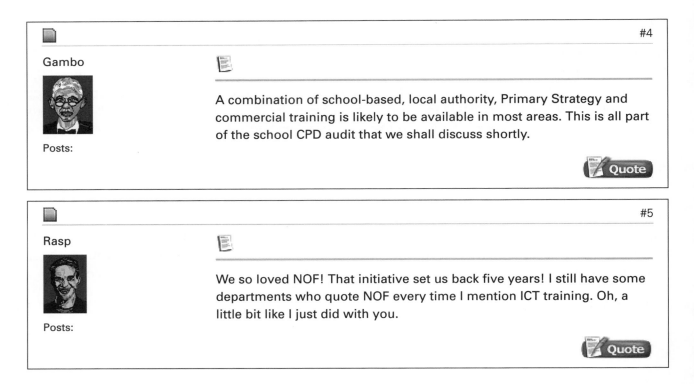

18th March

Management of information, transfer and transition

Management information system data is stored on the administration server and is managed and updated by the deputy headteacher. This is the central pupil data source and is backed up nightly. The system is supported by local authority (LA) technical services and is monitored by the head teacher. National data evaluation tools including RAISEonline and Fischer Family Trust (FFT) evaluations are used in conjunction with the school's own tracking systems and are analysed by all teachers each term in line with the school's assessment and self-evaluation policies. The school is committed to the reduction of administrative tasks through the effective use of ICT. The MIS data will be available for school transfer purposes wherever applicable and fully integrated within the LA-supported transfer protocols.

All staff accessing the school's pupil databases must be clear and mindful about data protection issues regarding access to such data.

NaaceMark (the forerunner of the ICT Mark) guidelines for ICT policies incorporated cross-reference to MISs a number of years ago and so at that time I added it to my templates. Some schools will want to retain separation of the two systems in policy as in practice, although I think it does little harm to incorporate a paragraph here that sets out precisely what you do in school. Please do remind staff of their responsibilities regarding data protection when handling pupil data. This should be synchronized with your E-safety procedures which we shall review next year.

19th March

The silence surrounding the MIS section I shall take as a contented nod of agreement. Therefore let us progress to look at some pertinent legislation.

12 – Legislation

Staff should be mindful of appropriate legislation relating to ICT with respect to copyright and data protection issues. Transfer and storage of information on the network is governed by the school's data protection and E-safety policies. The school's Internet use policy governs use of Internet-based materials.

There is a raft of legislation that schools now need to be mindful of, all of which is increasingly falling under the heading of E-safety, copyright laws and so on. For now, you should check that your policy has a covering statement, such as the one above, that sensibly links to the E-safety procedures and policy prevalent in school at this time. If you have little in place in terms of E-safety then customize the statement to suit and place additional priority on next years root-and-branch review.

20th March

#1

Alex

Posts:

Gambo, stop talking about E-safety in this threatening semi-mystical manner, you are beginning to frighten me.

Quote

#2

Toby

Posts:

Alex, be afraid, be very afraid!

Quote

#3

Rasp

Posts:

You really don't want to get me going on that one again. You want to try talking E-safety within a secondary setting ... No, I said I wasn't going there.

Quote

22nd March

Week 28, Task 21 – Managing Breakdowns

In October we discussed a technical support audit in order to develop a sustainable long-term strategy that would effectively guard against technical breakdowns undermining staff confidence in the school's ICT systems. I hope that you now have in place a system of manageable support in which you have confidence. This week I aim to provide an opportunity to bore down into the day-to-day operational issues that arise when managing the support systems in order to answer the following questions:

1 What processes are activated when equipment does not work?
2 How do you effectively log and record problems in order to manage time and faults effectively?

If your systems are robust these will quickly lead you to the point at which technical support staff, whoever they may be, will take over responsibility for the problem.

Figure 7.1 is a simple template that you may adopt and adjust to suit your personal circumstances. Be clear about your capacity to support problems as they arise; hopefully, following our discussions from September, some responsibilities have been delegated to a trained teaching assistant who will take on much of the administration of the tasks within Figure 7.1. Let us talk through an example.

The main network printer within the ICT suite has been reported faulty. It is the only laser printer within the school and school reports to parents will need to be printed out by the end of the week, as will pupil portfolio examples intended for a special open-day ICT display. Following the flow chart we quickly decide that this problem lies within the curriculum network and qualifies as an emergency. As the manager involved, your decision is immediately to assign technical support to sort out the problem. It does not matter whether you have your own technician, you have a TA engaged, or are supported by the high school or commercially. Your role now is to act appropriately even though it may well be the teaching assistant who makes the calls and so on. If the demands for the printer is not as pressing then this becomes a non-urgent call that lies within the school network. It is hardware specific and involves a machine that is less than 12 months old. In this case, having established (again via your teaching assistant if available) that the problem cannot be easily remedied (that is, new toner, paper jam and so on) via in-house support, the designated member of staff would contact the manufacturer and a call would be logged accordingly. If the machine were not covered by warranty then you would require your own technical support to attempt a repair so that a call would be logged internally and priority assigned to this work as necessary. This brings us to the second question that I raised. How do you effectively log and record problems in order to manage faults and time effectively? I will take this up later in the week.

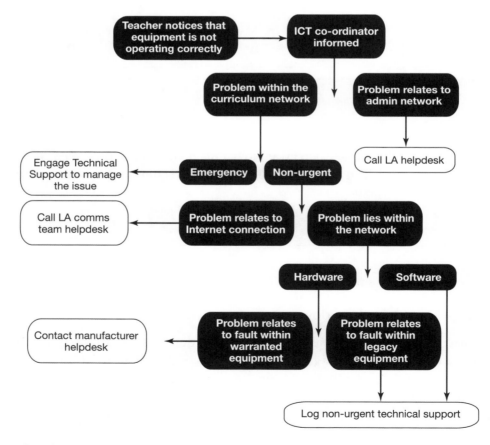

Figure 7.1 Technial support flow chart

Available on the net at http://www.sagepub.co.uk/wrightbk1

23rd March

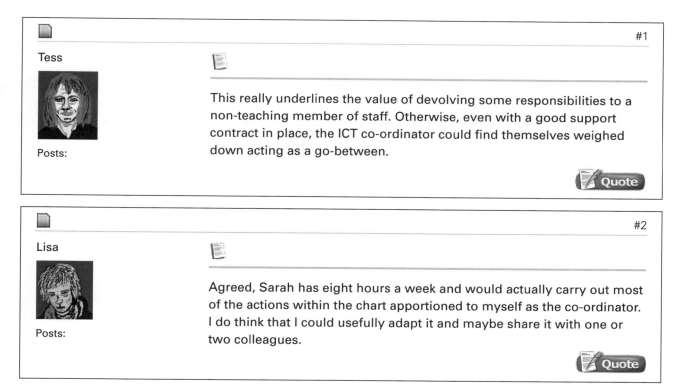

Tess

Posts:

#1

This really underlines the value of devolving some responsibilities to a non-teaching member of staff. Otherwise, even with a good support contract in place, the ICT co-ordinator could find themselves weighed down acting as a go-between.

Quote

Lisa

Posts:

#2

Agreed, Sarah has eight hours a week and would actually carry out most of the actions within the chart apportioned to myself as the co-ordinator. I do think that I could usefully adapt it and maybe share it with one or two colleagues.

Quote

24th March

Poor communication systems are going to undermine your best efforts at running an efficient school network. Staff have to understand that you cannot suddenly not have teaching commitments simply because their speakers are not working on the interactive whiteboard, no matter how charmingly they inform you during your coffee break. You have to have an effective logging system that works insomuch that staff are confident that they will get a timely response. This is where a local assistant is so crucial in being able to provide a relatively quick assessment of need and solution to a wide number of low-level problems. The first part of your system answers the question of how do teaching staff notify yourself or the relevant other staff member that a fault has occurred. Avoid verbal notifications, we are all very busy people and when multitasking are all capable of forgetting what someone has just offloaded onto us. If you have institutional use of email embedded within the school, set up an account for reporting jobs; you might even want to set up an MS Outlook form with a predefined support address on desktops or the school website that will facilitate a formal recording system and automatically produce a log or record of the problem. This is something to strive for but, if not available, then prepare a simple paper template that can be completed and forwarded on.

I do think that as co-ordinator you need to have sight of any requests for support in order to have an overview of the state of the network at any given time. I do not think that these should go directly to a technician, although clearly as circumstances vary this may be the desired outcome within some schools. You need to be at the hub, particularly if you are line-managing the technician and teaching assistant involved. The second aspect of communication involves notification of priorities to your technician. Each week support staff will need to have a calendar or diary into which calls can be assigned. It is not good practice to have systems so informal that a technician or support assistant is deciding in an ad hoc manner which job to peruse next. There has to be some shared understanding of how priorities are assigned.

Let us take the common scenario of an external technician making a fortnightly visit to your school. You may have three hours of their time and cannot afford to spend the first half-hour briefing them on what to do. Often they may need certain software to complete a job anyway, so understanding the nature of your problems before they arrive is ideal. Once again make use of MS Outlook if you have it established within your school. I think it is a good idea to set up a designated calendar for technical support into which you can quickly assign tasks for technical staff. This may be elaborated to include different types of support using the colour-coding task options and it enables you to quickly drag and drop tasks across the calendar as their urgency increases or wanes. Even if you do not have Outlook established across the network, there are many online calendar systems that you may choose to use. Google operate a free online calendar service (www.google.com/calendar) for which you may assign password access for selected staff or you may integrate this within your own website (Figure 7.2). This is available via the Internet and allows any technician to brief themselves about jobs before they even arrive at school. It also has the added advantage of importing data from Outlook, so could quite easily bridge intranet and Internet systems. Similarly, you can assign access so that a number of people may directly enter tasks. You could even look at allowing all staff access to this in order for any job to be logged this way. The possibilities are endless.

I hope that this enables you to think about the crucial area of communication when dealing with technical support issues. If you get the systems right you will save everyone an enormous amount of time, which is after all our most valuable and scarce commodity.

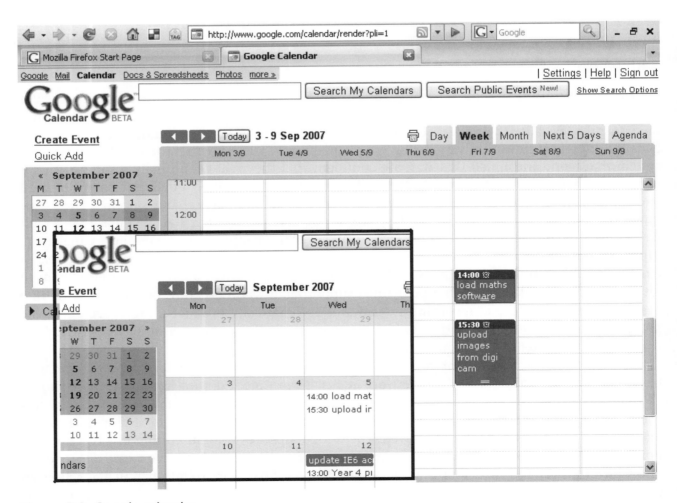

Figure 7.2 Google calendar

Available on the net at http://www.sagepub.co.uk/wrightbk1

25th March

#1

Alex

Posts:

Some very good ideas, Gambo, but I really just let the technicians get on with it now. They are in charge of the network and I think that we (the team) are in charge of the curriculum, the learning.

Quote

#2

Roman

Posts:

How do you separate the two though, Alex? Also isn't the tech support part of your team?

Quote

#3

Alex

Posts:

They are yes but they are the technical experts.

Quote

#4

Amina

Posts:

I don't think that Gambo was suggesting that you get overly involved in dictating how they go about their work, just that you need a clear overview of what is going on. As E-learning co-ordinator I directly manage the technicians' work in much the same way as I might for a teaching assistant or, indeed, aspects of some teachers' work.

Quote

#5

Alex

Posts:

I see your point although I'd sort of hoped that with the new wrap-around support that we now have I could forget about that side of things.

Quote

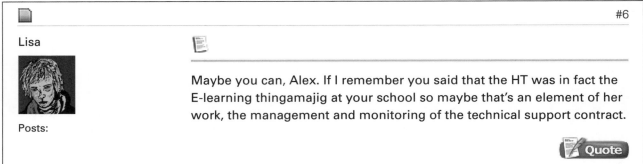

Lisa

Posts:

Maybe you can, Alex. If I remember you said that the HT was in fact the E-learning thingamajig at your school so maybe that's an element of her work, the management and monitoring of the technical support contract.

#6

26th March

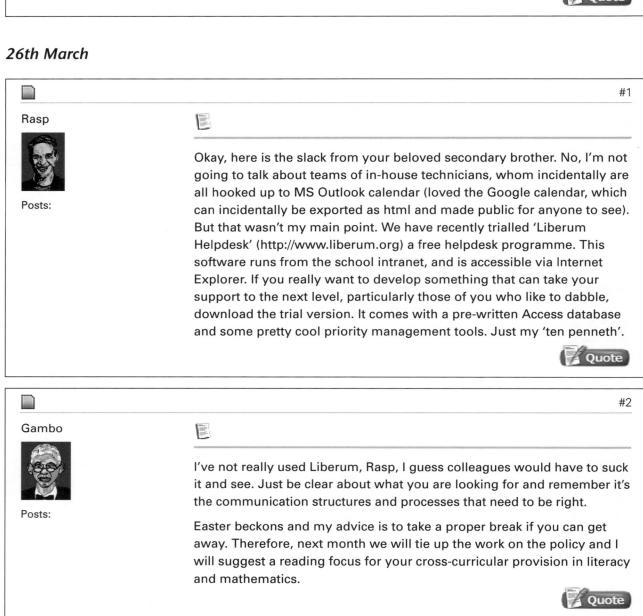

Rasp

Posts:

#1

Okay, here is the slack from your beloved secondary brother. No, I'm not going to talk about teams of in-house technicians, whom incidentally are all hooked up to MS Outlook calendar (loved the Google calendar, which can incidentally be exported as html and made public for anyone to see). But that wasn't my main point. We have recently trialled 'Liberum Helpdesk' (http://www.liberum.org) a free helpdesk programme. This software runs from the school intranet, and is accessible via Internet Explorer. If you really want to develop something that can take your support to the next level, particularly those of you who like to dabble, download the trial version. It comes with a pre-written Access database and some pretty cool priority management tools. Just my 'ten penneth'.

Gambo

Posts:

#2

I've not really used Liberum, Rasp, I guess colleagues would have to suck it and see. Just be clear about what you are looking for and remember it's the communication structures and processes that need to be right.

Easter beckons and my advice is to take a proper break if you can get away. Therefore, next month we will tie up the work on the policy and I will suggest a reading focus for your cross-curricular provision in literacy and mathematics.

Chapter 8 ● *April*

1st April

Week 29, Task 22 – Writing a Policy for ICT, Part 4

This is a busy time in school so I want to wrap up the policy within the first full week of April. Remember my core driver is to incorporate all elements that will guide schools towards ICT Mark standards within this area. We should therefore aim to encompass Internet safety arrangements, the broader health and safety agenda and arrangements to monitor the policy.

Child protection and Internet access

Computer networks, including those that may be accessed via the Internet, are an important aspect of information technology education. However, they present possible risks to the spiritual, moral and social development of pupils, particularly in terms of the nature of some of the material which may be obtained via the Internet. The school's E-safety procedures will be reviewed annually in order to stay abreast of technological developments. It is essential therefore that all staff are familiar with the procedures and that all pupil use of the network and in particular the school Internet is governed by the School Acceptable Use Policy (reference this document as an appendix here).

Pupil use of email is administered through e-pals monitored accounts and is governed by the School Pupil's Email Policy (reference this document as an appendix here).

All pupil use of the Internet is subject to the School Responsible Internet Code (reference this document as an appendix here).

*School's staff email and filtered Internet access is provided by the ******* local authority's local area network (LAN) and as such all staff use will be subject to the ********** Borough Council Email and Internet Usage Policy (reference this document as an appendix here).*

The guidelines have two core purposes. First, to flag up the significance of Internet safety, particularly within the light of the Every Child Matters strategy. Secondly, it guides staff towards any subsidiary policies that should be attached as appendices. Once again this will highlight the importance of the full E-safety review that we have pencilled in for the autumn term. For now, the amendments made in January to the Internet safety acceptable use policy will be sufficient so long as this is correctly cross-referenced. Arrangements regarding email and staff use should also be referenced if they vary significantly from those stated; be guided by your local authority. Staff at school may fall directly within the council's terms of Internet use procedures, and this too would be cross-referenced here.

2nd April

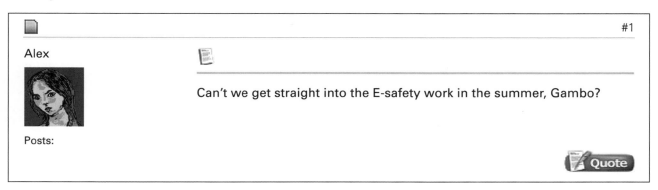

	#1
Alex	
Posts:	Can't we get straight into the E-safety work in the summer, Gambo?

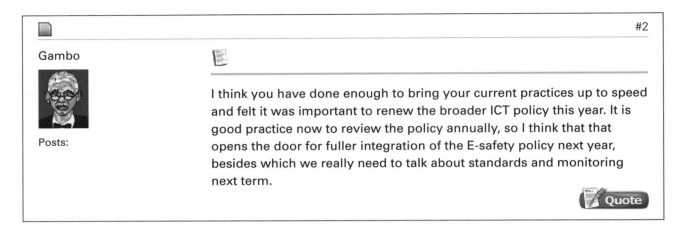

3rd April

Health and Safety procedures

The school recognizes the need for proper risk assessment to be carried out with regard to the incorporation of ICT across the broader curriculum. Health and Safety issues in ICT include: taking care with setting up and moving equipment; establishing appropriate working conditions and general electrical safety. All equipment installation and subsequent use will comply with prevailing local and national Health and Safety guidelines and the school's Health and Safety procedures.

General usage

Staff should be mindful of potential hazards and health concerns when using ICT. There should be sufficient space around any workstations for peripherals, papers, books and other materials to be used comfortably. Desk and floor space around workstations should be free of bags and coats, and gangways and exits must be kept clear at all times. When operating a workstation, pupils should look down at the screen, with the top of the screen roughly at eye level. The mouse should be held lightly in the widest part of the hand with pupils' fingers resting lightly on the mouse buttons so that a very small movement is needed to click a button. The arm or wrist should be supported on the table. In order to avoid eyestrain, pupils should take a break from the computer at least once every 20 minutes and should not constantly lean their head forward. Pupils sharing a computer should be encouraged to make sure that everyone in the group can see without straining.

Multimedia projectors

Pupils should be supervised at all times during the operation of multimedia projectors. Users should never stare directly into the beam of the projector and, when entering the beam, should not look towards the audience, or class, for more than a few seconds. If possible, users should keep their backs to the beam at all times.

Use of electrical appliances

It is imperative that all electrical equipment is kept in good working order. To ensure the health and safety of pupils and staff the following guidelines must be adhered to:

Pupils should not be allowed to switch on the power at the mains.
Equipment should be situated away from water.
Pupils should always be supervised when using electrical equipment.
All plugs, leads and equipment should be checked regularly and tested for electrical safety in accordance with council guidelines.
Pupils should not be allowed to carry equipment.
Computer systems will not be placed near magnets, radiators or have trailing wires, which can be tripped over.

Check that your own guidelines include most of these pertinent points. Teaching staff will need guidance regarding their concerns related to use of monitors and so on. This will also have implications for the amount of time any child is working at a computer. This does not mean that children cannot spend an hour in the ICT suite, but they should not be working for more than 20 minutes without a break at the monitor. I have included further guidance with regard to the multimedia projectors although you may prefer to bring this together with the extensive section we included under 'Resources'. Remember that each section needs to provoke debate within your team and your school. The electrical procedures are standard practice but may need to be brought to the attention of staff.

6th April

#1

Alex

Posts:

I was particularly interested in the section about time at the PC and posture. What are people's thoughts about children using backless stools in the ICT suite? We have just bought a set because those revolving chairs were driving staff to distraction. One colleague has already complained about posture and refuses to sit on them. They seem to think we could have a lot of problems in the future.

Quote

#2

Toby

Posts:

What was wrong with the swivel chairs?

Quote

#3

Lisa

Posts:

They swivel! I asked the premises manager to weld them to prevent this in our school.

Quote

#4

Roman

Posts:

They swivel precisely to discourage pupils from spending more than the 20 minutes staring at the screen. The swivel facilitates movement away, particularly with regard to a multi-part lesson.

Quote

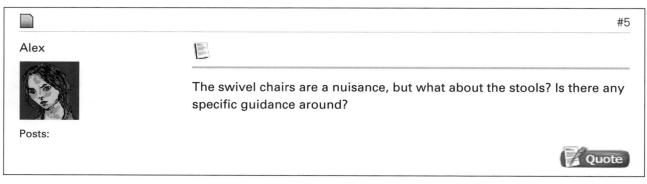

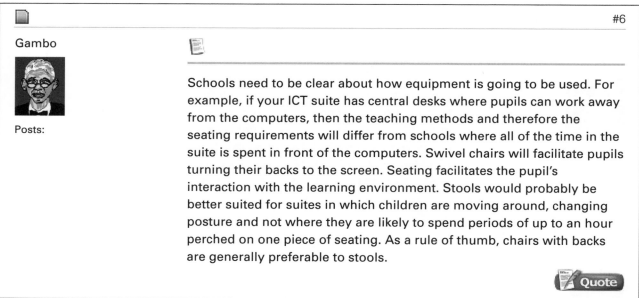

7th April

Anti-virus policy

*All networked computers are protected by ********* anti-virus protection. The ICT technician will regularly check all computer drives in order to ensure that the network remains virus-free, however, data can be irretrievably lost through the actions of some viruses and staff will be updated periodically by the ICT co-ordinator of any virus that is known to be a particular hazard to the school network. In order to reduce the risk of a virus infiltrating a school computer the following protocols should be observed by all staff.*

Staff transferring files into school systems via remote storage devices such as memory sticks or floppy disks from home computers should always run the anti-virus software prior to opening files onto school systems. If in doubt the ICT technician should be consulted prior to opening files.

Children should not introduce files from home into school systems without specific permission from a staff member who has adopted responsibility for running anti-virus checks on such files prior to their use.

Email attachments present a particular danger of virus infection and should not be opened when the identity of the sender is unknown. Any email that is received without the identity of the sender being known should be deleted immediately. If in doubt either the ICT co-ordinator or the ICT technician should be consulted prior to opening files.

Once again if you have been proactive with your E-safety procedures much of the network security arrangements will cross-reference with this section and it will therefore be adjusted accordingly.

Staff laptop computers

The use of laptop computers allows us to extend the use of ICT to the home, allowing staff to be more flexible in their use. A Microsoft Office package is installed upon each laptop, which allows word-processing and desktop publishing to be carried out. The computers are registered for a particular teacher's own use but remain the property of the school and are covered by the school's insurance policy. All software loaded onto a laptop is licensed to the school, not to the individual user. Copying of any software from the system is ILLEGAL and could lead to prosecution; likewise, software should not be added to a laptop without it being covered by the appropriate licence. The above guidelines are in place to protect the hardware and the user, any problems within an application should be referred to the ICT co-ordinator.

8th April

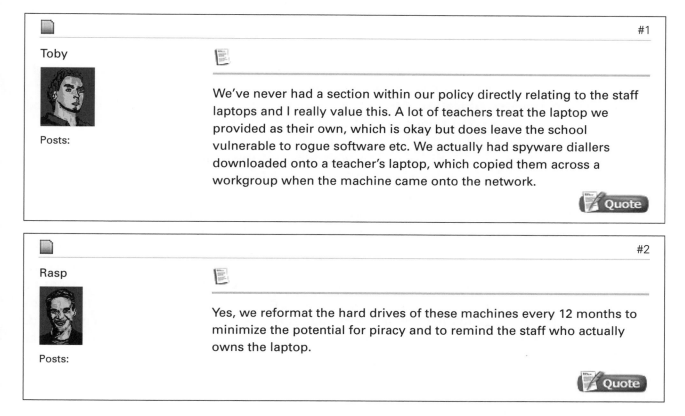

#1

Toby

Posts:

We've never had a section within our policy directly relating to the staff laptops and I really value this. A lot of teachers treat the laptop we provided as their own, which is okay but does leave the school vulnerable to rogue software etc. We actually had spyware diallers downloaded onto a teacher's laptop, which copied them across a workgroup when the machine came onto the network.

Quote

#2

Rasp

Posts:

Yes, we reformat the hard drives of these machines every 12 months to minimize the potential for piracy and to remind the staff who actually owns the laptop.

Quote

9th April

Monitoring, evaluation and review

The ICT co-ordinator in consultation with the headteacher and staff will monitor the effectiveness of this policy. It will be reviewed and updated by _____.

A standard reminder that the policy cannot gather dust having been agreed by staff and governors, it needs to be reviewed annually.

Remember to address each of the 18 sections within your own policy. Ideally the policy will come out of a robust discussion both within your ICT team and the senior management group of the school, and in so doing will be personalized to address the issues that are most pertinent to you. Obviously, each school will have its own timetable for policies to be revised. The E-learning co-ordinator should use their position within the senior management team (SMT) to negotiate at which point this policy will now be taken to staff and governors.

13th April

Week 31, Task 23 – ICT in the Primary Strategy – Literacy

The Easter break is an opportunity for subject leaders to again widen their study of subject and related links. The tasks for the remainder of the month will therefore offer opportunities to reflect upon the role of ICT within the national Primary Strategy, formerly the Literacy and Numeracy strategies and use this as a context for reconsidering the application of ICT within those two core subject areas. Within this chapter the two areas are considered separately, although there are more common features than individual ones and I shall aim to cover many of those here.

Let us discuss a few first principles with regard to the Primary Strategy, as I am aware that many relatively new ICT co-ordinators may currently have only a passive relationship with its structures. The first thing that you will notice whenever you approach the subjects of English and mathematics from an outside perspective is that they are not like any other subject area and that, as the two dominant core subjects, they are the 'sacred cows' that lie at the heart of primary education. The DfES, through the strategies, dominates education within both the primary and secondary sectors and controls the agenda when it comes to the teaching of literacy and mathematics.

The strategy permeates education through a national network of regional directors, local authority strategy managers and their teams of consultants directly to headteachers and literacy and maths (numeracy) co-ordinators within schools. They also control standards budgets, and so will have a well-established power base within your school. I think that this is significant to the manner in which you approach any review of ICT within these areas.

In October 2006 the national strategies released the revised frameworks for both literacy and mathematics. The initial intention to produce an ICT framework in 2005 was subsequently downgraded to a 'progression' which, when launched, will revise expectations within ICT to align with the revised frameworks for literacy and mathematics and is evidence of the strategy's commitment to ICT through the new frameworks. Between 2006 and September 2008 schools will need to audit their current provision within these two core areas and decide how and to what extent to adopt and adapt the new materials. As ICT subject leader, this may be an opportunity for you to have a voice within this agenda particularly with regard to the way in which ICT is embedded. The activities for the rest of the month are to spend some time reviewing the new frameworks at their web address, http://www.standards.dfes.gov.uk/primaryframeworks/, with particular regard to the ICT resources that each subject is offering. It will be of great value to your school for you to be familiar with these files, and to have an opinion regarding their suitability and any alternative resources available within the school.

Literacy resources

The literacy strategy has for some time had something of a love affair with the interactive whiteboard. Consequently, most of the resources that it has developed are teaching tools designed for use with the whiteboard. Generally speaking, these files will require either Smart or Promethean Active flip-chart viewers. These are offered as alternatives to match whichever product is used within school; you do not need to run both systems. In addition, you will require Microsoft Word and PowerPoint viewers and Adobe Acrobat reader to access materials if the computer upon which the resources are to be downloaded has not already got the appropriate software loaded and licensed. Finally, many of the files are downloaded as compressed or 'zipped' files, so you may want to consider the availability of generic 'unzipping' software. As ICT co-ordinator you should review network machines, particularly teacher laptops, to ensure that these 'readers' are all available.

The following links will offer you a free download for each of these products:

For SMART flipchart reader, http://www.smarttech.com/support/software/index.asp

For Active studio flip chart reader, http://www.promethean.co.uk

For MS Word reader, http://www.microsoft.com/downloads, then follow the link for MS Word 2003 viewer.

For MS PowerPoint reader, http://www.microsoft.com/downloads, then follow the link for MS PowerPoint 2003 viewer.

For Adobe Acrobat reader, http://www.adobe.com/downloads.

To decompress files (unzip), http://www.winzip.com.

The full list of ICT Literacy resource links may be located via the new Primary Strategy frameworks website via the library link to http://www.standards.dfes.gov.uk/primaryframeworks/library/Literacy/ict/ictks1 for Key Stage 1 resources and http://www.standards.dfes.gov.uk/primaryframeworks/library/Literacy/ict/ictks2/ for Key Stage 2.

Do spend some time this week familiarizing yourself with these tools (Table 8.1). If you've not already seen it, have a good look at the Year 5 'The Piano' resources which are exceptionally good.

15th April

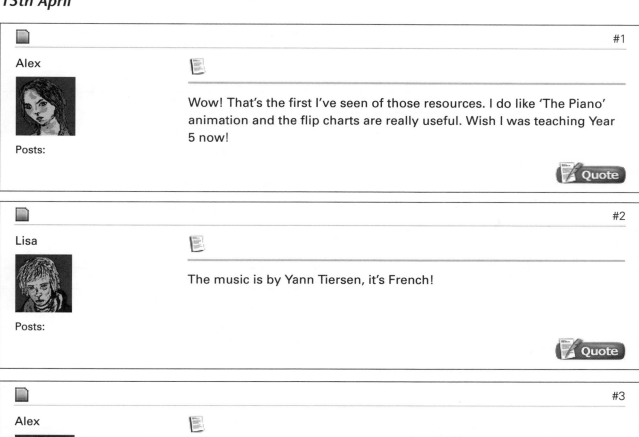

#1

Alex

Posts:

Wow! That's the first I've seen of those resources. I do like 'The Piano' animation and the flip charts are really useful. Wish I was teaching Year 5 now!

Quote

#2

Lisa

Posts:

The music is by Yann Tiersen, it's French!

Quote

#3

Alex

Posts:

What's it called?

Quote

Table 8.1 Revised primary framework, ICT Literacy resources

Year group	Unit title	File type		
		Text doc	**IW flip chart**	**Multimedia**
YEAR 1	**Non-fiction, Unit 5, Recount**			
	Life cycle resources		Smart/Prom	
YEAR 2	**Narrative, Unit 2, Little Red Riding Hood**			
	Written story	Word		
	3 x Slideshows			PPt.
	Character chart		Smart/Prom	
	Wolf chart		Smart/Prom	
	Non-fiction, Unit 2, Reports			
	Report grids	Word	Smart/Prom	
	Non-fiction, Unit 4, Reports			
	Report grids	Word/Acro		
YEAR 3	**Narrative, Unit 1, Stories in familiar settings**			
	Familiar settings		Smart/Prom	
	Poetry, Unit 2, Calligrams			
	Calligram flip charts		Smart/Prom	
	Narrative, Unit 2, Traditional stories			
	Myth setting		Smart/Prom	
	Myth analysis		Smart/Prom	
	Hyperlink instructions	Word		
	Myth frame			PPt.
	9 x Image files			Jpeg.
YEAR 4	**Narrative, Unit 2, Imaginary worlds**			
	Imaginary worlds		Smart/Prom	
	Non-fiction, Unit 3, The Shirt Machine – Explanation			
	Non-fiction flip charts		Smart/Prom	
	Movie resources			Quick / WMV
YEAR 5	**Narrative, Unit 2, Traditional stories**			
	Legends flip chart		Smart	
	18 x image resources			Jpeg.
	13 x sound resources			AIF.
	Poetry, Unit 2, The Highwayman			
	Narrative poetry flip chart		Smart/Prom	
	Narrative, Unit 5, The Piano			
	3 x Piano flip charts		Smart	
	Story modeller (embedded in fc)			Flash exe.
	Movie resources			Quick / WMV
	Audio resources			WMV /AVI/ MP4
	Narrative, Unit 4, Flashback Plan			
	Flashback flip charts		Smart/Prom	
YEAR 6	**Narrative, Unit 4, Paragraph analysis**			
	Paragraph analysis	Word/Acro		
	Non-fiction, Unit 2, Journalistic writing			
	Compare and contrast		Smart	

Available on the net at http://www.sagepub.co.uk/wrightbk1

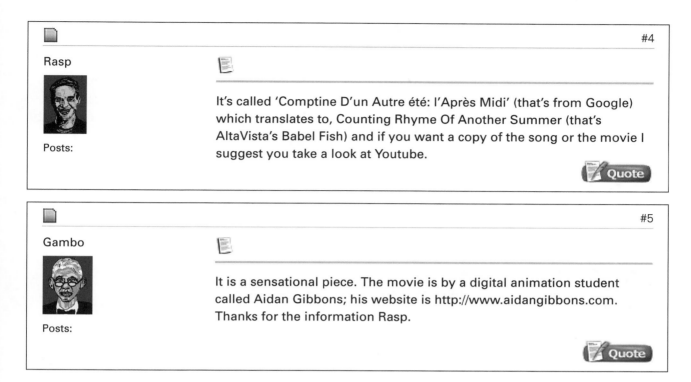

22nd March

Week 32, Task 24 – ICT in the Primary Strategy – Numeracy

Continuing the Primary Strategy theme this week we shall update our understanding of the mathematics materials. Understand that the old numeracy strategy was always far more proactive in making ICT resources available to schools. This was largely because of an early consensus regarding the value of the interactive teaching programmes first introduced as long ago as 2002. The programmes focused upon effective whole-class teaching, modelling, exposition and demonstration, prompting and questioning based around Flash exe files that could either be downloaded or used directly from the Internet. Consequently, from a very early stage the numeracy strategy had a very significant presence in terms of ICT that the literacy initiative could not replicate. This is interesting given that the IMPACT2 studies (an area that we shall look at more closely in Chapter 11) suggest that it is literacy where ICT has the most impact.

Within the revised national frameworks the ICT resources are divided into three categories. First, the ITPs (interactive teaching programs), then spreadsheets and, finally, interactive whiteboard (IW) files.

All the ITPs may be downloaded from the new frameworks resource area at http://www.standards.dfes.gov.uk/primaryframeworks/library/Mathematics/ICTResources/itps/.

As with any literacy resources I think that the ICT subject leader's job is, first, to ensure that the programmes will play when needed and, secondly, to ensure that colleagues are aware of what is available; many still are not.

The second set of resources are based around Microsoft Excel spreadsheets. Because this is proprietary software you will need to download the Microsoft viewer if you do not have adequate Office licences for using this software. It is also worth bearing in mind that Microsoft Office is not considered curriculum software for the purposes of Curriculum online and the spending of E-learning credits. For an MS Excel reader go to, http://www.microsoft.com/downloads, then follow the link for MS Excel 2003 viewer.

Excel offers teachers the facility to create templates of cells, which can be changed to present problems and explorations for children to solve and explore. The Excel files are flexible resources that can be used in many mathematics lessons, and accompanying each spreadsheet there is guidance which explains how to use the files and gives some suggested questions to be asked in lessons.

The Excel files may be downloaded from, http://www.standards.dfes.gov.uk/primaryframeworks/ library/Mathematics/ICTResources/spreadsheets.

The final section of resources refers to interactive whiteboard files, which consist of a whole series of SMART notebook flip charts for use as teaching aids. These are available from, http://www.standards.dfes.gov.uk/primaryframeworks/library/Mathematics/ICTResources/IWBs

All the numeracy resources refer to whole-class teaching tools, which may shed some insight into where the revised strategy is heading in terms of directing the impact of ICT. There are very few examples of pupils using ICT to enhance learning.

25th March

Chapter 9 • *May*

4th May

Welcome back, always good to get away at Easter. I do hope that you enjoyed the break and have returned refreshed and ready to continue your review of ICT and E-learning practices. This term we aim to tackle the fundamental question that should direct all of our work and which links together the fruits of each of our other ICT strategies: 'What is the standard of achievement within ICT at our school?' Only by answering this question may we begin to fully understand the impact of our strategies and investment in technological resources.

If your school is inspected, then, as subject leader, Ofsted will expect you to have a clear understanding of what the standards are and will wish to investigate your evidence base. It is vital therefore that you have self-evaluation processes in place that will accurately provide this information. Beyond that, standards should lie at the heart of everything you do. Often when I carry out consultancy work in primary schools I am asked about purchasing strategies, whether schools should invest in portable devices to develop their cross-curricular capabilities or consider renewing and upgrading an ICT suite. Consistently my answer comes back to standards. What are the standards of ICT in the school? What are the children achieving and attaining? If standards are good then it may be that the school is ready to develop its cross-curricular resources. However, if the core skills are not embedded then the school has to look at the means with which this can be improved, that is, perhaps investment is required within the core ICT suite. Unfortunately, more often than not schools do not have reliable evidence regarding standards and so all of its decisions are potentially flawed.

This pursuit will direct our work throughout the term, starting this month with an overview of the school's record-keeping systems and initial classroom visits to observe ICT lessons. Table 9.1 provides an organized plan for this term

Colleagues will see that August has been left for reflection. Hopefully by that time our work will be done providing a respite in which it's key conclusions can be properly evaluated.

Week 33, Task 25 – Review of Record-Keeping

Subject leaders should be clear about the systems that are operating within school that provide information about each child's attainment and achievement within their area. It will be helpful from the outset to understand the difference between record-keeping and assessment. For our purpose assessment refers to the processes through which a school makes judgements about what each child has learnt in terms of curricular objectives (attainment) and personal prior understanding (achievement). We then need to ask, how does the school record this activity and progress? What systems enable attainment and achievement to be passed on and used to inform future planning? When reviewing your current record-keeping systems you should decide whether or not they adequately record progress against identified criteria and in so doing facilitate a personalized learning cycle that prevents individual pupils from slipping through the net.

Review existing record systems critically using the following criteria:

Do they offer a simple means to record differential performance?
Do they allow for pupils' own self-assessment and peer assessment of progress?
Do they cover both the scheme of work used for delivering the discrete ICT curriculum and also for the acquisition of specific ICT skills related to the National Curriculum standards?

Table 9.1 Summer term plan

	SUMMER TERM			
MAY	**JUNE**	**JULY**		**AUGUST**
ASSESSING ICT In which co-ordinators will focus upon establishing a clear overview of standards in ICT. Including a review of record-keeping strategies, assessment and moderation procedures and the creation of an electronic portfolio of children's work				A graphical overview of the 33 tasks completed and short discussion of options for co-ordinators considering next steps
Assessing ICT – Record-keeping How does the school record what each child has learnt, including a review of pupil self-review statements?	**Assessing ICT – Summative Assessment Tasks** How individual units of work may be assessed using integrated tasks	**Assessing ICT – Working with Portfolios** The final piece within the assessment of ICT jigsaw providing each pupil with their own folder and the links with a school-wide portfolio		
MONITORING ICT In which co-ordinators will prepare a monitoring schedule to evaluate teaching and learning in ICT across each of the discrete ICT subject strands and across the broader curriculum				
Standards Classroom Observations What are the standards of ICT in the school? What are the children achieving and attaining? Preparation of a viable observation schedule and foci for observations	**Observing ICT in Other Subjects** Developing a plan to observe ICT across the curriculum in order to isolate and evaluate the development of key skills	**Moderating Standards and Creating a School Portfolio** In which we will examine the opportunities for pupil self-assessment through the development of portfolios		
The BBC Digital Curriculum – Implementation Strategy A review of the BBC National Digital Curriculum. How has it been adopted within your school? Is it providing resources that are better than you have used previously?	**CONTINUOUS PROFESSIONAL DEVELOPMENT**			
	CPD Audit of Need How do you identify individual staff skills and needs as well as whole-school ICT development priorities?	**CPD Training Opportunities** Consideration of how the various CPD needs identified through audit may best be met. Setting priorities for training on the basis of the impact that such training will have upon the quality of teaching and learning at school		

Available on the net at http://www.sagepub.co.uk/wrightbk1

It may be useful at this stage to get feedback from colleagues about their degree of confidence in your existing systems. Finally, ask how the information recorded is actually used in order to benefit the children. Often schools have refined and complex systems for gathering data yet fail to utilize the information that has been collated. Do not be afraid to question the validity of existing systems, I often question the purpose of extensive paper systems that are rarely reviewed by staff let alone the pupils and parents. Start with consideration of your scheme of work for ICT. How is your core curriculum being delivered? If a commercial scheme is being used, often this will provide its own systematic form of monitoring and recording of each pupil's activity. If so and this satisfactorily informs planning, there may be no need for the school to operate other parallel systems unless they add significantly to the planning process. Most schools implement the QCA national Scheme of Work for ICT, downloadable from http://www.standards.dfes.gov.uk/schemes2/it/. Schools often record progress against the learning outcomes provided within the scheme utilizing the guidance related to pupils who have made less or greater progress in order to differentiate the records. Table 9.2 demonstrates how the QCA learning objectives may quickly be incorporated into a simple chart to enable staff to identify higher- and lower-performing pupils.

There are a multitude of tracking and recording systems available via the various regional grids for learning. I like the simplicity of a basic system that enables staff to highlight marginal performance and accepts a standard that the bulk of the class will achieve. Any teacher should be able to integrate such a system into their teaching system and it embraces the ideals of assessment for learning. Remember that the core purpose of such records is to identify future planning needs and your review of your own systems should reflect upon how the record is impacting upon the learning cycle.

7th May

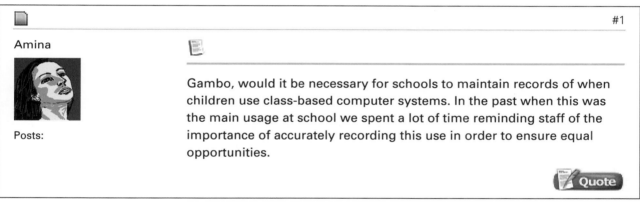

Amina
Posts:

#1

Gambo, would it be necessary for schools to maintain records of when children use class-based computer systems. In the past when this was the main usage at school we spent a lot of time reminding staff of the importance of accurately recording this use in order to ensure equal opportunities.

Quote

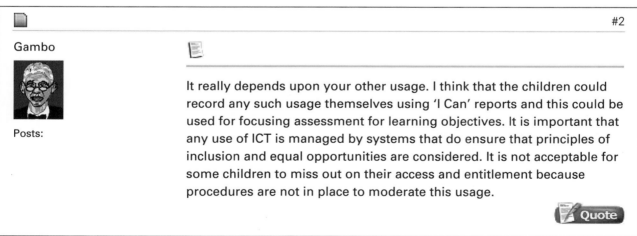

Gambo
Posts:

#2

It really depends upon your other usage. I think that the children could record any such usage themselves using 'I Can' reports and this could be used for focusing assessment for learning objectives. It is important that any use of ICT is managed by systems that do ensure that principles of inclusion and equal opportunities are considered. It is not acceptable for some children to miss out on their access and entitlement because procedures are not in place to moderate this usage.

Quote

Table 9.2 Exemplar QCA record sheet

ICT Class Record			
ICT Unit **: ********************			
Learning outcomes	**Children who have not made as much progress**	**Children who have progressed further**	**Comments**
INTEGRATED TASKS:			

Available on the net at http://www.sagepub.co.uk/wrightbk1

8th May

There are strong arguments for incorporating a record system that allows pupils to contribute to their own assessment and many schools will have 'I Can' systems that relate back to the scheme of work objectives. Once again it should be stressed that the value of such systems derives from their contribution to the child's understanding of the learning situation and to the steps that follow. Children should be allowed to contribute to their own understanding of ICT as a subject through self-evaluation, but in order for this to be effective it has to be integrated within an ethos of assessment for learning principles. This means that learning objectives have to be explicit in order for children to understand the criteria against which they may record their own progress. If colleagues already practise some form of self-report within record-keeping procedures then you should review the effectiveness of such systems. Do pupils' comments reflect learning objectives and suggest real understanding? Is peer comment encouraged and integrated? Do pupil entries lead to some real evaluation and conclusion regarding what has been learnt?

At worst, records are presented as the whole of a school's systems for assessment instead of simply being a part of that system. Also, there is no need for this to be a paper record. Many of the multitude of 'I Can' systems could easily be adapted within digital slides so that pupils can drag and drop statements or symbols onto appropriate learning objectives to indicate progress. The whole system could build into their own slideshow which could be stored on the school server or 'ultimately' online as part of an E-portfolio that may be accessed by parents at home (Figure 9.1).

Figure 9.1 Exemplar I Can electronic record

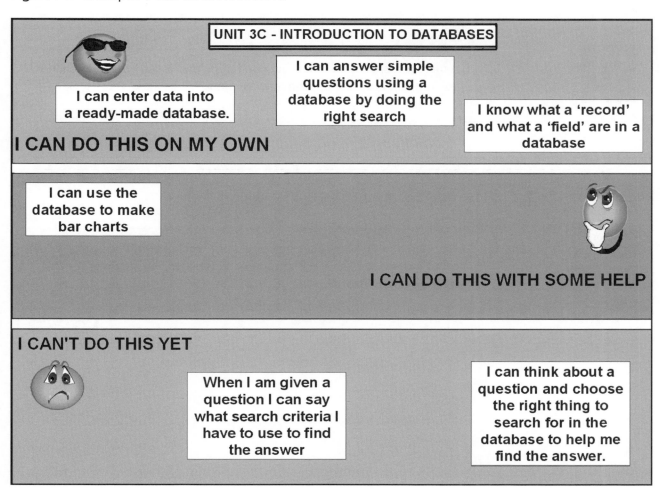

Available on the net at http://www.sagepub.co.uk/wrightbk1

9th May

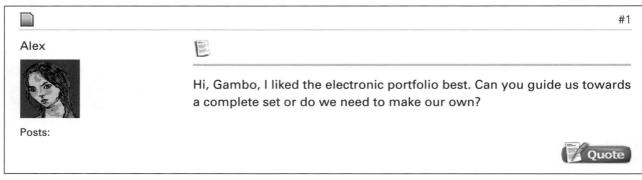

Alex

Posts:

Hi, Gambo, I liked the electronic portfolio best. Can you guide us towards a complete set or do we need to make our own?

#1

Quote

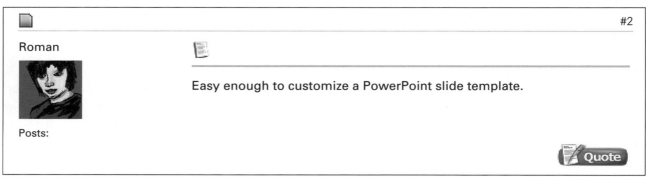

Roman

Posts:

Easy enough to customize a PowerPoint slide template.

#2

Quote

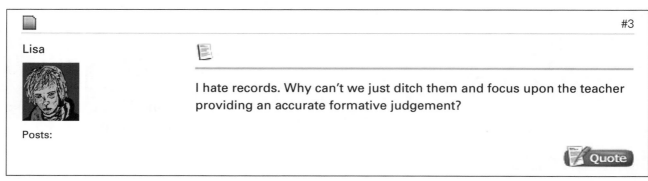

Lisa

Posts:

I hate records. Why can't we just ditch them and focus upon the teacher providing an accurate formative judgement?

#3

Quote

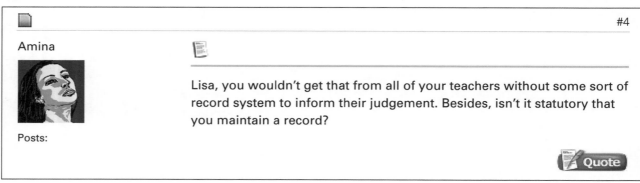

Amina

Posts:

Lisa, you wouldn't get that from all of your teachers without some sort of record system to inform their judgement. Besides, isn't it statutory that you maintain a record?

#4

Quote

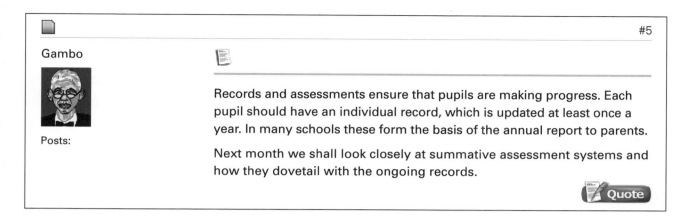

Records and assessments ensure that pupils are making progress. Each pupil should have an individual record, which is updated at least once a year. In many schools these form the basis of the annual report to parents.

Next month we shall look closely at summative assessment systems and how they dovetail with the ongoing records.

Quote

11th May

Week 34, Task 26 – Towards a National Digital Curriculum

Following on from last month's review of cross-curricular use of ICT, I feel it will be useful to take a look at the BBC National Digital Curriculum. How has it been adopted within your school? Is it providing resources that are better than you have used previously?

The days in which the government ploughed software funding into schools via E-learning credits have gone and schools have to formulate a revised strategy to implement use of the projected national digital curriculum that some time ago the BBC were commissioned to produce, and to consider how this fits in alongside existing content options, particularly when using ICT to support learning across the curriculum. Initial content was made available in January 2006 and the complete system, known as BBC Jam (www.bbc.co.uk/jam), will be phased in between that date and January 2009. The service supports key areas of the school curriculum for learners of all abilities and aims to bridge the home–school divide, providing a flexible tool for teachers and involving parents more fully in their children's education. Many practitioners regard the system as an ideal central tenet of a virtual learning environment's content provision. Table 9.3 demonstrates proposals for each subject's launch within the primary sector.

The table should support colleagues in negotiating a staged roll-out of the digital curriculum across each subject or phase area. It is worth reflecting on the BBC's remit when producing 'Jam' (the marketed title for these materials.)

Concerns from commercial software manufacturers about the proposed national resources have led to restraints being placed upon the scope of these materials, namely, that they should only:

'Cover up to a maximum of 50% of learning outcomes in each subject amenable to being taught by ICT.' (BECTA, 2004: 3)

BECTA made clear recommendations that the Jam materials should aim to break new ground and not simply replicate what was already available commercially. Hence the manner in which the resources that have come on-stream certainly lend themselves to home use and schools need to decide whether this will be their main remit locally. Certainly if activities are to be mapped within the cross-curricular matrix we worked upon last term, then colleagues should ensure that activities designed for one cohort group are not already being set for and completed for homework by an overzealous colleague in the previous year group. This is the main difference between the Jam materials and others in that they are freely available from the Internet without the need for special home licences.

If you have not already registered your school at the Jam website, please do so. Take some time to browse the resources available at present in order to get a clear idea of the quality, quantity and range of content before designing a strategy for implantation. As a focus for reference, I am going to talk about the KS1 history resources later this week, so please do look at those in particular.

Table 9.3 BBC digital curriculum subject launch schedule

2006			
	KS1	**Lower KS2**	**Upper KS2**
ENGLISH	▓	▓	
MATHS	▓		
SCIENCE	▓	▓	
ART			
DT			
GEOGRAPHY		▓	
HISTORY	▓	▓	
MFL FRENCH			
MFL SPANISH			
MUSIC		▓	▓
PE		▓	▓
RE		▓	▓

2007			
	KS1	**Lower KS2**	**Upper KS2**
ENGLISH	▓	▓	▓
MATHS	▓	▓	
SCIENCE			▓
ART			▓
DT			
GEOGRAPHY		▓	▓
HISTORY		▓	▓
MFL FRENCH		▓	▓
MFL SPANISH			
MUSIC		▓	▓
PE		▓	▓
RE			▓

2008			
	KS1	**Lower KS2**	**Upper KS2**
ENGLISH			▓
MATHS			▓
SCIENCE			
ART			
DT			▓
GEOGRAPHY	▓		
HISTORY			
MFL FRENCH			
MFL SPANISH			▓
MUSIC			
PE			
RE	▓		▓

Source: BBC (2004).

Available on the net at http://www.sagepub.co.uk/wrightbk1

13th May

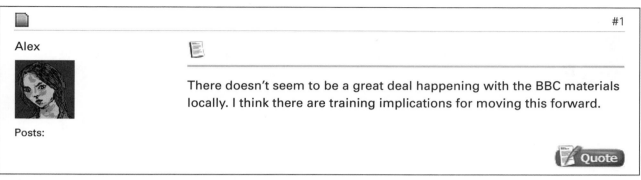

Alex

Posts:

#1

There doesn't seem to be a great deal happening with the BBC materials locally. I think there are training implications for moving this forward.

Quote

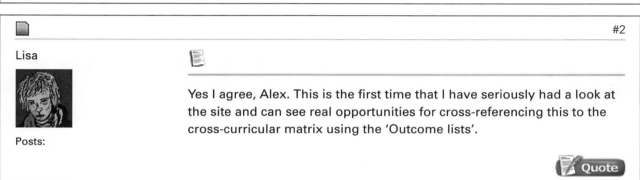

Lisa

Posts:

#2

Yes I agree, Alex. This is the first time that I have seriously had a look at the site and can see real opportunities for cross-referencing this to the cross-curricular matrix using the 'Outcome lists'.

Quote

14th May

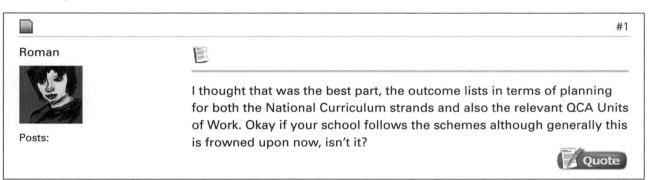

Roman

Posts:

#1

I thought that was the best part, the outcome lists in terms of planning for both the National Curriculum strands and also the relevant QCA Units of Work. Okay if your school follows the schemes although generally this is frowned upon now, isn't it?

Quote

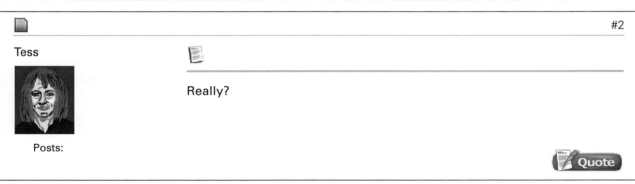

Tess

Posts:

#2

Really?

Quote

#3

Roman

Posts:

Doesn't agree with assessment for learning principles, apparently.

Quote

#4

Tess

Posts:

But that's all about personalization. I should have thought that this site was aimed particularly at schools looking to personalize.

Quote

#5

Amina

Posts:

Where is the differentiation?

Quote

#6

Gambo

Posts:

You can set differentiated parameters using the 'preferences' within each activity. For example pupils may or may not need to read subtitles etc. What did colleagues think of the units themselves? Did you find them 'different' from other resources already available? Any comments about the KS1 History units?

Quote

#7

Rasp

Posts:

Vladimir the Russian was cool!

Quote

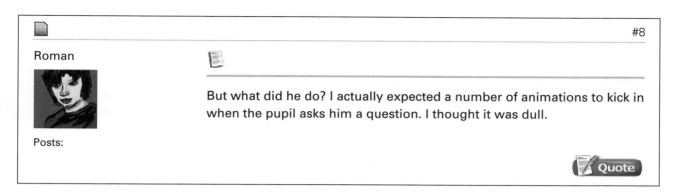

Roman

Posts:

But what did he do? I actually expected a number of animations to kick in when the pupil asks him a question. I thought it was dull.

#8

Quote

15th May

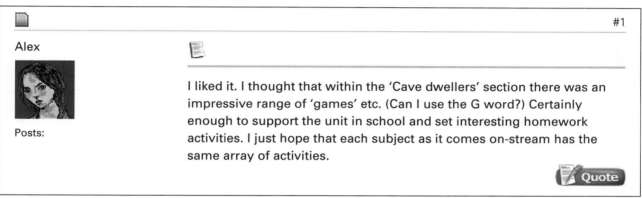

Alex

Posts:

I liked it. I thought that within the 'Cave dwellers' section there was an impressive range of 'games' etc. (Can I use the G word?) Certainly enough to support the unit in school and set interesting homework activities. I just hope that each subject as it comes on-stream has the same array of activities.

#1

Quote

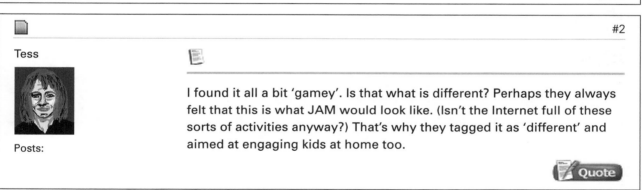

Tess

Posts:

I found it all a bit 'gamey'. Is that what is different? Perhaps they always felt that this is what JAM would look like. (Isn't the Internet full of these sorts of activities anyway?) That's why they tagged it as 'different' and aimed at engaging kids at home too.

#2

Quote

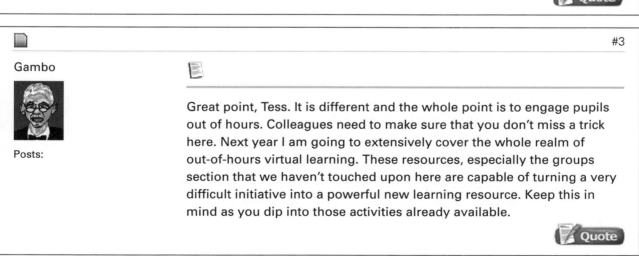

Gambo

Posts:

Great point, Tess. It is different and the whole point is to engage pupils out of hours. Colleagues need to make sure that you don't miss a trick here. Next year I am going to extensively cover the whole realm of out-of-hours virtual learning. These resources, especially the groups section that we haven't touched upon here are capable of turning a very difficult initiative into a powerful new learning resource. Keep this in mind as you dip into those activities already available.

#3

Quote

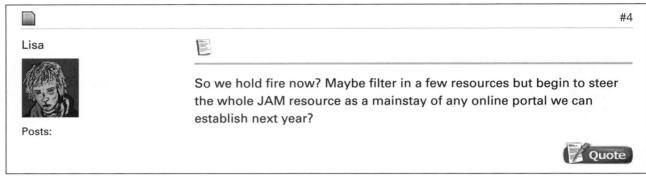

Lisa

Posts:

#4

So we hold fire now? Maybe filter in a few resources but begin to steer the whole JAM resource as a mainstay of any online portal we can establish next year?

Quote

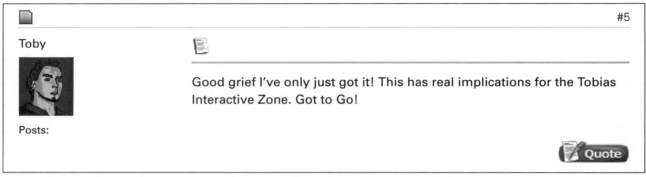

Toby

Posts:

#5

Good grief I've only just got it! This has real implications for the Tobias Interactive Zone. Got to Go!

Quote

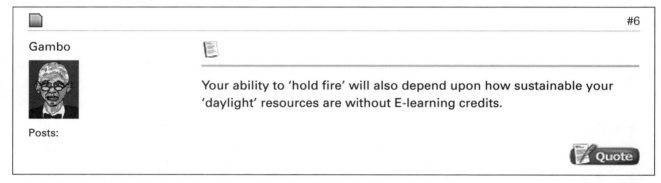

Gambo

Posts:

#6

Your ability to 'hold fire' will also depend upon how sustainable your 'daylight' resources are without E-learning credits.

Quote

18th May

Week 35, Task 27 – Monitoring Standards in ICT

For the next two weeks we are going to return to our focus of standards, resurrecting the core questions introduced at the start of the month:

What are the standards of ICT in the school?
What are the children achieving and attaining?

During this fortnight you are going to carry out a number of lesson observations as part of your subject leader monitoring role in order to inform your judgement about how well the subject is being taught, how well pupils learn. It is likely that your school already practises a system based around Ofsted principles, and inevitably your work from an ICT perspective has to dovetail tightly with your school model. The first thing to do is to decide upon a focus for your work. Remember that you are not simply observing teachers, your primary focus is standards. I suggest that over the year you aim to complete a range of observations targeting various themes.

In Chapter 4 you spent some time growing familiar with the level descriptors. Take another look at Table 4.2 that looks at the level descriptors by theme. This will provide a very useful focus for planning your lesson observations. In effect you have four core observation foci: Word-processing and Multimedia; Data Handling; Simulation and Modelling; and Control and

Monitoring. The fifth theme, 'Using ICT in the Real World', can be monitored through pupil interviews and will form a fifth activity.

Table 9.4 provides a focus for observations based upon lesson monitoring for one day each term. Over the 18-month cycle co-ordinators would be able to conclude an across-the-board review of standards. This is an important point when considering any assessment of ICT related to levels of attainment. The ICT level should reflect a pupil's ability across all of the ICT strands, taking account of strengths and areas of relative weakness. Obviously the schedule should be adjusted to match when units of work are delivered within your own school. If complete strands are not taught concurrently then the schedule should be adjusted to accommodate this, however, do monitor standards across strands. Your first task will be to prepare a viable observation schedule, hopefully one that allows you to complete your first observations next week.

Table 9.4 ICT lesson observation schedule

Autumn Y1		**Focus: Word-processing and Multimedia**
	Year 1	^{1B} Using a word bank
	Year 2	^{2A} Writing stories: communicating information using text
	Year 4	^{4A} Writing for different audiences
	Year 6	^{6A} Multimedia presentation
Spring Y1		**Focus: Simulation and Modelling**
	Year 1	^{1A} An introduction to modelling
	Year 3	^{3D} Exploring simulations
	Year 5	^{5A} Graphical modelling
	Year 6	^{6B} Spreadsheet modelling
Summer Y1		**Focus: Data Handling**
	Year 2	^{2C} Finding information
	Year 3	^{3C} Introduction to databases
	Year 5	^{5B} Analysing data and asking questions: using complex searches
	Year 6	^{6D} Using the Internet to search large databases and to interpret information
Autumn Y2		**Focus: Control and Monitoring**
	Year 1	^{1F} Understanding instructions and making things happen
	Year 2	^{2D} Routes: controlling a floor turtle
	Year 5	^{5E} Controlling devices
	Year 6	^{6C} Control and monitoring – What happens when … ?
Spring Y2		**Focus: Using ICT in the Real World**
	Year 1	Pupil interviews
	Year 2	Pupil interviews
	Year 4	Pupil interviews
	Year 6	Pupil interviews

Available on the net at http://www.sagepub.co.uk/wrightbk1

20th May

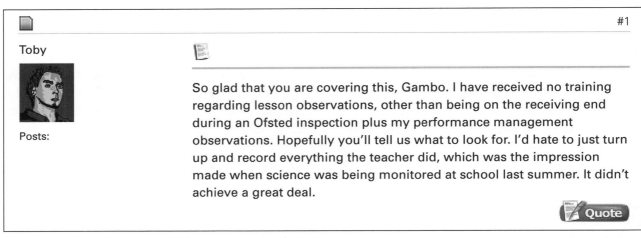

Toby

Posts:

#1

So glad that you are covering this, Gambo. I have received no training regarding lesson observations, other than being on the receiving end during an Ofsted inspection plus my performance management observations. Hopefully you'll tell us what to look for. I'd hate to just turn up and record everything the teacher did, which was the impression made when science was being monitored at school last summer. It didn't achieve a great deal.

Quote

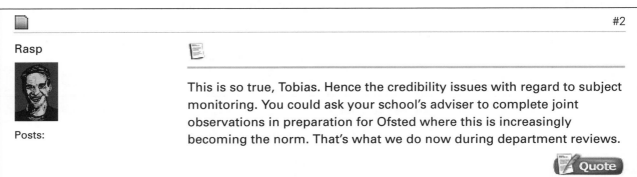

Rasp

Posts:

#2

This is so true, Tobias. Hence the credibility issues with regard to subject monitoring. You could ask your school's adviser to complete joint observations in preparation for Ofsted where this is increasingly becoming the norm. That's what we do now during department reviews.

Quote

22nd May

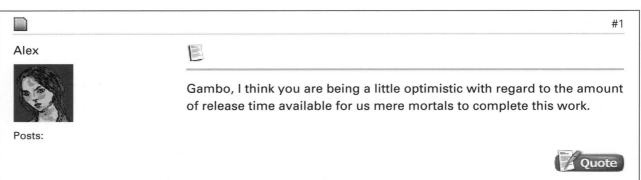

Alex

Posts:

#1

Gambo, I think you are being a little optimistic with regard to the amount of release time available for us mere mortals to complete this work.

Quote

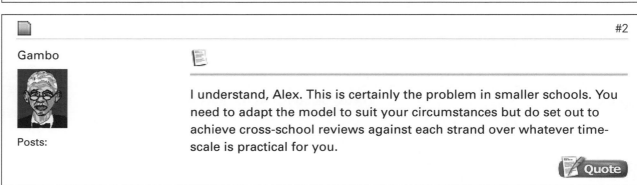

Gambo

Posts:

#2

I understand, Alex. This is certainly the problem in smaller schools. You need to adapt the model to suit your circumstances but do set out to achieve cross-school reviews against each strand over whatever time-scale is practical for you.

Quote

25th May

Having created a schedule for your observations, you are ready to begin this aspect of your monitoring. Do let colleagues know what to expect and point out that your primary focus is to make a judgement regarding the standard of work demonstrated within the lesson across a range of ability groupings and any evident progress across a Unit of Work. It is then the observer's role to identify and attribute any existing causal relationship between teaching, resources, learning environment, pupil attitudes and any achievement demonstrated. Do not just passively observe the teacher; it is the children that you are interested in. Be aware of the journey that the class will have been on prior to this lesson. Is this the beginning, middle or towards the end of the Unit of Work? Clearly there are advantages to it being the latter. Also, prepare yourself beforehand so that you know what you are looking for in order to attribute levels of understanding, you can use the level descriptors we used in Chapter 4 as guidelines, taking great care to ascertain who are the middle-ability children as well as any high or lower achievers within the room.

If you have a standard observation form in school then use that one. My view is that, increasingly, schools need to align their systems to Ofsted's, so if nothing else is available you could use a download of Ofsted's evidence form (HMI 2506) available from Ofsted publications (https:// ofsted.gov.uk/publications). More important is the manner in which you go about your monitoring role. Do not rush to write things down; take several minutes to take in the classroom climate and to establish in your own mind what the groupings are and what are the key factors either contributing to or getting in the way of learning. Once you are confident that you understand the dynamics of the lesson, then you can begin to exercise your judgement with regard to attainment and achievement. Do not get distracted, particularly if things begin to go awry in terms of the technical demands of the lesson. You are not there to facilitate the lesson or to support the teacher as a proxy technician. You are an objective observer, and if learning fails to take place as a direct result of a teacher failing to respond effectively or to plan around a technical glitch then this needs to form part of your evaluation.

In terms of note-taking, your form should have two clear sections. The first is where you will notate any significant observation regarding learning and attempt to relate this back to provision. For example, most children were able to use sequences of instructions to control devices as a direct result of the teacher's careful modelling of this procedure. The second section provides an opportunity to summarize the main points observed and begin to indicate potential barriers to learning which would normally be fed back to the teacher. If nothing else, you have to make a judgement about the standard of learning that you observe within each lesson and relate this to national expectations. This is the whole purpose of your observation so do not leave without it.

When you have completed each set of lessons, you can make an overall evaluation of the standards being attained across a complete strand. This information will then inform your judgement about the overall health of ICT as a subject in your school. If you have made effective notes it will also begin to guide you as to what you need to do next in order to raise standards further.

A final word of wisdom. In my experience the single biggest contributing factor to underachievement in ICT is low expectations both on behalf of the teacher within an individual lesson and the structured demands of the lesson itself. Because many teachers still lack expertise with regard to ICT, lessons may still 'dumb down' to the lowest common denominator. If your scheme of work is effective, then teachers have to present children with the right level of challenge in order to achieve reasonable standards. It is not acceptable for Year 4 to be pitching in with Year 2's 'control' objectives any more than it would be for a Year 6 teacher to decide that the main focus for their creative writing lesson was to reinforce full stops and capital letters. At some point we have to burst out of the comfort zone. Hopefully, colleagues will have arranged some release time this week to begin their monitoring work. I look forward to hearing from you.

26th May

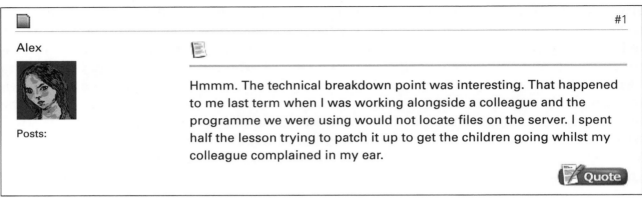

Alex

Posts:

#1

Hmmm. The technical breakdown point was interesting. That happened to me last term when I was working alongside a colleague and the programme we were using would not locate files on the server. I spent half the lesson trying to patch it up to get the children going whilst my colleague complained in my ear.

Quote

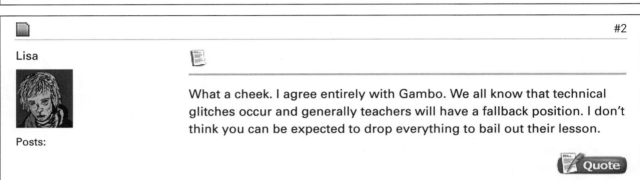

Lisa

Posts:

#2

What a cheek. I agree entirely with Gambo. We all know that technical glitches occur and generally teachers will have a fallback position. I don't think you can be expected to drop everything to bail out their lesson.

Quote

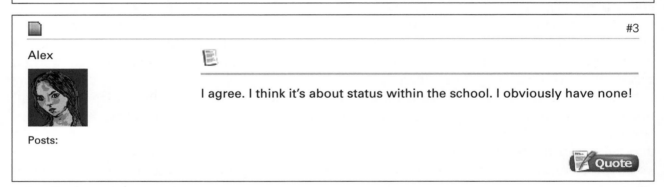

Alex

Posts:

#3

I agree. I think it's about status within the school. I obviously have none!

Quote

29th May

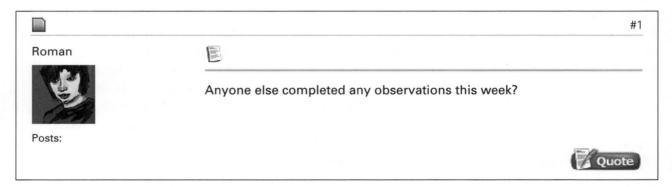

Roman

Posts:

#1

Anyone else completed any observations this week?

Quote

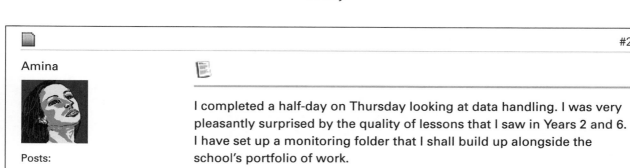

Amina

Posts:

I completed a half-day on Thursday looking at data handling. I was very pleasantly surprised by the quality of lessons that I saw in Years 2 and 6. I have set up a monitoring folder that I shall build up alongside the school's portfolio of work.

Quote

#2

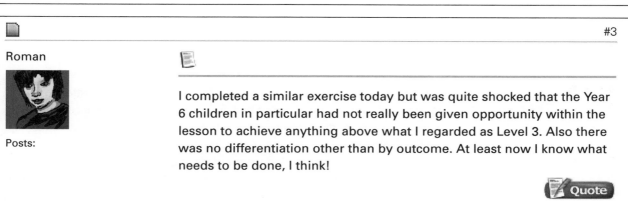

Roman

Posts:

I completed a similar exercise today but was quite shocked that the Year 6 children in particular had not really been given opportunity within the lesson to achieve anything above what I regarded as Level 3. Also there was no differentiation other than by outcome. At least now I know what needs to be done, I think!

Quote

#3

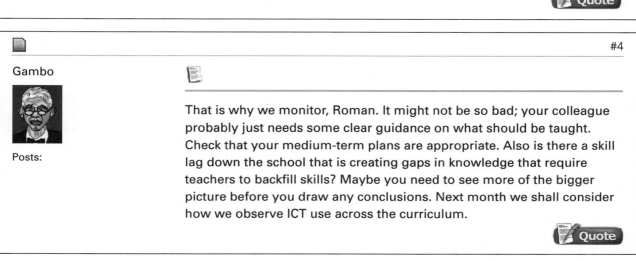

Gambo

Posts:

That is why we monitor, Roman. It might not be so bad; your colleague probably just needs some clear guidance on what should be taught. Check that your medium-term plans are appropriate. Also is there a skill lag down the school that is creating gaps in knowledge that require teachers to backfill skills? Maybe you need to see more of the bigger picture before you draw any conclusions. Next month we shall consider how we observe ICT use across the curriculum.

Quote

#4

Chapter 10 • June

1st June

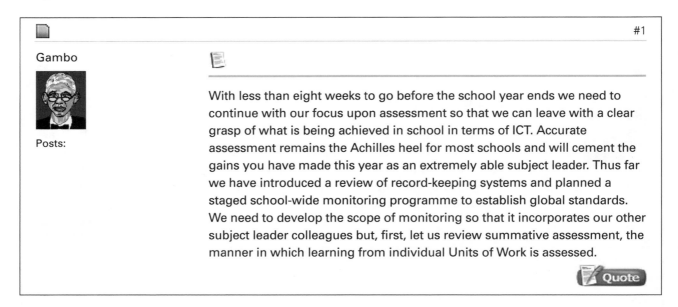

In the image forum post:

> **Gambo**
>
> Posts:
>
> #1
>
> With less than eight weeks to go before the school year ends we need to continue with our focus upon assessment so that we can leave with a clear grasp of what is being achieved in school in terms of ICT. Accurate assessment remains the Achilles heel for most schools and will cement the gains you have made this year as an extremely able subject leader. Thus far we have introduced a review of record-keeping systems and planned a staged school-wide monitoring programme to establish global standards. We need to develop the scope of monitoring so that it incorporates our other subject leader colleagues but, first, let us review summative assessment, the manner in which learning from individual Units of Work is assessed.
>
> Quote

1st June

Week 37, Task 28 – Assessing ICT using Summative Assessment Tasks

Summative assessment has become somewhat unfashionable in primary settings in recent years, largely in the wake of the 'assessment for learning' revolution. Championed by the national strategies and numerous celebrated authors it is the formative 'ongoing' review of individual learning that rules the day in terms of assessment. Teachers have had a prodigious raft of training that quite rightly directs their attention towards the need to engage children with their learning objectives and to develop effective strategies for ongoing formative assessment. We shall look at the manner in which such techniques can impact upon the successful teaching of ICT next month, however, for now I should like to champion the cause of summary review in ICT as the most effective means of tracking pupil progress across the Units of Work through periodic and systematic summative assessments.

Ideally every Unit of Work, be it taught via a commercial scheme or through your own adaptation of the QCA scheme, should end with an integrated task that allows pupils independently to apply the skills, knowledge and understanding taught within that unit. Creative tasks can introduce real fun into the last few weeks of a topic and encourage independent work patterns vital for the rapid development of IT literacy. Your first task is quite straightforward therefore: to review the quality and consistency with which summative tasks are used at school and the degree to which they produce levelled exemplars of pupils work. Where this works best in each year group pupils will complete over the course of the year a series of these tasks that will provide evidence of achievement across each strand of the subject area. Consider whether this is the case within your own school. You may wish to complete the pro forma outlined in Table 10.1 as a quick monitoring activity.

Your aim is to establish an overview of the culture within school both for using the tasks as a teaching aid and as a means to making accurate assessment judgements. Having established where the current teaching strengths lie you can begin to devise a strategy for developing these further across the school.

Table 10.1 Summative assessment pro forma

Year Group	Unit Title	Assessment Task		
		Fully Levelled	Part Levelled	No Task
YEAR 1	1A An introduction to modelling			
	1B Using a word bank			
	1C The information around us			
	1D Labelling and classifying			
	1E Representing information graphically: pictograms			
	1F Understanding instructions and making things happen			
YEAR 2	2A Writing stories: communicating information using text			
	2B Creating pictures			
	2C Finding information			
	2D Routes: controlling a floor turtle			
	2E Questions and answers			
YEAR 3	3A Combining text and graphics			
	3B Manipulating sound			
	3C Introduction to databases			
	3D Exploring simulations			
	3E Email			
YEAR 4	4A Writing for different audiences			
	4B Developing images using repeating patterns			
	4C Branching databases			
	4D Collecting and presenting information: questionnaires and pie charts			
	4E Modelling effects on screen			
YEAR 5	5A Graphical modelling			
	5B Analysing data and asking questions: using complex searches			
	5C Evaluating information, checking accuracy and questioning plausibility			
	5D Introduction to spreadsheets			
	5E Controlling devices			
	5F Monitoring environmental conditions and changes			
YEAR 6	6A Multimedia presentation			
	6B Spreadsheet modelling			
	6C Control and monitoring – What happens when … ?			
	6D Using the Internet to search large databases and to interpret information			

Available on the net at http://www.sagepub.co.uk/wrightbk1

2nd June

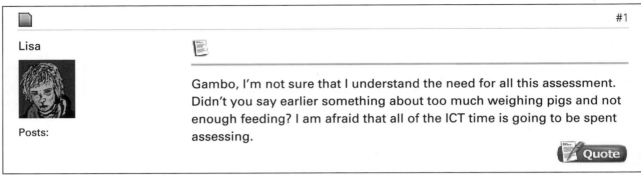

Lisa

Posts:

Gambo, I'm not sure that I understand the need for all this assessment. Didn't you say earlier something about too much weighing pigs and not enough feeding? I am afraid that all of the ICT time is going to be spent assessing.

#1

Quote

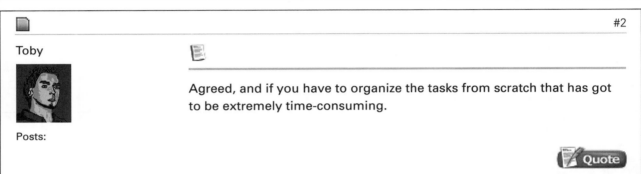

Toby

Posts:

Agreed, and if you have to organize the tasks from scratch that has got to be extremely time-consuming.

#2

Quote

4th June

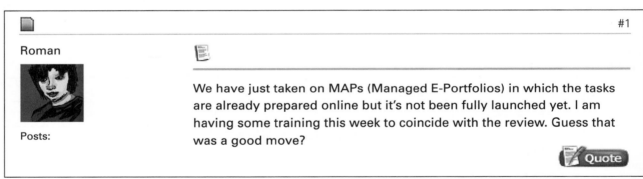

Roman

Posts:

We have just taken on MAPs (Managed E-Portfolios) in which the tasks are already prepared online but it's not been fully launched yet. I am having some training this week to coincide with the review. Guess that was a good move?

#1

Quote

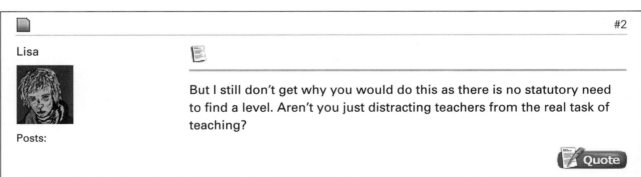

Lisa

Posts:

But I still don't get why you would do this as there is no statutory need to find a level. Aren't you just distracting teachers from the real task of teaching?

#2

Quote

#3

Gambo

Posts:

Lisa, you are right to question unmanageable systems that detract from a teacher's core purpose, that of bringing about learning. In ICT like any other subject area, assessment systems are designed to establish what actually is being learnt. We cannot simply assume that all children are achieving their objectives and then move on to the next unit of work. Each school has to develop a broad and balanced range of procedures that reliably capture the performance of each pupil and impact upon planning in order that it is effectively aligned to pupils' needs.

Quote

#4

Alex

Posts:

Can't this be achieved through the teacher's records we looked at last month?

Quote

#5

Lisa

Posts:

I agree with everything you said, Gambo, but a separate summative task for each unit?

Quote

#6

Gambo

Posts:

First, I think that the tasks go a long way towards validating the teacher records that tend to be stronger in some areas than others. I also think that it is possible to have an effective combination of systems that cover the breadth of the curriculum. However, each unit should contain an integrated task in order to reinforce its key elements and to develop independent learning. It should be a reasonably short step into developing these tasks into assessment opportunities. The problems arise where the units are not being taught robustly, thus denying children the opportunity to engage in the task; similarly where teachers are not accustomed to providing feedback to the children upon the quality of the ICT work. Unlike traditional book-based subjects it is rarely marked and so a transition to a robustly assessed system can seem daunting.

Quote

Best practice occurs when the tasks are completely integrated within the lesson structure and do not rely upon additional procedures or overbearing administrative requirements. Roman talked about the MAPs system as a commercial scheme suitable for summative assessment. MAPs not only provides web-based tasks for children across KS2 and indeed KS3 to complete, but also provides a relatively straightforward structured system by which teachers can review the work and assign levels. However, it also sits within a web-based portal, which requires individual pupil and teacher logins (www.maps-ict.com). This can be a real plus for many schools looking to develop E-portals and to benefit from the home–school links that this facilitates. However, for many staff this is placing ever greater demands upon their own ICT confidence levels than the completion of the tasks themselves. Some schools may wish to pursue such an all-embracing system if they felt that existing records and so on and other levelling activities were ineffective. If a school chose to design its own tasks, the key questions would be:

1 Does the task allow sufficient opportunity for pupils to demonstrate higher-level attainment? Many exercises if poorly planned will restrict the potential for more able pupils to shine.
2 Is the task equally accessible to all insomuch as it is not going to penalize less able readers, particularly if adequate support is not available?
3 Are the assessment criteria clear so that teachers may easily make judgements based upon both process and pupil outcomes?

Any system should be judged against each of these criteria. Schools may wish to consider whether they need to take a revised look at their whole Scheme of Work when considering how it is being assessed. It might be that an all-embracing scheme such as RM's ICT Alive (www.rm.com/ictalive), which includes its own integrated assessment tasks, may be the way forward. In either case, colleagues are going to require prolonged and sustained training support in order for the introduction to be effective.

Therefore, to conclude, I invite colleagues to consider to what extent their present system is fit for purpose and, if revision is required, the extent of such a move and its impact upon current teaching practice within the school. Finally, it is not okay to do nothing. Go back to the fundamental question that you need to answer as subject leader. What are the standards of work in ICT? Remember that a levelled judgement refers to a pupil's ability as demonstrated across all the ICT strands. If you do not know what those standards are, or if you are not confident that those standards are based upon secure assessment, then you need to consider revising your current systems and that rigorous system of summative assessment tasks may be one means of moving forward.

10th June

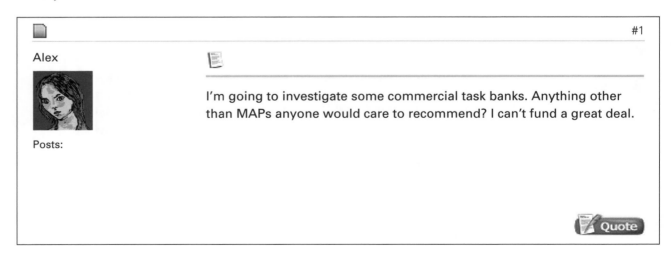

Alex

Posts:

I'm going to investigate some commercial task banks. Anything other than MAPs anyone would care to recommend? I can't fund a great deal.

#1

Quote

Amina

Posts:

#2

We are currently using 'GOAL' test systems for a number of subjects including ICT. I particularly like the fact that the children enjoy doing the tests. They are also easy to administer and provide useful information that forms part of our teacher's assessment repertoire. I also think they enable us to answer your key questions regarding standards, Gambo.

Quote

Tess

Posts:

#3

Personally I don't like this sort of multiple-choice test, I'm also not convinced that it is ICT that is being tested rather than reading comprehension or mathematics data-handling skills.

Quote

Gambo

Posts:

#4

GOAL is another option; remember that a school needs to look at how a range of systems is workable within their context. I do have reservations regarding the lack of process within this sort of assessment, after all it is the ICT process that needs to be assessed and developed. The children are actually 'doing' less ICT here. You can trial the product at the GOAL website: www.goalonline.co.uk.

Quote

Rasp

Posts:

#5

I know it's off topic but what are your thoughts about the QCA KS3 test, Gambo?

Quote

Gambo

Posts:

Rasp, I think it's ground breaking and a stunning piece of software that could potentially transform online assessment across all sectors. Colleagues may want to take a look for themselves (www.rm.com/qca) but it is off topic.

#6

Quote

15th June

Week 39, Task 29 – Observing ICT in Other Subjects

Hopefully, you are building a raft of resources and strategies to address the two core questions I posed last month, namely:

What are the standards of ICT in the school?
What are the children achieving and attaining?

As we now consider the monitoring of ICT usage within other National Curriculum subject areas, let us be clear that this ideally will be done not by the ICT co-ordinator but as an aspect of each subject leader's monitoring role within their subject area. Therefore, your activity is to prepare colleagues so that they are able to take on that monitoring role. I recommend that you access a staff meeting in order to deliver a common message or this may be part of a broader school agenda INSET (in-service training) day related to subject leadership and monitoring. The thing is to seize every opportunity to promote the use of ICT.

Take another look at Table 4.2 (Chapter 4) that looked at the level descriptors by theme. Introduce this to colleagues and ask them to identify where this might overlap within their subject areas and begin to identify progression across individual strands. Make a point of highlighting to colleagues where expectations lie. For example, with regard to word-processing, 'Pupils use ICT to generate, develop, organize and present their work' is indicative of Level 3 skills. This should be challenged if it makes up the majority of a Year 6 history assignment. Highlight the Year 4 requirements in terms of amending work, use of a variety of sources, for example combining Internet-based study with evidence collected using a digital camera or sound recorder. An awareness of audience and the potential for using email will further extend project outcomes.

Proper consideration of such ideas will not only lift the potential for ICT skills to exceed the expected Level 4 but will clearly enhance the history project. It is also useful for staff to get the opportunity to see a variety of ICT use in order to practise their observation techniques. Remember to incorporate all of the key points that were central to the discrete ICT monitoring activities:

1 Primary focus is the judgement regarding standards.
2 Identify and attribute any relationship between teaching, resources, learning environment, pupil attitudes and achievement.
3 Be aware of the journey that the class will have taken prior to the lesson.
4 Prepare beforehand in order to attribute levels of understanding.
5 Beware of low expectations.

In October 2004 the DfES produced the Primary National Strategy's *Learning and Teaching Using ICT Example Materials from Foundation Stage to Year 6* (DFES0315-2004G), which took the form of a series of CD-ROMs that were delivered to every school in the country. They provide a number of lesson examples, which are very useful for shared moderation work. If not readily available in school, they can be ordered at no charge to schools via the Teachernet online publications web-site. Alternatively materials are available for download from http://samples.lgfl.org.uk/primary.

A selection of four or five vignettes should be sufficient to demonstrate best practice. Choose a selection that crosses age ranges and subject areas. The Year 1 Geography example shows a class in which the small group of children are guided to use Pixie to follow a route around school and to drop off characters at agreed points along that route as part of a locality Unit of Study. The video demonstrates the children using ICT to 'explore what happens in real and imaginary situations', indicative of Level 2 simulation and modelling. Discussion may focus upon the extent to which this level of attainment might be assigned to the entire group, some of the group or none. Similarly, colleagues could discuss the value of the activity in providing evidence of children being able to 'plan and give instructions to make things happen and describe the effects' in terms of the control and monitoring aspects of the activity.

Have a look at a selection of the videos available and begin to prepare this training session for colleagues. It will be far more useful than simply asking subject leaders to complete the observations and far more efficient than trying to complete these yourself.

18th June

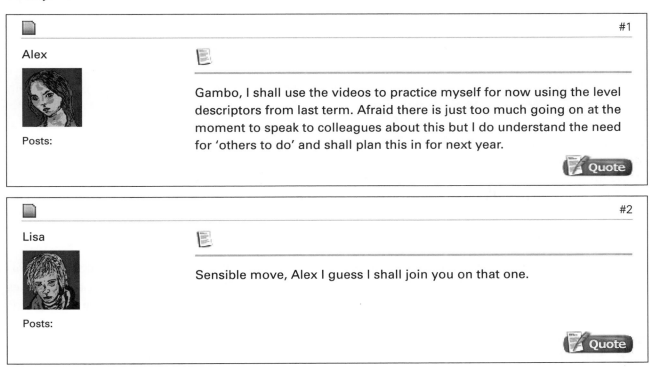

#1

Alex

Posts:

Gambo, I shall use the videos to practice myself for now using the level descriptors from last term. Afraid there is just too much going on at the moment to speak to colleagues about this but I do understand the need for 'others to do' and shall plan this in for next year.

Quote

#2

Lisa

Posts:

Sensible move, Alex I guess I shall join you on that one.

Quote

19th June

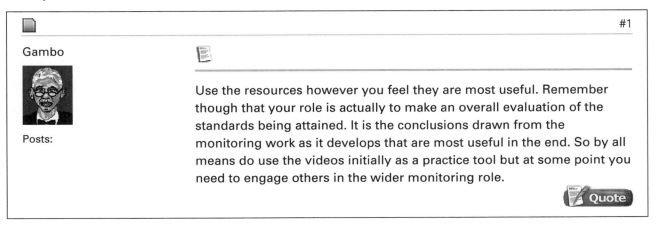

#1

Gambo

Posts:

Use the resources however you feel they are most useful. Remember though that your role is actually to make an overall evaluation of the standards being attained. It is the conclusions drawn from the monitoring work as it develops that are most useful in the end. So by all means do use the videos initially as a practice tool but at some point you need to engage others in the wider monitoring role.

Quote

25th June

Week 40, Task 30 – CPD – a Needs Analysis

For a school to become truly E-enabled it is essential that staff are properly trained to meet the needs of a twenty-first-century curriculum. Of course, as ICT co-ordinator you cannot choose the staff but you do have to ensure that those staff that you do have are provided with every opportunity possible.

Many schools have not undergone a thorough ICT staff skills review since the New Opportunities Fund (NOF) ICT training programme of 2000 to 2003 and it is worth spending a little time here considering some of the lessons of the past.

The NOF programme most notably emphasized the development of an appropriate pedagogy rather than ICT skills as the means to make a fundamental step change in a teacher's ability to use ICT as a teaching and learning tool. It focused upon ICT in the classroom and much of the training was online. The initiative is estimated to have cost around £230 million across the UK and was accessed by around 395,000 teachers using 47 English approved training providers (ATPs) at a cost of £450 per teacher. Even now, looking back, the scope and ambition of the project are staggering yet one would struggle to find anyone in the field of ICT in schools who would laud its impact. Most criticism of the scheme references the matter of teacher readiness for this type of advanced online CPD. Many staff lacked the prerequisite ICT skills and many schools had not got the broadband or hardware infrastructure required. Therefore the audit that precipitated training was generally ill matched to the work that followed.

The official Teacher Training Agency commissioned report conducted by Mirandanet, which evaluated perspectives on NOF, noted that:

'From the quality assurance perspective, the most successful schools seemed to enjoy good strategic leadership and collegiate work patterns. The programme flourished where senior managers valued this opportunity and wanted to make sure that their school benefited from it, even if they weren't particularly ICT literate themselves. In these schools ring-fenced time, technical support and general encouragement, contributed to staff enthusiasm. The schools used strategies like regular workshops, informal problem solving pairs and groups that helped to balance staff strengths and weaknesses.' (Mirandanet, 2003: 7)

This was certainly my own experience at the time when training involved working alongside colleagues in order to 'hand-hold' and to plug the gaps with additional in-house skill-based surgeries as the need arose. This highlights two key facets essential for future training initiatives: first, that schools undertake a clear audit of need and, secondly, to ensure that teacher and teaching assistants future needs are dovetailed within the school's strategic plan for E-learning and ICT.

The fifth element of BECTA's self-review framework looks specifically at the continued professional development opportunities provided by schools and offers a good starting point for discussion. In particular with regard to strand 5A of the framework which considers the extent to which the school plans its future provision. Let us consider the requirements at Level 2 of the framework, which is the ICT Mark threshold for this strand.

Aspect 5a-1 Identifying individual staff skills and needs
'There is a regular and systematic audit of staff skills and needs in relation to ICT. This covers both ICT competence and the effective use of ICT in learning and teaching.'

5a-2 Identifying whole-school ICT development needs
'Development needs are closely linked to the school's ICT priorities and planning and include a focus on the use of ICT in learning and teaching.'

5a-3 Planning to meet school and individual needs
'Plans for professional development are based on a systematic audit. They provide a mix of activities and take account of individual and whole-school needs.'

Therefore we have to audit staff capability. The most forward-thinking schools will begin to profile areas of school in terms of staff ICT competencies.

When developing a profile of staff strengths it is essential to place this within the broader context of the school's needs and those of the phase or year group in which that person works. Table 10.2 can be used to log training gaps from a variety of sources. Examples of curriculum requirements might include core ICT content training, for example, QCA-related workshops or training specific to other curriculum areas such as Numeracy ITPs appropriate to that age range. School phase requirements would link to initiative development such as enhanced use of interactive whiteboards, developing the use of ICT to support children with special educational needs or developing virtual learning modules. Such targets may be generic across a phase or may affect the whole school. Table 10.2 also allows for the identification of basic ICT competencies, which was a key flaw identified from the NOF training, whilst another section relates to the use of management and information software or systems. Finally, it is worth logging access to school laptops or home broadband facilities particularly with the development of E-portals and schools' virtual learning facilities.

Remember that teaching assistants should be included alongside teachers and there may also be performance management related issues for senior managers. In terms of the actual auditing tools, be wary of simply issuing staff with questionnaires and so on as a means of establishing skills deficits. These are frequently self-fulfilling and rarely identify specific areas that can readily be addressed. Question the value of staff league tables; it is not a competition and once again they are largely self-fulfilling, rarely shedding fresh light upon what you already know. Best practice would be to create a bespoke survey based upon your own school's specific needs and related to the particular teacher's year group and so on. More important here, I think, is an understanding of the demands upon any particular teacher in the coming year and what that will mean in terms of effective CPD. The pro forma in Table 10.2 should lead to a meaningful conversation with individual teachers to establish what those needs are. It is also often useful to then issue staff with a training profile card such as the example in Figure 10.1.

This training profile card may be adapted to suit the range of your school targets. In essence it is a bit like a performance management review in that three targets are probably enough to focus upon effectively.

Table 10.2 Staff ICT training audit

Phase	Name (Teacher or TA)	Curriculum/ QCA requirements	School/phase requirements	Basic skills	Teacher MIS	Home use, laptop allocated
Foundation Stage						
Key Stage 1						
Key Stage 2 (Lower)						
Key Stage 2 (Upper)						

Available on the net at http://www.sagepub.co.uk/wrightbk1

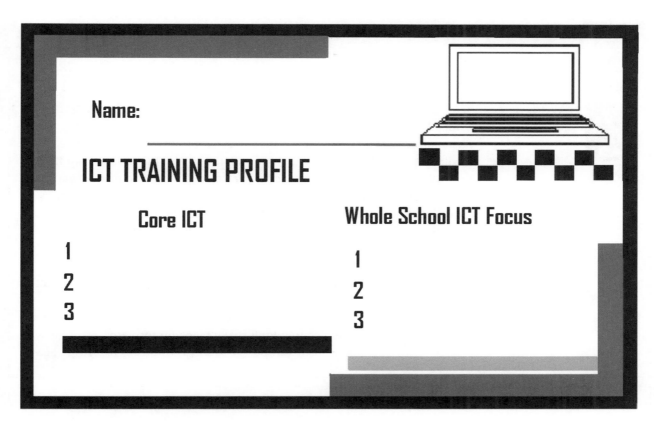

Figure 10.1 ICT training profile card

Available on the net at http://www.sagepub.co.uk/wrightbk1

25th June

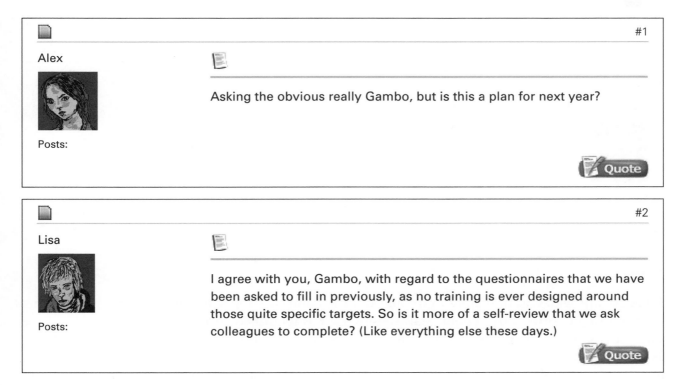

26th June

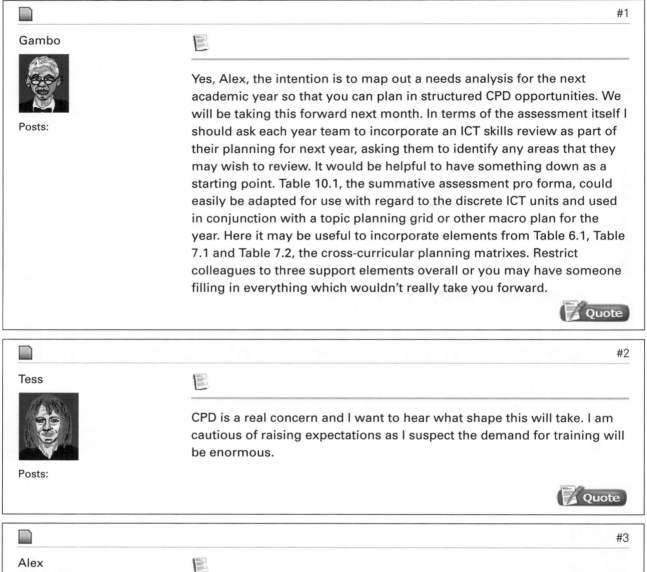

#1

Gambo

Posts:

Yes, Alex, the intention is to map out a needs analysis for the next academic year so that you can plan in structured CPD opportunities. We will be taking this forward next month. In terms of the assessment itself I should ask each year team to incorporate an ICT skills review as part of their planning for next year, asking them to identify any areas that they may wish to review. It would be helpful to have something down as a starting point. Table 10.1, the summative assessment pro forma, could easily be adapted for use with regard to the discrete ICT units and used in conjunction with a topic planning grid or other macro plan for the year. Here it may be useful to incorporate elements from Table 6.1, Table 7.1 and Table 7.2, the cross-curricular planning matrixes. Restrict colleagues to three support elements overall or you may have someone filling in everything which wouldn't really take you forward.

Quote

#2

Tess

Posts:

CPD is a real concern and I want to hear what shape this will take. I am cautious of raising expectations as I suspect the demand for training will be enormous.

Quote

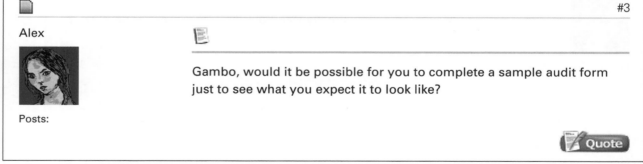

#3

Alex

Posts:

Gambo, would it be possible for you to complete a sample audit form just to see what you expect it to look like?

Quote

27th June

Table 10.3 provides an outcomes example from the audit, with specific reference to lower juniors within a single form entry school. Staff self-review has identified specific curriculum areas where support is sought. The phase will be introducing pupil email next year, so this has been identified as a generic target whilst one member of staff, Carol, the Year 4 teaching assistant, has responded to the offer of basic skills training. Phase leader, Sarah Hardman has been identified within the SMT as the staff member who will lead subject strand assessment analyses using the RAISEonline portal. Both have been allocated laptops for home use.

Next month we shall use this exemplar as the basis for planning appropriate CPD provision.

Table 10.3 Exemplar section from staff ICT training audit

Phase	Name (Teacher or TA)	Curriculum/ QCA requirements	School/phase requirements	Basic skills	Teacher MIS	Home use, laptop allocated
	Sarah Hardman Y4	4C Branching databases – Spr	Introducing pupil email		RAISEonline	LfT
		Geog Database – Spr				
Key Stage 2 (Lower)	Carol Fletcher Y4 TA	4C Branching databases – Spr	Introducing pupil email	Support requested		
		Music–Composition software – Aut				
	Mike Pearson Y3	Science Database – Sum	Introducing pupil email			LfT
	Mahesh Patel Y3 TA	3E Email – Sum	Introducing pupil email			
		Science Database – Sum				

Available on the net at http://www.sagepub.co.uk/wrightbk1

147

29th June

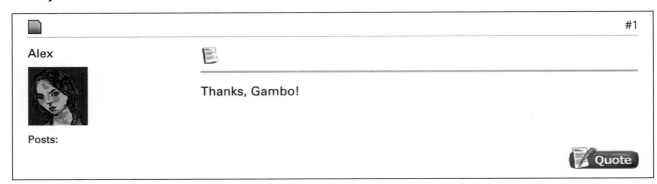

Alex

Posts:

Thanks, Gambo!

#1

Quote

Chapter 11 • *July*

2nd July

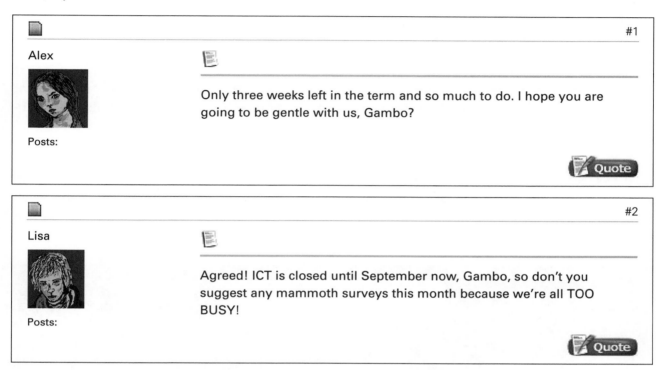

#1

Alex

Posts:

Only three weeks left in the term and so much to do. I hope you are going to be gentle with us, Gambo?

Quote

#2

Lisa

Posts:

Agreed! ICT is closed until September now, Gambo, so don't you suggest any mammoth surveys this month because we're all TOO BUSY!

Quote

2nd July

Week 41, Task 31 – Planning CPD Provision

Having completed your audit of staff in terms of future CPD, I'd like to spend a little time considering how the various needs may be met. The next few weeks are time in which you may wish to quietly complete the audit if it has not been possible to do so before now. The BECTA self-review offers the following target areas in terms of best practice.

5b-1 Range of development opportunities
'A wide range of development opportunities are provided both within and out of school which meet the individual needs and styles of most staff.'

5b-2 Quality of professional development
'Professional development activities for most staff are consistently timely and closely linked to the school's ICT resources, current practices, and school and individual needs. They are well focused, engaging, and effective and address the confidence levels of individuals.'

5b-3 Sharing effective practice
'Individual staff development incorporates the sharing and wider adoption of effective practice within the school.'

5b-4 Coaching, mentoring and individual support

'Individual mentoring and coaching is provided as a part of planned ICT professional development for most staff, according to need.'

5c-1 Monitoring and evaluation

'The school has systems to monitor and evaluate the quality of professional development in ICT and has begun to link this to outcomes for learning and teaching.'

5c-2 Linking to future professional development planning

Plans for professional development in ICT take good account of the results of monitoring and evaluation and assess likely value for money and impact on learning and teaching.

Figure 11.1 pulls together the key elements cited within the framework. It demonstrates that first and foremost there are a wide range of CPD opportunities open to schools and it is not simply a matter of booking teachers onto courses as these arise. That option is not generally economical and any model that you are recommending to your school's senior management needs to be costed within your development plan. The second core point is that of timings, as these are critical. There is no point sending a staff member off to a 'control' workshop next January if they need to teach the unit this September; it seems an obvious point but one that is very pertinent. Figure 11.1 also highlights the fact that whatever form of professional development is undertaken there should be structures within school through which it can be disseminated and the impact of the training evaluated.

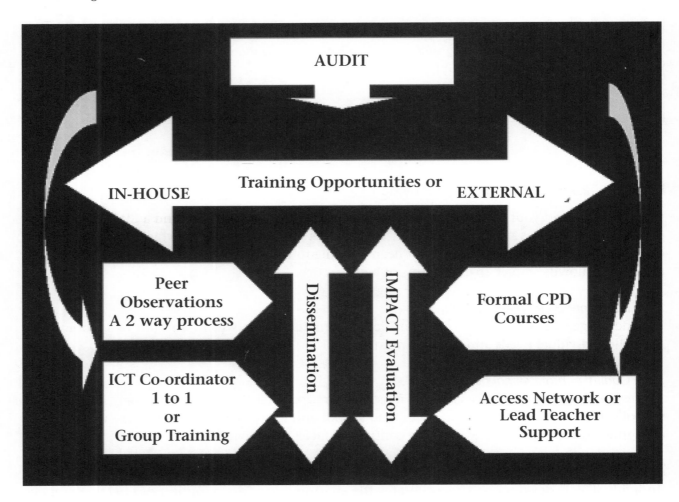

Figure 11.1 Planning CPD for ICT

Available on the net at http://www.sagepub.co.uk/wrightbk1

I am going to use the exemplar audit (Table 10.3) as a context for CPD review.

It is generally helpful to set priorities for training on the basis of specific criteria based around the impact that such training will have upon the quality of teaching and learning at the school. On this basis I should prioritize training for ICT in the following form:

1 Whole-school/phase initiatives
2 Specific individual curriculum teaching requirements
3 Specific individual essential systems training
4 Additional ICT skills training.

Any whole-school initiative has to have impact and as co-ordinator it will be your responsibility not only to organize but also probably to deliver this training. In the example given, the core focus for the phase was introducing pupil email. One might aim to deliver this training in-house, possibly as a twilight session. Generally if you have the support of a teaching assistant then this may be something they can follow up providing in-class support. Be clear about this though – providing teacher support should not equate to teaching the unit whilst the teacher prepares something else. The only way to avoid this is to build in structures that demand participation.

For email I should correlate the pupil launch with a roll-out of staff email activities, maybe arranging briefing notes, memos and so on to be emailed to encourage active participation. That should accommodate part of Mahesh, the Year 3 TA's curriculum needs. In addition, it certainly looks like the lower junior staff require some database training. If there is expertise within school then the logical step here would be to organize peer observations with colleagues taking it in turns to observe and be observed. Also try to get to the hub of the problem; it is a good opportunity to flag up the central role of objectives and to be clear how these are to be addressed. This could be supported by yourself offering an after-school workshop if a number of staff, as is the case in the example, had all identified the same area of need. The two staff who additionally want support in the branching database QCA unit may be able to get that support via the general database workshop. More likely the teachers will need to attend local in-service training if it is available. If not, contact the local authority and request it; in the age of self-evaluation and responding to the needs of users you may find that they welcome such a call. It is probably not practical to send both staff members along though. Avoid the temptation to send the TA even though that would be the cheapest option. It is the teacher, in this case Sarah, who is responsible for provision within that classroom and I should expect her to pass on the skills to the TA and not the other way around, although I do accept that there are some exceptionally able teaching assistants gaining recognition for their talents and taking responsibility for leading large groups of children, when covering PPA time for example. The Year 4 TA, Carol, should be provided with an opportunity to shadow a colleague elsewhere in school where music composition software is being used, ideally further up the school. In this way she will get a sense of the progression and feel comfortable teaching at a less challenging level.

The MIS training related to RAISEeonline may be addressed either through local authority training or, if the school is engaged within a primary network, there may well be expertise within a cluster partner school and a facility for this linkage to be utilized. Affording colleagues the opportunity to work in other similar settings can be extremely empowering. That leaves us with Carol's request for an IT skills training package. This is the request that generally gets left off the INSET plan, especially when it originates from a teaching assistant, however, if we accept that a teacher's confidence in using ICT at a basic level remains a barrier to the development of the E-learning school then you should have a policy in place for dealing with such requests. Perhaps you could introduce something in-house or across a local primary network, in which case the Training and Development Agency for Schools' (TDA) own generic ICT skills test has very useful downloadable practice applications available from: http://www.tda.gov.uk/skillstests/practicematerials/ict.aspx.

Alternatively you may wish to co-ordinate accredited support from any of the leading ICT training organizations such as EPICT, ECDL or CLAIT:

The European Pedagogical ICT Licence (EPICT), http://www.epict.info.
The European Computer Driving Licence (ECDL) for Educators, http://www.educatorsecdl.com.
Computer Literacy and Information Technology (CLAIT), http://www.clait2006.co.uk.

In order to be prepared for the array of training requests that may arise once 'Pandora's box' is opened you should consider how best to implement personal whole-school training, a cross-fertilization of skills through both in-house and across-school clusters peer support and the setting up of a standard accreditation procedure with regard to basic skills training via an established and accredited skills provider.

5th July

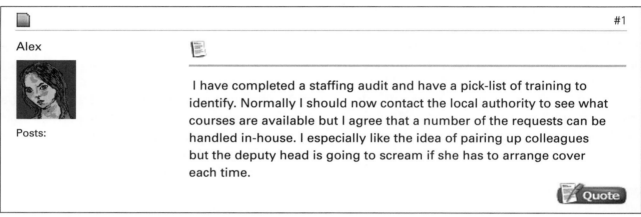

#1

Alex

Posts:

I have completed a staffing audit and have a pick-list of training to identify. Normally I should now contact the local authority to see what courses are available but I agree that a number of the requests can be handled in-house. I especially like the idea of pairing up colleagues but the deputy head is going to scream if she has to arrange cover each time.

Quote

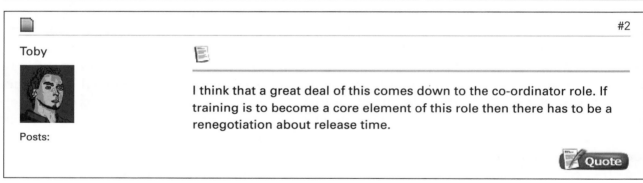

#2

Toby

Posts:

I think that a great deal of this comes down to the co-ordinator role. If training is to become a core element of this role then there has to be a renegotiation about release time.

Quote

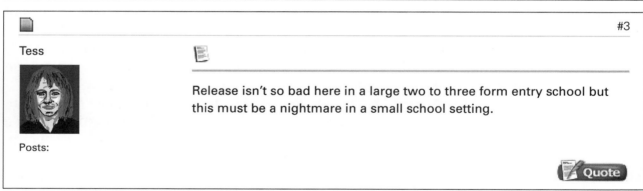

#3

Tess

Posts:

Release isn't so bad here in a large two to three form entry school but this must be a nightmare in a small school setting.

Quote

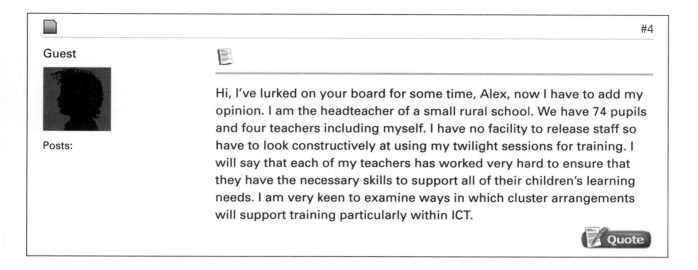

Guest

Posts:

Hi, I've lurked on your board for some time, Alex, now I have to add my opinion. I am the headteacher of a small rural school. We have 74 pupils and four teachers including myself. I have no facility to release staff so have to look constructively at using my twilight sessions for training. I will say that each of my teachers has worked very hard to ensure that they have the necessary skills to support all of their children's learning needs. I am very keen to examine ways in which cluster arrangements will support training particularly within ICT.

#4

9th July

Week 42, Task 32 – Moderating Standards and Creating a School Portfolio

The final piece within our assessment of ICT jigsaw deals directly with the concepts of assessment for learning and, in particular, with a shared understanding of learning goals and outcomes in order to produce a clear understanding of the next steps for learning between pupil and teacher. To that end, it is recommended that each pupil has access to their own electronic folder into which all of their ICT-related work is collected. Furthermore, they should be encouraged from a very early age to take ownership of that system and to operate folders that relate directly to their tasks and learning objectives as demonstrated in Figure 11.2

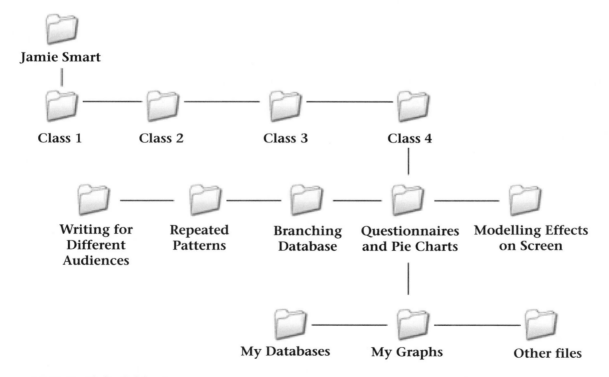

Figure 11.2 Portfolio folder tree

Available on the net at http://www.sagepub.co.uk/wrightbk1

School procedures and structures with regard to the development of pupil portfolios will immediately impact upon pupils' understanding of their ICT journey and the manner in which the often disparate Units of Work link together. With the arrival of online portals in 2008 this should be seen as a real opportunity to reinforce this type of architecture.

Once pupils are familiar with their folder structure they should be encouraged to collect work and to begin to annotate it with reference to their learning objectives. This not only presents an excellent assessment for learning opportunity, but will provide essential evidence of process in order for teachers and subject leaders to make a judgement regarding the level of the work.

As we reach the end of the academic year it is a good time to plan provision for next year. How are pupil files transferred? Are they archived? If your own system lacks the pupil ownership of the one suggested, then this is a good time to change it. Do not be put off by technicians either, there should be no technical reason why this cannot be established and if there are objections then bring forward plans for presenting pupils with online file storage so that the folders may also be accessed from home.

Such a structure allows each pupil to develop his or her own portfolio, which in turn should feed into a school portfolio of exemplar work. At the end of each half-term pupils should be encouraged to go back over their work and pick out the best examples that match the learning objectives with which these are associated, in effect forming a filter system that self-elects work for the school portfolio.

10th July

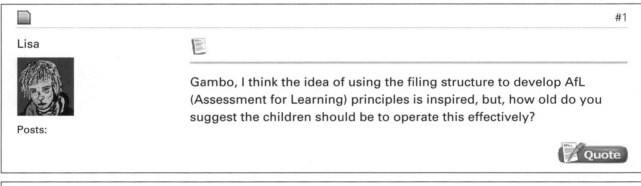

#1

Lisa

Posts:

Gambo, I think the idea of using the filing structure to develop AfL (Assessment for Learning) principles is inspired, but, how old do you suggest the children should be to operate this effectively?

Quote

#2

Gambo

Posts:

Hi, Lisa, its going to depend on the school, but I think that from Year 3 onwards the pupils can manage their folders autonomously. Prior to that the system may need to be 'managed' by the school but infant children will still respond to the structure.

Quote

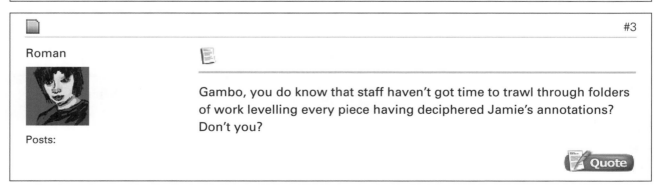

#3

Roman

Posts:

Gambo, you do know that staff haven't got time to trawl through folders of work levelling every piece having deciphered Jamie's annotations? Don't you?

Quote

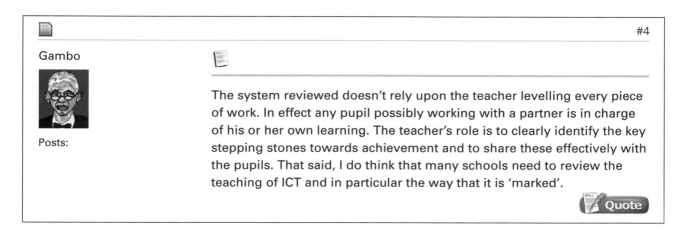

Gambo

Posts:

#4

The system reviewed doesn't rely upon the teacher levelling every piece of work. In effect any pupil possibly working with a partner is in charge of his or her own learning. The teacher's role is to clearly identify the key stepping stones towards achievement and to share these effectively with the pupils. That said, I do think that many schools need to review the teaching of ICT and in particular the way that it is 'marked'.

Quote

11th July

It was stated in an earlier chapter that effective assessment of and for ICT would require a combination of records, summative tasks and ongoing formative assessment. This will involve teachers and the subject leader periodically reviewing the pupil portfolio and assigning a level to recent work. In order for this to be manageable it is not necessary for every piece of work to receive multiple assessments.

Using the earlier example, Jamie Smart had completed five Year 4 Units of Work from the QCA scheme. Let us assume that for Unit 4A Writing for different audiences, Unit 4B Developing images using repeating patterns, and Unit 4E Modelling effects on screen, the class records (Table 9.2) and I Can records (Figure 9.1) were used as a basis for recording pupil progress. Unit 4C, the branching database activity, was assessed via a summative end of unit task and levelled by the class teacher. The final unit, 4D Collecting and presenting information: questionnaires and pie charts, is to be assessed with Jamie during a portfolio review. During this session the teacher or teaching assistant will ask the pupil to talk through their work and their annotations that have been gathered whilst referencing each point against the learning outcomes established in Table 4.2 or directly from the QCA scheme materials.

A simple web search will uncover numerous examples of levelled ICT work that could be used for guidance or as a focus for school-based INSET. The most useful probably remains the National Curriculum in Action site (www.ncaction.org.uk). Use the site to model the process of assessment with staff. It includes a wide range of screenshots of pupils' work alongside commentary of how the work was arrived at and a rationale for any level that was allocated.

As subject leader you may wish to create a schedule for perusing folders in order to have examples to add to a class portfolio representing learning at each level. Dovetail this schedule with your classroom monitoring work so that you have a rolling programme by which new materials may be added. Do remember that, ultimately, accurate levelled assessment relates to breadth and pupils' ability across all strands of the ICT curriculum. When you effectively capture that breadth you have established effective assessment within your subject, which will in turn drive up standards. Good luck!

13th July

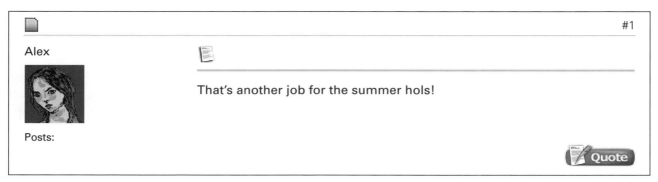

Alex

Posts:

#1

That's another job for the summer hols!

Quote

#2

Toby

Posts:

What is?

Quote

#3

Alex

Posts:

Compiling my levelled school portfolio.

Quote

#4

Toby

Posts:

You not got one of those already? Shame on you. Tobias Interactive has an online version you may wish to peruse.

Quote

#5

Alex

Posts:

I'll pass for now, thanks all the same.

Quote

16th July

Week 43, Task 33 – Reflections on Impact

The final task for this term, and indeed this academic year, is a request that you put aside a little time to reflect upon the impact of all of your hard work. Your school, like most others, will have enjoyed massive government investment in ICT resources, which clearly will have had a marked impact upon access to resources and the levels of ICT use. However, this is not an end in itself. The goal ultimately has to be to raise standards of achievement. As subject leader your ultimate evaluation is to understand the educational value of the ICT investment and its impact upon pupil attainment. Government studies from the groundbreaking Impact2 research (BECTA, 2002) onwards has concluded that something positive happens to the attainment of pupils who make (relatively) high use of ICT in their subject learning and that school standards are positively associated with the quality of ICT resources and quality of their use in teaching and learning, regardless of socio-economic characteristics. Furthermore findings noted within the DfES 'Big pICTure' review (2003) indicated that ICT can play an important role in motivating pupils and encouraging them to engage in learning, within and beyond the classroom.

Information and communication technology has the potential to deliver new forms of teaching and learning in schools and to revolutionize pupils' approaches to learning, however, there are still fundamental questions to be answered regarding the capacity of ICT to promote inclusiveness rather than simply to increase divisions both within the classroom and the broader community. In terms of gender, boys are more likely to report a positive impact of using ICT upon their attainment, and ICT is widely perceived by teachers to help engage boys and to maintain their attention for longer periods of time.

In simple terms each school should begin to evaluate its provision for ICT against each or any of the five core elements within Figure 11.3. Try to develop an understanding of what impact means for your school and how this can best be generated.

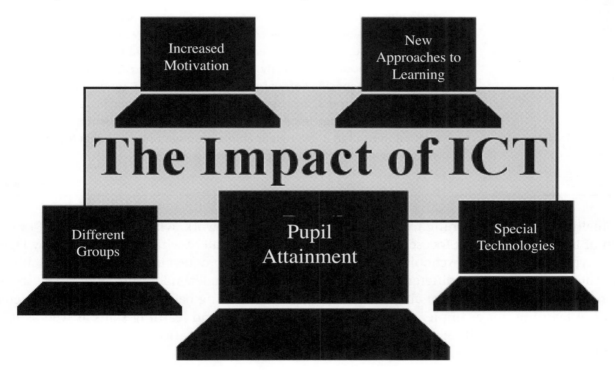

Figure 11.3 The impact of ICT

Available on the net at http://www.sagepub.co.uk/wrightbk1

18th July

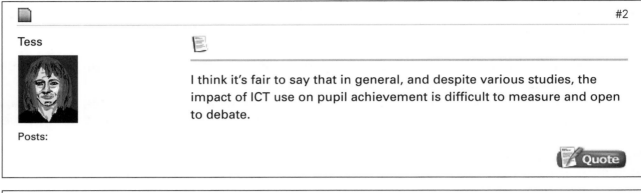

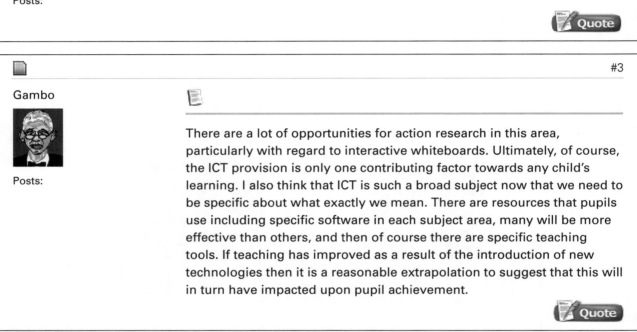

Finally, it is worth returning to the BECTA self-review framework, which featured a self-evaluation of impact. The matrix focuses upon a variety of elements all of which were covered by Figure 11.3, typically stating that schools will review pupils' year-on-progress in ICT as a discrete subject, and the progress made by different groups in ICT and pupils independent use of ICT. The second strand anticipates a judgement about how ICT improves learning before reflecting upon different types of learning, for example, the development of thinking and learning skills as well as ICT's contribution to creativity. Finally, it addresses the issue of motivation in terms of self-esteem, pupil attitudes towards their work, and pupil behaviour.

Chapter 12 • *August*

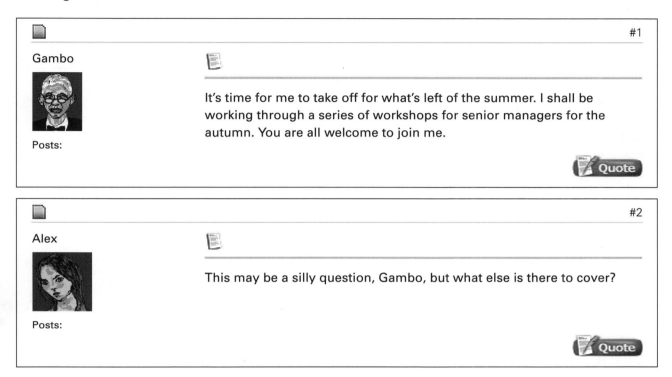

The Road Goes Ever On and On

Having completed this year's programme any co-ordinator will have a very strong strategic view of their subject area. Next year I want to take a number of core issues forward at an even deeper level and particularly address concerns I have had expressed by senior school managers regarding the long-term consequences of supporting a modern IT network.

In the first term we will undertake a complete review of E-safety procedures in the light of the Every Child Matters agenda. We will also consider their funding model in order to plan for ICT developments with due regard to the true total cost of ownership. This will be supported by a broader ICT action planning review to embed a revised E-learning vision through a series of long-term sustainable actions, including and leading onto an analysis of local area networks and the issue of maintaining network security. In the spring term I intend to undertake a fresh review of the curriculum in order to examine how the E-learning community will adapt its core practices to facilitate this new technology. We consider the evolving role of school websites as they assume Web 2.0 interactivity and we examine the place of E-learning within the extended schools agenda. The use of ICT as a tool for management systems is reviewed and we discuss how ICT can be used to support different groups of children. Finally, in the summer term co-ordinators will examine self-evaluation strategies linked to the school's SEF, the Ofsted Section 5 Framework and Every Child Matters. They will consider application for the ICT Mark and National Best Practice awards. A series of new technologies will be examined with regard to their impact upon schools and various virtual learning strategies will be put to the test.

7th August

Figures 12.1, 12.2 and 12.3 provide an overview of everything we have covered. I think you will agree that it is an extensive list. Actually some co-ordinators may wish to rerun the whole 33 tasks next year to see how each one looks a year down the line. Any initiative will take a two-year cycle to embed after all and, of course, to accommodate the inevitable changes that our exciting subject of information and communication technology guarantees to serve up.

Have a good break!

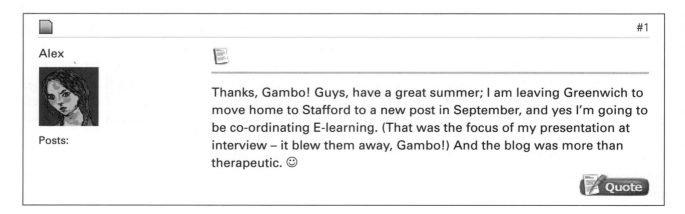

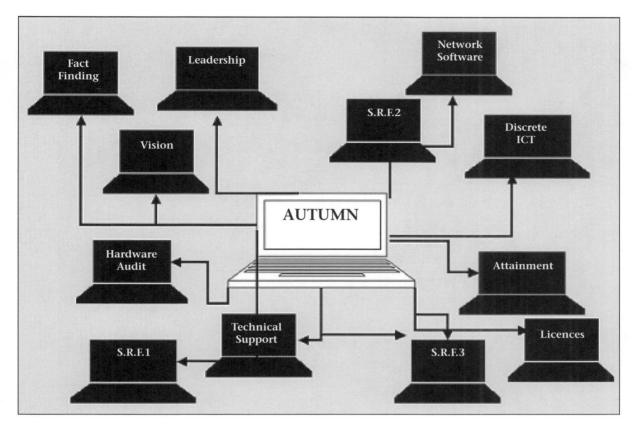

Figure 12.1 Autumn overview

Available on the net at http://www.sagepub.co.uk/wrightbk1

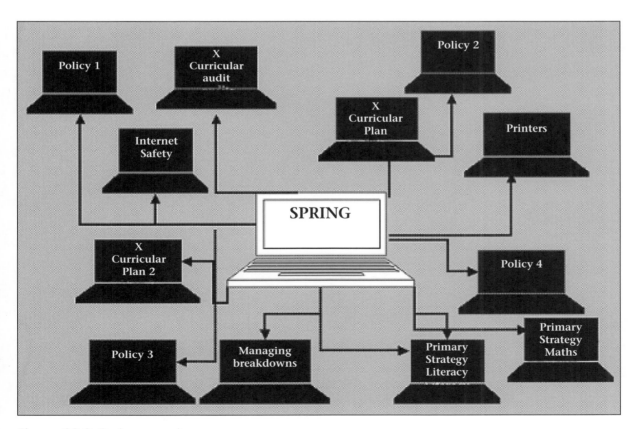

Figure 12.2 Spring overview

Available on the net at http://www.sagepub.co.uk/wrightbk1

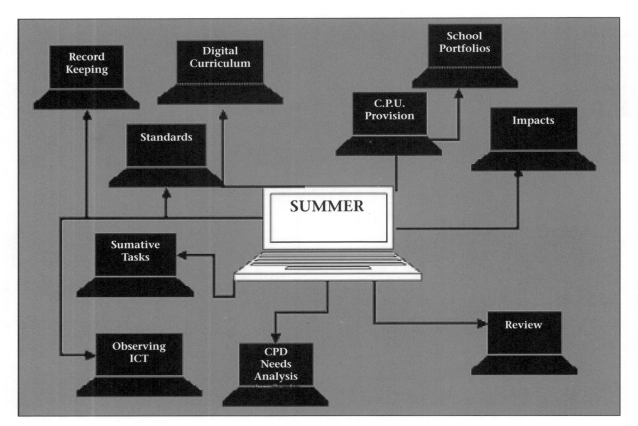

Figure 12.3 Summer overview

Available on the net at http://www.sagepub.co.uk/wrightbk1

References

Adobe, Acrobat Reader and Macromedia Flash Player downloads, http://www.adobe.com/downloads.

Aidan Gibbons, Digital animation movie, *The Piano*, http://www.aidangibbons.com.

BBC (2004), *Digital Curriculum Service, 5-Year Outline Commissioning Plan – England*, 30 July.

BBC, Online digital curriculum, www.bbc.co.uk/jam.

BECTA (2005), *E-safety, Developing a Whole-School Approach to Internet Safety*, ref. 15327.

BECTA (2005) *The BECTA Review 2005, Evidence on the Progress of ICT in Education.*

BECTA, Framework for ICT technical support, http://www.becta.org.uk/tsas.

BECTA (2004), *ICT, Amenability and the BBC Digital Curriculum Service in England: BECTA's Report to the DCMS.*

BECTA (2002), *Impact2, The Impact of Information and Communication Technologies on Pupil Learning and Attainment.*

BECTA Planning to purchase an interactive whiteboard, http://www.becta.org.uk/leaders/leaders.cfm?section=3_1&id=3173.

BECTA, Self-review framework matrix, http://www.becta.org.uk/schools/selfreviewframework.

BECTA, Software licensing catalogue, http://procurementtools.becta.org.uk/.

CLAIT, Computer Literacy and Information Technology, http://www.clait2006.co.uk.

DfES (2003), *The Big pICTure: The Impact of ICT on Attainment, Motivation and Learning.*

ECDL, European Computer Driving Licence for Educators, http://www.educatorsecdl.com.

EPICT, European Pedagogical ICT Licence, http://www.epict.info.

GOAL, Assessment software, www.goalonline.co.uk.

GOOGLE, On-line calendar, www.google.com/calendar.

Health and Safety Executive, HSE advice on the use of interactive whiteboards, http://www.hse.gov.uk/radiation/nonionising/whiteboards.htm.

Liberum, Helpdesk download, http://www.liberum.org.

MAPs, Managed E-portfolios, www.maps-ict.com.

MICROSOFT, Licence comparison table, http://www.microsoft.com/uk/education/how-to-buy/licensing-comparison/.

MICROSOFT, Licensing compliance: overview, http://www.microsoft.com/uk/education/how-to-buy/compliance/.

MICROSOFT, Microsoft school agreement estimated retail price calculator, http://www.microsoft.com/education/sacalculator.aspx.

MICROSOFT, Office suite readers, http://www.microsoft.com/downloads.

Mirandanet (2003), *Learning to Use ICT in Classrooms: Teachers' and Trainers' Perspectives Part One: A Summary of the Evaluation of the English NOF ICT teacher Training Programme 1999–2003.*

National Curriculum, Attainment Targets for ICT, http://www.nc.uk.net/nc/contents/ICT---ATT.html.

National Curriculum, Programme of Study for ICT, http://www.nc.uk.net/nc/contents/ICT-1--POS.html.

National Curriculum in Action, ICT Level descriptions, http://www.ncaction.org.uk/subjects/ict/levels.htm.

National Curriculum in Action, Progression in ICT, http://www.ncaction.org.uk/subjects/ict/progress.htm.

Ofsted, (2005), *Embedding ICT in Schools – a Dual Evaluation Exercise*, HMI 2391, December.

OFSTED, Evidence collection form, HMI 2506, https://ofsted.gov.uk/publications.

Primary National Strategy, Key Stage 1 Literacy ICT resources, http://www.standards.dfes.gov.uk/primaryframeworks/library/Literacy/ict/ictks1.

Primary National Strategy, Key Stage 2 Literacy ICT resources http://www.standards.dfes.gov.uk/primaryframeworks/library/Literacy/ict/ictks2/.

Primary National Strategy (2004) *Learning and Teaching Using ICT Example Materials from Foundation Stage to Year 6*. (DFES0315-2004G), http://samples.lgfl.org.uk/primary.

Primary National Strategy, Mathematics Excel resources, http://www.standards.dfes.gov.uk/primaryframeworks/library/Mathematics/ICTResources/spreadsheets.

Primary National Strategy, Mathematics interactive teaching programs, http://www.standards.dfes.gov.uk/primaryframeworks/library/Mathematics/ICTResources/itps/.

Primary National Strategy, Mathematics IWB resources, http://www.standards.dfes.gov.uk/primaryframeworks/library/Mathematics/ICTResources/IWBs.

Primary National Strategy, *Primary Framework for Literacy and Mathematics*, http://www.standards.dfes.gov.uk/primaryframeworks.

Promethean, *Active studio flip chart reader*, http://www.promethean.co.uk.

QCA (2000), *ICT in Other Subjects: a Reference Guide to Indicate ICT Provision in the Programmes of Study for Other Subjects in the National Curriculum.*

QCA, KS3 ICT onscreen test, www.rm.com/qca.

QCA, Scheme of Work for ICT, http://www.standards.dfes.gov.uk/schemes2/it.

Research Machines, ICT Alive software suite, www.rm.com/ictalive

SMART, Flipchart reader, http://www.smarttech.com/support/software/index.asp.

Training and Development Agency for Schools, ICT skills test, http://www.tda.gov.uk/skillstests/practicematerials/ict.aspx.

Underwood, J. with Ault, A., Banyard, P., Bird, K., Dillon, G., Hayes, M., Selwood, I., Somekh, B. and Twining, P. (2005) *The Impact of Broadband in Schools*. BECTA Sponsored Investigation of Broadband Technology Impacts in Schools.

WINZIP, Compression utility tool, http://www.winzip.com.

Index